JAPAN'S TRADE POLICY

Despite the constant criticisms of its major trading partners, Japan continues to run massive trading surpluses. Will foreign pressure ever force it to open up?

This book argues that there is a complex relationship between the conduct of Japan's trade policy and external pressure. It takes as a case study the US/Japan trade talks of the mid-1980s. These focused on four key areas: pharmaceuticals, telecommunications, electronics and forestry products. The outcomes of these talks demonstrate the danger of generalizations and the relative constraints and importance of different ministries. The US exerted most pressure in the cases of telecommunications and forestry: whereas they achieved significant results in terms of opening the market in the former, they had almost no impact in the latter. Similarly, the moderate pressure exerted in pharmaceuticals and electronics brought the almost complete removal of trade barriers in the former, but very moderate results in the latter.

By exploring the process of policy making in some of the ministries which are increasingly involved in determining Japan's trade policy, this book provides valuable insights for both academics and policymakers.

Yumiko Mikanagi was born in Tokyo and has studied in both Japan and the US. She is Assistant Professor in Politics and International Relations at the International Christian University, Tokyo. She is the author of 'Sekai keizai hendō no naka no nihon' (Japan in a Changing World Political Economy) and 'Haken suitaiki ni okeru kyōchō' (Cooperation During the Era of Hegemonic Decline) in *Kokusai Seiji*.

ROUTLEDGE STUDIES IN
THE GROWTH ECONOMIES OF ASIA

1   THE CHANGING CAPITAL MARKETS OF EAST ASIA
Edited by Ky Cao

2   FINANCIAL REFORM IN CHINA
Edited by On Kit Tam

3   WOMEN AND INDUSTRIALIZATION IN ASIA
Edited by Susan Horton

4   JAPAN'S TRADE POLICY
Action or reaction?
Yumiko Mikanagi

5   THE JAPANESE ELECTION SYSTEM
Three Analytical Perspectives
Junichiro Wada

JAPAN'S TRADE POLICY

Action or reaction?

Yumiko Mikanagi

London and New York

First published 1996
by Routledge
11 New Fetter Lane, London EC4P 4EE

Simultaneously published in the USA and Canada
by Routledge
29 West 35th Street, New York NY 10001

Routledge is an International Thomson Publishing company

© 1996 Yumiko Mikanagi

Typeset in Garamond by Poole Typesetting (Wessex) Ltd, Bournemouth
Printed and bound in Great Britain by
TJ Press (Padstow) Ltd, Padstow, Cornwall

British Library Cataloguing in Publication Data
A catalogue record for this book is available from the British Library

Library of Congress Cataloguing in Publication Data
Mikanagi, Yumiko.
Japan's Trade Policy : Action or reaction? / Yumiko Mikanagi.
p.   cm. — (Routledge studies in the growth economies of Asia; 4)
Includes bibliographical references and index.
ISBN 0–415–13735–7 (alk. paper)
1. Japan—Commercial policy. 2. Japan—Foreign economic
relations. I. Title. II. Series.
HF1601.M534   1996
382'.3'0952—dc20   95–23841

ISBN 0-415-13735-7 (hbk)
ISSN 1359-7876

For my mother and father

CONTENTS

List of figures and tables   ix
Preface   x
Acknowledgements   xii
A note on convention   xiv

1 INTRODUCTION   1
  Is Japan like 'us'?   7
  Changing global context and Japan's policy responses   9
  About the MOSS talks   14
  Argument in brief   18
  Design of the book   18

2 *EXPLAINING JAPANESE FOREIGN ECONOMIC POLICY*   19
  Contending approaches to Japanese foreign economic policy   19
  A gap in the existing literature   25
  A ministry-centred approach   26
  Explaining cases   37

3 *GAIATSU* AND THE MOSS TALKS   38
  Effects of Gaiatsu   38
  Effective agenda-setting   40
  Non-linear relationship between Gaiatsu *and results*   45
  Conclusion   52

4 *THE THREE ELEMENTS OF THE CAPACITY OF MINISTRIES*   54
  Autonomy of ministries   54
  Policy instruments   58
  Institutional objectives   62
  Conclusion   73

5 *RELATIONSHIPS WITH THE PRIVATE SECTOR*   74
  Types of relationship and shared interests   74

Why MITI failed to be responsive in the MOSS talks   83
Explaining an exceptional case: forest products   85

6 *CONCLUSION*   93
Direct implications: a 'snapshot' view   93
Indirect implications: a long-term view   97
Policy suggestions for the US and Japanese governments 101
Conclusion   113

Appendices   115
Notes   125
Bibliography   146
Index   159

FIGURES AND TABLES

FIGURES

5.1 Growth of world telecommunications equipment export
    market and Japan's market share   79
5.2 Distinction between upstream and downstream industries   85

TABLES

1.1 Comparison of US exports of products negotiated under
    the MOSS talks to US total exports   17
2.1 Types of relationship and the obstacles they pose for market
    liberalization   35
3.1 Tariffs on computers before the MOSS talks   43
3.2 Amount of pressure and achievement   46
3.3 Forest product tariff reductions schedule   49
3.4 US–Japan pharmaceuticals trade before the MOSS talks   51
4.1 Number of approval grants in 1981   60
4.2 Comparison of tariffs on forest products (1985)   62
4.3 Forest product tariff reductions   71
5.1 The size of VAN carriers   81
5.2 The *Gokanen Keikaku* proposal   90
5.3 The final draft of the *Gokanen Keikaku*   91

PREFACE

This book began as a long discussion with Professor Kenneth A. Oye in the spring of 1987. The puzzle that led me to focus on Japan's foreign economic policymaking was that while Japan's foreign policy seemed to be a mere response to international pressure, the response was not uniform. In my general studies on Japan's foreign economic policies, I noticed that Japan responded well to international pressure in some cases such as citrus fruits and textiles but showed resistance to cases such as rice and semiconductors. The very fact that I was unable to come up with a convincing answer to the questions of why and under what conditions Japan responds to international pressure motivated me to continue pursuing this project.

Researchers in social sciences who do not possess means to conduct laboratory experiments frequently encounter problems of controlling variables. However, in my preliminary studies, I was fortunate to discover a set of four cases – pharmaceuticals, telecommunications, forest products and electronics – discussed under the Market-Oriented Sector-Selective (MOSS) talks. Among the four cases, Japan responded relatively well in the pharmaceutical and telecommunications talks and showed resistance in forest products and electronics cases. That these cases were all nego-tiated between 1985 and early 1986 mostly eliminated a number of factors such as changes in exchange rates and international distribution of power as explanatory variables. The fact that they all occurred within the frame-work of the MOSS talks also meant that all negotiations were done with the same goal, i.e. removal of all types of barriers to trade, which in turn eliminated the potential effect of negotiation format on negotiation out-comes.

Initially, I had no intention to write a book on the Japanese bureaucracy. However, the MOSS talks directed my attention to the ways in which the Japanese bureaucracy responds to foreign pressure, primarily because the bureaucracy dominated the policymaking process in which Japan's response was generated. To be more specific, it was the different responses of various ministries in the bureaucracy that drew my attention.

While the strength of this study is that readers will find how various ministries such as the Ministries of Health and Welfare, and Posts and Telecommunications – which have attracted little attention from policymakers and scholars in the past – behave in international trade negotiations, I am aware of the limits of this study deriving from the fact that it places central focus on the Japanese bureaucracy. Given the current political fluidity in Japan it is unlikely that the bureaucracy will lose all of its influence over policy formation soon. However, there is a rising call among political, business, and intellectual leaders for administrative reform in order to restrict the power of the bureaucracy and in the long run, the Japanese policymaking process will shift its weight away from the bureaucracy toward political leaders. Thus, further studies on Japan's foreign economic policy formation must shift their attention to roles played by non-bureaucratic actors and institutions.

Although there may be other limitations to this study in addition to the one stated above, it is my hope that it offers useful insights for students of Japanese politics and international relations as well as foreign policymakers and trade negotiators about the ways Japan behaves in the face of foreign pressure.

Yumiko Mikanagi
Mitaka-shi, Tokyo

ACKNOWLEDGEMENTS

This book could not have materialized without the help of many people. It is impossible to list all the names of teachers, advisors, colleagues, and friends who helped me during the long duration of this project and I understand that expression of my gratitude in this limited space will inevitably risk omitting some who supported this project at various stages. Nevertheless, with this risk in my mind, I cannot complete this book without thanking the following people for their generous help. To be sure, people who are listed deserve credit, but I bear the responsibility for all the faults and criticisms.

While I am heavily indebted to many professors at the Politics Department of Princeton University, I particularly would like to thank Professors Kent E. Calder and Robert Gilpin for overseeing this project from its inception to the end. I also owe my thanks to Ken Oye, who inspired me to initiate this work, Keisuke Iida, and Ezra Suleiman who read the manuscript at various stages of this project and gave me helpful comments. I am indebted to other members of the Department, of course, but I am particularly indebted to Mildred Kalmus who helped me on various needs related to this project. The Center for International Studies and the Center of Regional Studies of Princeton University provided me with financial assistance for this project.

Although I could not have conducted research without the help of many in the Japanese government, I am particularly thankful to the generous help offered by Hoshino Shinyasu, Toshida Seiichi, Sakai Tatsu, and Gotō Kenji.

Without the support of the Brookings Institution, I could never have completed this project. Among the members of the Institution, Ken Flamm, Ed Lincoln, Pietro Nivola, Janne Nolan, and Bert Rockman assisted me on parts or all of the earlier manuscript. I am also indebted to Bruce MacLaury, John Steinbruner, Charlotte Baldwin Brady, Susanne Lane, and Yuko Iida Frost.

ACKNOWLEDGEMENTS

I would like to thank friends and colleagues for their support and helpful comments. Among those, I must express my thanks to Kathy Moon, Murakawa Ichiro, Andrew Richards, Chiba Shin, and Neil Waters. Arno Janssen assisted me with notes and the bibliography. I would also like to thank editors from Routledge, Nicholas Gillard and Alan Jarvis, for their continuous help.

I am dedicating this book to my parents, Mikanagi Eiko and Kiyoyasu. My mother, for all these years, has been enthusiastic and supportive of my work. My father, as a government official, provided me with an inside view of the world of bureaucrats and thus inspired me to work on this book. My deepest gratitude and apology goes to Jeff Young, who has not only tolerated my totally unorganized lifestyle but also offered me unconditional assistance. His help included extensive discussions on the nature of Japanese politics, and editing and proofreading endless versions of this manuscript. To thank him for his support, I must write another book for him with a promise not to disturb the peace at home again.

A NOTE ON CONVENTION

Following the recent stylistical change in Western literature on Japan, all Japanese names in this book take the Japanese form of family name first followed by given name. Names of those who lived and published overseas for a long time, however, follow Western tradition.

Most translations from Japanese, including titles of books and articles, are mine. However, I adopted the English translations of text and titles whenever translations were given by the authors themselves.

1

INTRODUCTION

Japan is going through its largest political changes in the postwar period. After thirty eight years of relative stability under the domination of the Liberal Democratic Party (LDP), Japanese politics now faces a high degree of unpredictability and confusion.

On 9 August 1993, Mr Hosokawa Morihiro of the Japan New Party succeeded in forming an anti-LDP coalition government. The government changed twice within less than a year. In late April, 1994, the parliament (Diet) elected Mr Hata Tsutomu of the Japan Renewal Party as the prime minister following the resignation of Mr Hosokawa. However, due to the almost immediate withdrawal of the Socialist Party (Social Democratic Party of Japan, SDPJ) from the ruling coalition, the government lost majority support in both houses of the Diet. Only two months later, having faced the threat of a no-confidence resolution, the Hata government resigned. To everyone's surprise, after the Hata government's resignation, the LDP and the SDPJ, long-time rivals since the formation of these parties, succeeded in forming a coalition together with the small Harbinger Party. The new LDP–Socialist coalition elected Mr Murayama Tomiichi of the SDPJ as the first socialist prime minister since 1948.[1] In December 1994, opposition parties such as the Japan Renewal Party, the Clean Government Party, and the Democratic Socialist Party formed a new party, the New Frontier Party.

These political changes have raised expectations of Western observers that Japan will become more like 'us', i.e. a mature democracy where the government is both internationally responsible and internally accountable to its citizenry. Currently, no one denies that Japan is now a highly developed economy. However, despite the level of economic development Japan has achieved over the last four decades, the Japanese government does not look much like that of other industrialized democratic nations. Internally, Japanese politics and policymaking do not seem to

1

fully respond to developments in the economy and the society. Internationally, the government has taken few spontaneous 'actions' in becoming more like a normal power, i.e., a state that bears large responsibility in relation to the global community. Instead, Japanese policymaking, foreign policymaking in particular, has been trapped in a cycle of 'reaction' to foreign pressure.

To the disappointment of these observers, though, the recent political changes may not lead to immediate policy changes. This is because, as many argue, the bureaucracy has been as powerful as political leaders in Japan's policymaking since the end of the second world war.[2] Therefore, the recent political changes and resulting changes in policy programmes pursued by winning coalitions may face strong resistance by the bureaucracy. To be sure, in the long run, political changes should lead to policy changes. However, for issues that need immediate attention, the effect of political changes will be buffered by the workings of the bureaucracy. Thus, if we want to know whether the Japanese state can formulate policies that are consonant with Japan's economic power, we should not be misled by the current political change, but instead, we need to focus on policymaking mechanisms within the Japanese bureaucracy.

This book is about the Japanese bureaucracy. More specifically, it proposes that despite the continuing centrality of the bureaucracy in policymaking, its components, namely, individual ministries and agencies, face varying degrees of constraints which limit their capacity to bring about open markets in Japan. There are two reasons for focusing our study on the bureaucracy. Contrary to Weberian formulations, bureaucracy does not only administer but also takes an active part in policymaking. This has been particularly true in postwar Japan, where the bureaucracy has been the main vehicle for policymaking while politicians engaged in a game of musical chairs for politically important posts. In addition, the bureaucracy has so far been investigated from a narrow viewpoint. Unlike the common perception, the Japanese state is not composed of three unified actors, that is, the ruling party, big business, and the bureaucracy. Just as the LDP was shown to have internal conflicts through its breakup, the bureaucracy is replete with conflicting objectives and interests. What this book tries to offer is a cross-sectional study of the ministries in order to understand the constraints and opportunities each ministry faces when deciding on policy changes.

What kind of changes should we be looking for? In today's Japanese political context, two types of change are needed. First is a political change. Japan's political system must change in order to make the state more accountable to voters' interests and preferences. Because this change requires reduced roles for the bureaucrats, it is not in the interest of the bureaucracy. Therefore, this type of change is unlikely to be launched from the bureaucracy.

2

While political change stirs the curiosity of foreign observers, what is more directly relevant to Japan's diplomatic and trading partners is the second type of change: redefinition of Japan's national goals and reorientation of the policies needed to fulfil them. Japan needs to establish some form of long-term global policy. Japan was a passive follower of American leadership throughout the Cold War period. But with the end of the Cold War and the rise of Japan's economic and technological strength, Japan faces both internal and external pressure to have its own policy in order to take responsibility in maintaining global order.

This global responsibility has two pillars. One is maintenance of global peace and the other is maintenance of global economic welfare. In terms of the first responsibility, the direction Japan should take is not yet clear. With the end of the Cold War, the possibility of another all-out war has been drastically reduced. Ongoing conflicts, such as the wars in the former Yugoslavia and Rwanda, are all regional. The response of the international community to such regional conflicts has been to involve the United Nations in mediating settlements. The Japanese government recently expressed its willingness to become a permanent member of the Security Council as a first step to fortify its contribution to United Nations activities.

However, whether Japan will decide to overhaul its long-term security policy is uncertain for three reasons. Most importantly, Japanese politicians and bureaucrats have not discussed security issues thoroughly. For example, while Japanese policymakers have been paying a lot of attention to gaining a permanent seat on the UN Security Council, they have not debated or publicized the meaning of or the necessity for this objective. Many problems are left unanswered. Most importantly, political leaders from both the SDPJ and LDP have emphasized that Japan will stay out of UN military engagements. If that is the case, then, will Japan not face a major dilemma when the Security Council has to decide on a military action, in which Japan will not participate despite its veto power? If a permanent seat in the Security Council is a symbol to assert a change in Japan's security policy, what is the orientation of the change? How should the Japanese government adjust its security relations with the United States and its Asian neighbours? Does the Japanese government have a comprehensive view on whether or how it should increase its involvement with the United Nations? For instance, does the Japanese government also plan to increase its financial contributions and send more staff to the United Nations?

In addition, any sort of expanded military role for Japan would not only face strong opposition from neighbouring nations, but would also require a change in article nine of the Japanese constitution, and thus will not happen easily. (A change of the constitution requires the support of two-thirds of the members of both houses of the Diet and a majority in a national referendum. The constitution has not been amended since its enactment in 1947.) Finally, while an increasing number of Japanese citizens are in favour of a more active Japanese role in peace-keeping operations, national opinion over the orientation of Japan's security policy is still divided.

Progress on the second pillar of Japan's global responsibility is more likely to occur first. As in the case of Japan's role in maintaining global peace, Japan has no blueprint yet for the types of policies it needs to adopt in order to fulfil the responsibilities of an economic power. However, there is an emerging awareness among policymakers – politicians and bureaucrats – that Japan needs to become a more open economy. Faced with increasing criticisms from abroad, Japan's policymakers are convinced that if Japan continues to record large annual trade surpluses, its trading partners will adopt retaliatory measures. Thus, although the motivation seems to be self-centred (avoidance of punishment) Japan is beginning to take an active role in the maintenance of the global free trade system through greater efforts to open its markets.

In this book, we will focus on the Japanese bureaucracy precisely because of the increased need for market openness. When we refer to barriers to trade, we are thinking about two different obstacles to imports. The most common barriers are tariffs and quantitative restrictions to trade. The second type of barriers are regulations. In theory, regulations are not trade barriers since they do not discriminate against foreign products in favour of domestic products. However, regulations tend to work against foreign products because of the high cost of adjusting the products to meet rules and standards that are different from those of the home market.

After several GATT-sponsored rounds of multilateral trade negotiations, few products are protected by either high tariffs or import quotas in most industrialized nations. However, other types of measures such as export subsidies and 'voluntary export restraints', still limit foreign producers' market access. For instance, as became salient in the recent process of US–EC (European Union, or EU, today) trade negotiations, agricultural products receive heavy export subsidies in the EU according to its Common Agricultural Policy (CAP). The subsidies, in addition to surcharges on agricultural imports from non-EU countries, give price competitiveness to EU agricultural products and virtually exclude foreign products from the EU market. Between the US and Japan, exports of Japanese-made automobiles have been 'voluntarily' restricted to certain numbers.

In Japan, very few products are protected by high tariffs and import quotas (except for some agricultural products).[3] However, regulations and private sector commercial practices pose major obstacles for foreign (as well as domestic) businesses. Once regulations are created, the bureaucracy has the largest role in their day-to-day application, and the most discretionary power in their expansion or withdrawal. Therefore, in order to determine the extent to which Japan can open its markets, we need to investigate the possibility that the bureaucracy can undo the regulations it has created.

Because a complete study of policymaking in the Japanese bureaucracy is a rather ambitious undertaking, this project can only provide a starting point. Nonetheless, we hope to attain two goals by way of studying subjects dealt with in this book. The first goal is a general and academic one: to improve our understanding of Japan's policymaking process. Another goal is aimed at policymakers of Japan's trading partners and is intended to be more practical. This book tries to indicate to Japan's trading partners how various ministries behave and what strategies to adopt in relation to each ministry.

This second goal is designed to avoid a typical mistake a policymaker or a scholar is likely to make when dealing with Japan. One tends to assume that the Japanese bureaucracy is synonymous with the Ministry of International Trade and Industry (MITI). Even those with more experience in trade negotiations with Japan may be able to list only the three best known ministries, namely, MITI, the Ministry of Finance (MOF), and the Ministry of Foreign Affairs (MOFA). While it is undeniable that these ministries, especially the first two, are the most powerful and prestigious within the Japanese bureaucracy, it is a grave mistake to assume that only these ministries are relevant in Japan's policymaking.

Until the early 1980s, MITI has been the central actor in international trade negotiations. This is because industries under MITI's jurisdiction, such as steel and automobiles, successfully expanded their exports, which in turn caused trade friction with other countries. For example, MITI led trade negotiations on textiles in 1970–71, steel in 1977, and automobiles in 1980–81. In addition to the fact that MITI frequently became the most important international trade negotiator, the increased scholarly attention to MITI's industrial policy created a belief that MITI was the only important trade policy ministry in Japan.

However, by the mid-1980s, the focus of American trade policy shifted from controlling Japanese exports to the US to securing overseas markets for American products. Indeed, the 1985–86 Market-Oriented Sector-Selective (MOSS) talks we will study in the following chapters mark the turning point of American trade policy not only in relation to the Japanese government but also in relation to other trading partners. In relation to Japan, the MOSS talks laid the ground for later trade negotiations, such as the Structural Impediments Initiative (SII) talks held between 1989 and 1990, and the 'Framework' (Bilateral Comprehensive Economic) talks that began in September 1993.[4] In both talks, the goal of the US government was to expand American exports to Japan. The US government's effort to establish the North American Free Trade Agreement (NAFTA) is also a reflection of this new American trade strategy to open overseas (in this case, Mexican) markets to American exports. Finally, the strategy to pursue open markets abroad is seen in the US government's active participation in the Uruguay Round and its support for the establishment of the World Trade Organization (WTO).

If the MOSS talks marked a turning point in US trade strategy, the same was true for Japanese trade policy. The MOSS talks were the first cross-sectoral trade talks to make the Japanese government accept the principle of open markets through removal of all trade barriers. To be sure, the Japanese government negotiated with the US government about US exports to Japan before the MOSS talks. For instance, between 1977 and 1978, the US negotiated with Japan to liberalize Japanese imports of oranges and beef. Between 1978 and 1979, the procurement policy of the Nippon Telegraph and Telephone Corporation (NTT, then the national public monopoly of domestic telecommunications service) became the target of US–Japan trade negotiations. However, these talks were all about simply expanding American exports to Japan, within the context of a closed market. By contrast, the MOSS talks were not just about increasing American exports; they were about making Japanese markets more open.

Thus, the Japanese government faced strong pressure to accept the principle of comprehensive open markets, for the first time in its history. Japan faced two options: 'action' or 'reaction'. Japan could have taken an active free trade policy and opened markets of crucial importance to Japan's trading partners, in addition to the sectors negotiated in the MOSS talks. The MOSS talks gave Japan a great opportunity to become more like a normal capitalist power. Alternatively, Japan could have taken the option of reaction, as it had historically: respond to pressure only on the issues on the negotiation agenda and reduce trading partners' frustration temporarily.

This book demonstrates which option Japan took and which options it is likely to take in future. To put the conclusion briefly, as far as the MOSS talks are concerned, the Japanese government took the second option of reaction, with varying degrees of success. However, when we look at the MOSS decisionmaking process and current political changes that may undermine the power of the bureaucracy, we may be able to expect that the Japanese government may move to take action in making the Japanese economy more open.

The shift in American trade strategy changed more than just the options the Japanese government faces. Due to the inclusion of previously non-traded sectors, such as telecommunications and construction, into trade negotiations, the number of actors engaged in trade policymaking has increased. Historically, internationally traded sectors belonged to MITI's jurisdiction. Conversely, sectors that did not engage in international trade usually fell under other ministries' jurisdiction. However, the shift of

American trade strategy brought 'domestic' ministries such as the ministries of Health and Welfare and Construction onto the international scene.

Studies on policymaking in these domestic ministries are underdeveloped. For Japan's trading partners, inadequate information gives rise to wrong expectations, assumptions, and trade strategies. (These expectations and assumptions tend to be based on former negotiations done with MITI.) A practical goal of this study is to correct these expectations and assumptions and provide strategies.

As we expand the scope of our study to include ministries other than MITI, we must also set a limit to the current study. Because this project is only one of the many steps we must follow to increase our understanding of the Japanese bureaucracy, this book cannot offer an exhaustive study of the bureaucracy. Thus, two caveats must be made. The first caveat is on the unit of analysis. Typically, a Japanese ministry is divided vertically according to the types of industries and issue areas the ministry oversees. While sections are the smallest unit of division, bureaus, which encompass several sections, act as a coherent unit in making budgets and policies. Accordingly, intra-ministerial conflict, centring around inter-bureau disagreements, is common. However, for reasons of simplicity, this study will look mainly at ministries as the basic unit of analysis. Second, while an increasing number of ministries and even agencies (organizations without full ministerial status or ones affiliated with and overseen by other ministries) are important in shaping Japan's public policies, this book does not cover them all. It will examine ministries and agencies that have been influential in the recent past and present international trade negotiations.

IS JAPAN LIKE 'US'?

In this book, we will look at how and why ministries promote or stall market liberalization. In the course of explaining this process, this book will touch upon a highly contemporary but at the same time historical question regarding the relationship between state and society in Japan. 'Is Japan like us?' is a question that Western scholars have asked, either explicitly or implicitly, for a long time.[5] This question has at least two parts. It can ask whether Japan is democratic or not. In other words, the question asks whether the Japanese state is accountable to the preferences of its citizenry. Another interpretation of this question derives from an American perspective on the relationship between state and society. According to a theory based on this perspective, namely, group theory, interest groups bargain with each other and determine policy outcomes.[6] Assuming that the Japanese state has a large role in policymaking, the question concerns the extent to which various interest groups are allowed to compete with one another and influence politics and policymaking within the state.

By investigating patterns of market liberalization policy, we hope to attain a key to answering these questions. If ministries are the central actors for market liberalization in Japan, to what extent are they responsive to the needs of Japanese society? Conversely, to what extent do these ministries make policies based on their own objectives and interests, ones which may conflict with the interests of Japanese society? In other words, to what extent are non-state actors allowed to influence policymaking in the ministries? What are the possibilities and limits to Japanese efforts to open markets?

Answering these questions is important in determining trading partners' policy toward Japan. If there is a clear limit to ministries' ability to open Japanese markets, some trading partners may well conclude that Japan must be 'contained', or that Japan must be forced to open through 'managed trade'.[7] However, if some ministries are able to promote market liberalization, our question is when and under what circumstances will they do so?

The pattern of politics and policymaking in Japan has also stimulated a policy debate in countries with a laissez-faire tradition. The main debate is whether it is good to have an active state or a passive state in relation to the economy. This debate derives its origin from Chalmers Johnson's proposal that the Japanese state is fundamentally different from other Western states as regards its economic policies. In this view, the Japanese state's concern is the effective attainment of its goals, which was almost exclusively the attainment of industrial growth, and not the efficient use of resources.[8] This idea contrasts sharply with the American celebration of efficiency attained through maximum market competition.

Johnson concluded that active state involvement was largely successful in meeting its goal of industrial growth.[9] In part based on the presumed success of Japan's industrial policy, some recent scholars of economic policy have suggested that the US government adopt policies to foster industrial competitiveness.[10] However, while Johnson's 'developmental state' model is useful in underscoring the different roles played by the state in the West and in Japan, it is a mistake to assume that active state intervention always leads to successful industrial growth. The model does not explain why some cutting-edge industries, such as aerospace and computer software, have failed to develop in Japan even with substantial state involvement. In addition, the causal argument that Japan's industrial growth was due to industrial policy is difficult to test. The success of many industries such as textiles, steel, and automobiles cannot be attributed solely to industrial policy. The period in which these industries grew coincided with the period when the world economy was rapidly expanding, in part thanks to the American free trade policy.

Moreover, while we must agree that MITI played a large role in Japan's economic policymaking in the high-growth period (setting aside for the moment the argument about whether such intervention was effective), it is difficult to say that MITI remained central over the last decade. In contrast to the 1950s and the 1960s, when all important industries such as steel and automobiles were under MITI's jurisdiction, the most competitive industries such as telecommunications and satellites now fall under the jurisdiction of several ministries. For instance, telecommunications falls under the jurisdiction of both the Ministry of Posts and Telecommunications (MPT) and MITI, and satellites fall under the jurisdiction of the Science and Technology Agency in addition to the MPT and MITI. As we will see in this book, the diversification of ministries involved in economic policymaking means an end to the single-minded pursuit of economic expansion. The main reason is that ministries other than MITI are not always interested in Japan's industrial growth, which has been MITI's main objective throughout most of the postwar period. In addition, the increase in the number of actors involved in economic policy formation has made the policymaking process much more complex over the last twenty years.

CHANGING GLOBAL CONTEXT AND JAPAN'S POLICY RESPONSES

Over the last decade, three major changes occurred in the global economic setting faced by Japan, which in turn require Japan to change its foreign economic policies. The first change is that the US has become less tolerant of countries which try to benefit from the open American economy while closing their own markets to US exports. While the US has for the most part avoided an overt shift to protectionism, its rising trade deficit and the repeated perception of failed trade negotiations with its trading partners, Japan in particular, have made the US more aggressive in securing overseas markets for US-made products.[11] The end of the Cold War has accelerated this tendency. With the dissolution of the Soviet Union, the US lost a major incentive to give priority to the coherence of the Western alliance, and instead began to pay more attention to its own economic welfare.

President Bill Clinton – the first Democratic president in twelve years – has been focusing on the economic well-being of American citizens since his presidential election campaign, mostly out of a need to underscore perceived differences from the Republican emphasis on security issues. In terms of trade policy, increased economic well-being of American citizens meant increased openness of overseas markets for American products. In addition to the Congressional approval of the North American Free Trade Agreement (NAFTA), the Clinton administration's initiatives to secure overseas markets for American exports was seen in the Uruguay Round talks and in its trade negotiations with Japan (the 'Framework' talks). In these talks, trade negotiators of the Clinton administration repeatedly referred to the use of 'qualitative and quantitative indicators of success', 'objective indicators' or 'measures of success' for market access in Japan. While US government officials have left the meaning of these 'indicators' or 'measures' unclear, the repeated use of these terms raises legitimate fears among US trading partners, Japan in particular, that the US government is not afraid to adopt managed trade, perhaps demanding market shares, when market opening measures do not work to increase American exports.

Another change in the global economic setting has occurred in the perceptions of policymakers in industrialized nations. Policymakers now face increased constraints on alternatives for boosting their economies. A majority of the advanced industrialized nations experienced severe economic downturns since the late 1980s, in the form of zero to minus GDP growth rates, often accompanied by double-digit unemployment rates. However, by the end of 1994, most of these economies managed to reverse their recessions and began to demonstrate stronger growth of GDP by mid-1994. The problem for policymakers in these nations is, then, not recovery from recession *per se*.

The problem is that they must *sustain* economic growth. However, policymakers possess a reduced number of policy alternatives to attain this goal because of the need to avoid inflation. Therefore, the traditional tools for promoting economic growth, namely, fiscal and monetary policies, cannot be used without caution because of the danger of igniting inflation. This need to be extremely careful about inflation derives from the fact that the economic and political disaster of stagflation – recession accompanied by high inflation – which occurred in many industrialized nations in the aftermath of the first oil crisis is still fresh in the minds of economic policymakers and politicians in these countries. The collective memory of the experience of the 1970s places a constraint upon the alternatives of these policymakers. Faced with such constraints, policymakers are beginning to search for ways to stimulate domestic demand without causing inflationary pressure.

Japan's option for sustained growth without causing inflation is to deregulate its markets. While the recession in Japan has not caused major social instability due to a lack of large-scale loss of jobs, recession has hit Japan badly, causing the slowest growth rate since the early 1970s and the largest postwar downturn. On 8 September 1995, the Bank of Japan reduced the official discount rate to 0.5 per cent, the lowest in the postwar period. After five major economic packages of government spending, a long period of low interest rates, and the adoption of income tax cuts, one last structural measure Japan needs to pursue is deregulation.

However, the Japanese government has been slow in acting upon the growing perception that deregulation can promote non-inflationary growth. For instance, Prime Minister Hosokawa's initiative to form a committee to produce a 1990s version of the Maekawa Report,[12] as well as his emphasis on the need for 'economic reforms', indicated that the government has decided that long-term growth must rely more on domestic demand, which requires deregulated and open markets. Despite his emphasis on such reforms, however, Hosokawa's short-lived government achieved little to deregulate the economy. While the succeeding governments, led by Hata and Murayama, have upheld the goal of deregulation, these two governments have not done anything significant – in terms of both scope and duration – partially because of the current political turmoil.

The final change in the global economic setting is the acceleration of regional economic integration. While global multilateralism stagnated during seemingly endless GATT Uruguay Round negotiations, industrialized nations moved toward regional cooperation of their economies. Even with the conclusion of the Round, it is uncertain whether the ultimate goal of GATT, namely global free trade, will be attained. The European Union is emerging as one economic unit, as members of the EU are making solid efforts to remove barriers to any type of economic transaction within the region. In addition, the size of the EU market will increase over the next decade due to the ongoing process of enlargement.

Another effort to create a continent-wide market is seen in North America. Although the Clinton government faced strong opposition from labour unions and some environmentalists, the US Congress approved NAFTA in November 1993. However, the scope of integration created by NAFTA will be much less than what the Maastricht Treaty envisions for the EU. Most importantly, NAFTA does not aim at eventual political integration as the EU does. In addition, NAFTA is not a tariff union and thus each government reserves the authority to adjust tariffs against extra-regional trade. Furthermore, because of the deep concern for loss of employment in the US, the integration of the North American economy will not proceed to include provisions to allow the free movement of labour across borders.

The point of concern here is not whether it is possible for Europe and America to become completely integrated economies, though. What is relevant is how regional integration affects the choices faced by Japan's foreign economic policymakers. It is unclear to what extent regional integration will have a negative impact on the global free trade system. To our relief, the current rise of regionalism is of a different nature from that of the 1930s. The memory of protectionism and the rise of bloc economies in the 1930s, which might have been a contributing factor to the Second World War, is still present in the minds of the policymakers of the industrialized world. This collective memory serves to support the norm

11

of free trade held by the Western nations. Thus, the current rise of regionalism should not be mistaken for a recurrence of the 1930s.

While the current regional integration may not signify a rise of protectionism, regional integration will have both 'trade-creative' and 'trade-divertive' effects.[13] The trade-creative effect is the increase of trade from reduction of intra-regional trade barriers and promotion of uniformity of product standards and regulations. However, there will be a trade-divertive effect. Regional integration will raise the relative cost of extra-regional trade for local companies by offering opportunities for economy of scale for businesses done within the region. Also, intra-regional trade will increase relative to extra-regional trade because of the reduced transaction costs among companies within the region.

However, non-member states are most worried about the protectionist measures these regions may adopt against external trade. GATT prohibited raising extra-regional trade barriers, both tariffs and quantitative restrictions, in cases of regional integration. However, there were measures that either 'bypass GATT's rule of law', such as voluntary export restraints, or 'those that "capture" and pervert it' such as the imposition of countervailing duties and the use of anti-dumping provisions.[14]

Even after the establishment of a more comprehensive international trade organization, the World Trade Organization (WTO), in January 1995, unilateral measures against 'unfair' trade seem to persist. The problem is the lack of effective multilateral means to prevent the use of such measures. The unilateral measure announced by the US government on 16 May 1995 in retaliation for the failed US–Japan talks on automobile parts exemplifies the weakness of the WTO.

Moreover, trade policymakers, the lawyers specializing in GATT laws in particular, can always find a legal loophole. The agreement between an American and Japanese firm on Japan's cellular phone market is a case in point. Under heavy pressure, Motorola and IDO (Nippon Idō Tsūshin) agreed to expand Motorola's market access in March 1994. While the agreement is similar to a Voluntary Import Expansion (VIE), not a VER, the Motorola–IDO formula between private firms, rather than governments, signifies the possibility of a virtual market share agreement without the appearance of a VER agreement.[15] Thus, because there are many possibilities of legal loopholes in the Uruguay Round agreements and the WTO, it is still possible that a regional free trade zone will become more protectionist, if external trade increases to the point of threatening industries of member nations (the recent increase in the number of anti-dumping cases within the EU suggests that this possibility is real).

Japan has three options in response to emerging regional arrangements: do nothing, create an exclusive regional arrangement with its Asian neighbours, or increase its openness, either unilaterally or within a multilateral form such as Asian Pacific Economic Cooperation (APEC). (Notice that increased protection is not an option. As a result of rounds of multilateral trade talks, Japanese policymakers do not consider raising protection as a legitimate trade policy.) The choice Japan will make will have a deep impact on both the Japanese economy and Japan's political power in global affairs.

Because of the sheer size of the EU and NAFTA markets – over six trillion dollars each in terms of GDP – Japan has a large stake in keeping these markets open. Because the first two choices may produce adverse results such as adoption of retaliatory measures by the members of the EU and/or NAFTA or increased pressure for managed trade, it is rational for Japan to choose the third option, that is, to increase its openness.

No nation closes its market to imports without a clear reason. This reluctance is due to widespread awareness among industrialized nations of the cost of protectionism. Yet, if Japan decides either to create its own regional trading bloc and exclude non-Asian trading partners or 'do nothing' and continues to record large trade surpluses, two options are available to Japan's (non-Asian) trading partners.

They may decide to demand that the share of their exports in the Japanese market increases. This option has already been tried in the US–Japan semiconductor negotiations held in the mid-1980s and more recently in the US–Japanese talks on automobile parts. A variation of this approach was seen in the aforementioned Motorola–IDO agreement, and is likely to be adopted in more sectors in the near future. The reasons are quite clear. If the Japanese market is closed to newcomer firms and does not have free market competition, it means that the Japanese observe 'managed trade' at home. If the Japanese observe 'managed trade' at home, then it is hard for Japanese officials to criticize their trading partners' demand that the Japanese government should agree on market shares with foreign governments. Therefore, as the case of semiconductor negotiations indicates, no matter how much Japan resists the idea of 'managed trade', Japan can do little but acquiesce to the demand for higher market shares.

Or, Japan's trading partners, the US in particular, may increase the use of retaliation threats. Even though retaliatory measures are seldom adopted, Japan needs to avoid this scenario because exporting firms' production plans are seriously affected by such threats. However, as long as Japan keeps its markets closed, Japan will have little political leverage over its trading partners to change their policies. As the experience of the US and its leadership in creating GATT and the postwar world free trade system indicates, unless Japan lifts barriers to foreign exports, it has no legitimate claim over other governments to do the same.

The reasons why Japan is vulnerable to decisions made by its trading partners are multifold. As we will see in the next chapter, hegemonic power, international regimes, and market dependence explain partially why Japan must yield to foreign pressure. However, the bottom line of all these three reasons is that thanks to the prevalence of GATT norms in the postwar period, liberal trade policy has become the universal norm. Thus, if any country practises trade policy that differs from this norm, be it high trade barriers or tight regulations, the country has very little legitimacy in claiming that its policy must persist. Thus, today's trade negotiations between Japan and other nations tend to give less political leverage to Japan than to its trading partners.

ABOUT THE MOSS TALKS

So far, we have looked at the need for Japan to liberalize its markets in the light of Japan's relations with the global economy. However in the following chapters, we will focus primarily on US–Japan economic relations. To be sure, over the last decade, Japan's economic ties with other nations, Asian neighbours in particular, have been strengthened, in part due to the rising yen. However, I am focusing on the bilateral relations because for Japan, its relations with the US have been by far the most important, both economically and politically, since the end of the Second World War and they continue to be so today.

The cases I use in the following chapters all appeared in the set of US–Japan trade negotiations called the Market-Oriented Sector-Selective (MOSS) talks which took place between 1985 and 1986. The MOSS talks were initiated after several series of trade negotiations to control Japanese exports which served but little to reduce the US trade deficit with Japan. The US decided to shift its focus from imports from Japan to American exports to Japan and launched a new type of trade negotiation aimed at a thorough removal of all the governmental trade barriers in selected sectors.

The MOSS talks were initiated at the Reagan–Nakasone meeting on 2 January 1985. In this book, I will deal with the four sectors, namely, telecommunications, electronics, pharmaceuticals, and forest products that were the original MOSS-negotiated issues.[16] The method of focusing on one sector and aiming at removing all barriers to trade was modelled after the 1984 US–Japan Yen–Dollar agreement, which, in the opinion of at least part of the US government, 'contributed to the liberalization of Japanese financial markets'.[17] The MOSS talks were concluded on 8 January 1986. The outcome of the talks varied from one sector to another. While most of the issues in the talks on telecommunications and pharmaceuticals were resolved by 8 January, the talks on electronics and forest products did not produce the outcomes expected by the US negotiators. (For a detailed account of the talks' progress, please see appendices at the end of this book.)

There are several reasons why I chose cases from the MOSS talks. The

14

first and most important reason is that the MOSS talks marked a significant shift of US trade policy toward Japan as I mentioned earlier, which in turn changed Japan's foreign economic policy agenda. Since the early 1970s, when the US bilateral trade deficit with Japan became rather sizeable, the US had pressured Japan to reduce its trade surpluses through a correction of its export strategy to the US (except for agricultural trade in which Japan restricted imports of products such as beef, oranges and rice). However, as the steel and automobile voluntary export restraint agreements indicate (first negotiated in 1977 and 1980, respectively), the attempt to control Japanese exports had limited effects on the US trade deficit with Japan. Having experienced frustration over such failures, the US shifted its focus from imports from Japan to American exports to Japan. MOSS was adopted in order to remove all the governmental trade barriers in selected sectors. Thus, removal of barriers to exports in Japan began with the MOSS talks. These talks laid the ground for following trade negotiations, such as the Structural Impediment Initiative of 1989–90 and the Framework talks, starting in 1993.

The MOSS-type trade negotiation signalled a shift in American trade policy. Contrary to the idea that the US is becoming increasingly protectionist, the fact that it has chosen to pursue open overseas markets (instead of unilaterally closing its own markets) indicates that the US is still upholding the principles of free trade. It is true that the recent tendency for the American government to insist on 'qualitative and quantitative indicators of success' for market access signifies a deviation away from free trade principles. A full examination of the topic is outside the scope of this book, but we must bear in mind that managed trade has not become the primary norm for the American government, as seen in its effort to establish NAFTA and push the Uruguay Round to conclusion. The US' use of rhetoric that at times sounds consistent with 'managed trade' is mostly a response to Japanese markets, which do not seem to operate in the same way as other overseas markets.

Another reason for examining the MOSS talks is that the MOSS cases represent a counter-intuitive case of market liberalization. The dominant explanation of Japanese trade policy, that is, mercantilism, tells us that a government will not liberalize markets for non-competitive products.[18] According to this theory, several of the sectors negotiated under the MOSS talks were 'most-likely' to receive continued protection and therefore 'least-likely' to be liberalized.[19] However, as a result of the talks, most sectors, if not all, were liberalized. Thus, the cases of the MOSS talks represent 'crucial' cases to reassess the theory that Japanese trade policy is mercantilist.

Additional reason is that the MOSS talks offer a set of cases for meaningful comparison with one another. They are similar in that, as mentioned above, all requests for liberalization were expected to meet continued protectionism. They are also similar in that US pressure produced some response by the Japanese government. They are different, and hence interesting, in that outcomes varied across issues. This combination of similarities and differences shows clearly the impact of independent or intervening variables, such as bureaucratic policymaking mechanisms.

If international pressure was the independent variable that explains overall Japanese willingness to accept market liberalization in the MOSS talks, two facts suggest the existence of intervening variables. (Some might think policy changes made during the MOSS talks were due to the rise of the yen. Exchange rate fluctuations are not studied in this book because the rapid rise of the yen did not occur until after the Plaza Accord reached in September 1985. Moreover, interviews suggested that the perceptions and decisions of trade policymakers and private sector representatives involved in the talks were not affected by the exchange rate changes.) First, the initial level of market closure had little to do with Japan's responsiveness. In other words, we cannot conclude that Japan was responsive in sectors which were already relatively open. The US exported relatively more pharmaceuticals to Japan (measured as the ratio of exports to Japan to exports to the world) than it did other products. The other sectors in the MOSS talks did not show equally high export ratios (Table 1.1). However, in telecommunications, for instance, Japan showed high responsiveness despite a relatively closed market.

Another fact is that the amount of pressure applied to Japan did not correlate with Japan's responsiveness. For instance, the US showed stronger interest and thus pressed harder in the talks on forest products and telecommunications than in the talks on pharmaceuticals and electronics. However, high pressure in the case of forest products did not yield significant results, whereas Japan's responsiveness was high in the talks on pharmaceuticals, which received relatively low pressure from the US.

The MOSS talks are important not only for their theoretical value but also for their policy implications. The initiation of the Structural Impediments Initiative (SII) in 1989 seemed to have suggested that the *modus operandi* of trade talks between the US and Japan has shifted from talks focused on individual sectors to cross-sectoral ones. SII involved structural problems spanning several sectors of the Japanese economy, such as *keiretsu*,[20] as well as issues of the macro economy, such as public investment. However, the recent shift back to sectoral discussions, as seen in the Framework talks, suggests that sector-specific negotiations remain significant for several reasons. One reason is that cross-sectoral discussions such as SII, even if successful, do not necessarily resolve politicized US trade problems with Japan. Measures such as expansionary macro-economic policy and change in land policy may increase exports to and investment in Japan. However, there is no guarantee that US exports in sectors of special interest to the US government and the private sector, such as automobiles and telecommunications, will increase. Instead, it is likely that Japanese firms will increase imports of US products that are much less politically important, such as US-made Hondas, or increase imports from other countries, such as computers made in Malaysia.

Further reason that sector-specific talks remain important is that the US is likely to continue setting agendas that are strongly influenced by sectoral interests, as evidenced by the current discussions over automobiles and auto parts. Accordingly, in order to mitigate sectoral pressure, the US administration will continue to be sector-specific instead of dealing with cross-sectoral issues, of which the consequence on the trade balance is not at all clear.[21] Thus, sector specific talks continue to be an important form of US–Japan trade negotiations. Therefore, it is important to investigate the conditions under which such talks successfully achieve market liberalization in Japan.

Table 1.1 Comparison of US exports of products negotiated under the MOSS talks to US total exports (million US dollars)

	1982	1983	1984	1985
Total US exports to the World (A)	210,929	199,144	216,008	211,420
Total US exports to Japan (B)	20,663	21,561	23,162	22,166
(B)/(A) x 100	9.8%	10.8%	10.7%	10.5%
MOSS sectors				
Pharmaceuticals (SITC 54)				
Export total (C1)	2,390	2,612	2,759	2,843
To Japan (D1)	500	526	534	567
D1/C1	20.9%	20.1%	19.3%	19.9%
Forest Products (SITC 63)				
Export total (C2)	226	281	221	189
To Japan (D2)	17	18	18	19
D2/C2	7.8%	6.3%	8.3%	9.9%
Electronics (SITC 75)				
Export total (C4)	10,431	12,116	15,149	15,707
To Japan (D4)	780	843	1,093	1,199
D4/C4	7.5%	7.0%	7.2%	7.6%
Telecommunications Equipment (SITC 76)				
Export total (C5)	4,111	4,015	4,324	4,679
To Japan (D5)	277	294	307	271
D5/C5	6.7%	7.3%	7.1%	5.8%

Sources: Data compiled from United Nations, *International Trade Statistics Yearbook*, 1985 and OECD, *Foreign Trade by Commodities*

ARGUMENT IN BRIEF

The argument of this book is that the bureaucracy is the central actor in Japan's market liberalization. However, what is more important is despite its centrality, the bureaucracy faces a number of constraints placed on its ability to liberalize markets. Most importantly, the bureaucracy is not a unified actor that single-mindedly pursues industrial growth. Rather, the bureaucracy is a complex mosaic of various ministries with diverse goals which the Japanese government must satisfy. In addition, each ministry has varying degrees of autonomy and ranges of policy instruments which may further constrain its ability to carry out market liberalization. Furthermore, the types of relationships ministries maintain with the private sector may increase or decrease ministries' ability to implement policies that conflict with the interests of the private sector.

DESIGN OF THE BOOK

This book is divided into three sections: a theoretical framework, case studies, and a concluding chapter that explores both theoretical implications and policy recommendations for the US and Japanese governments. In Chapter 2, I will lay out several approaches to understanding foreign economic policymaking in Japan. I contend that while international factors, *gaiatsu* or foreign pressure in particular, are important in creating incentives for policy change in Japan, both the state (ministries) and the private sector must be incorporated in order to explain why Japan demonstrates varying responsiveness to *gaiatsu*. In Chapters 3, 4 and 5, I will examine cases from the MOSS talks in order to investigate factors that are important in determining Japanese foreign economic policy formation. In Chapter 3, I will demonstrate the relevance of *gaiatsu* in soliciting policy changes in Japan, while showing that there is no linear relationship between the amount of *gaiatsu* and Japan's responsiveness. In order to understand why Japan responded more in some MOSS cases but less in others to *gaiatsu*, in Chapters 4 and 5, I will investigate the elements of the capacity of ministries and the ministries' relationship with the private sector. In the final chapter, I will discuss direct and indirect implications of the MOSS talks on both the state and society relationship in Japan and the power of the bureaucracy. In addition, I will make several policy recommendations to both the US and Japanese governments in order to promote cooperative economic relationships between the two countries.

2

EXPLAINING JAPANESE FOREIGN ECONOMIC POLICY

In this chapter, I will first lay out several approaches for explaining Japanese foreign economic policy. I will begin with international systems-level analyses in order to demonstrate the importance of foreign pressure in explaining Japanese foreign economic policy. Then, I will move on to state-level approaches. In general, Japan's policymaking is well explained by approaches of this level. However, by indicating the increasing importance of ministries other than MITI, I will indicate a gap in existing state-level approaches. In addition, I will outline a society-level approach that focuses on interest groups. The strength of this approach is its consideration of social input. However, the main purpose of this section is to indicate its weakness, even in explaining American foreign policy (which is usually portrayed as the result of bargaining among various interest groups). The second half of this chapter will be an attempt to construct a new theoretical framework that helps to explain the foreign economic policymaking of various Japanese ministries. The approach taken in this framework aims at underscoring variations of the 'capacity of ministries', which determines the extent to which a ministry can pursue market liberalization on a given issue.

CONTENDING APPROACHES TO JAPANESE FOREIGN ECONOMIC POLICY

Hegemony, international regimes, market dependence, and *gaiatsu*

International systems-level approaches are relevant in explaining Japan's foreign economic policy, because they help us understand why Japan responds to *gaiatsu*, or foreign pressure. Despite the common international recognition that Japan keeps its markets closed to foreign entrants, Japan has lifted the majority of its formal trade barriers, such as tariffs, quantitative restrictions, restrictions on foreign direct investment, and controls on international capital transactions. These policy moves are in part explained by US requests that Japan liberalize its markets, a cycle of reaction common since the 1970s. On the international systems level, there are three main reasons why Japan has responded and still responds to *gaiatsu* to liberalize its markets.

The most important reason is that the US has been a hegemonic power, and therefore Japan has had to respond to pressure exerted by the US. According to hegemonic stability theories, if a state has an overwhelmingly strong economy – namely, if the state is a hegemon – its interest is to establish an international free trade system in order to ensure overseas export markets.[1] While the 'benevolent hegemon' version of this theory holds that the hegemonic state will unilaterally open its markets – with the expectation that other states will reciprocate and open their markets – it is often the case that other states try to free ride and exploit the hegemon's open markets while closing their own. Thus, as the 'coercive hegemon' version of this theory maintains, the hegemonic state must pressure others to open their markets. For the less powerful states, there is no choice but to acquiesce in the demands of the hegemonic power, out of fear of punishment.

In addition, the reason why Japan responds to *gaiatsu* is the existence of international regimes. Although the topic is debatable, many scholars maintain that US hegemony has already declined.[2] The relevant question, then, is that if US hegemony has already declined, why does Japan try to meet US demands to open its markets? The adherents of international regimes theory suggest that international regimes, defined as 'sets of implicit or explicit principles, norms, rules, and decision-making procedures around which actors' expectations converge in a given area of international relations', have persistent effects on the decisions of member states even after the initial international distribution of power has changed.[3] In the international trade area, it is difficult to distinguish the effects of the two factors, that is, US hegemony and the free trade regime exemplified by the GATT, when Japan responds to *gaiatsu* for more open markets.

But there is no doubt that the rules and norms of the GATT regime have had a lasting effect on the ideas lying behind Japan's trade policy formation. For instance, during the Uruguay Round, the Japanese government tried to strengthen the authority of the GATT panel for conflict resolution.[4] The goal of the Japanese government was to prevent unilateral use of anti-dumping measures by GATT members. The Japanese proposal included a provision to allow the panel to consider data submitted by firms when investigating a case of dumping. The final Uruguay Round agreement failed to include this provision because the US government was the primary opponent of this provision. While the US government is not willing to give up its authority to unilaterally rule on anti-dumping,

Japan's proposal indicated that the Japanese government supports multi-lateralism, a pillar of GATT norms. Of course, in the past, Japanese industries frequently became targets of anti-dumping measures; thus, the high likelihood that Japanese industries may become targets in the future is probably the foremost reason why Japan opposes unilateral use of anti-dumping measures. However, it is also true that Japan will increasingly want to levy anti-dumping duties on products such as textiles and colour TVs from newly industrializing economies (NIEs), Asian NIEs in particular. Given that the Japanese government also has a stake in maintaining lax enforcement of anti-dumping measures, Japan's proposal is not neces-sarily due to short-term interests related to its own industries. It is an indicator that the Japanese government prefers multilateral conflict resolution to unilateral measures.

The final reason why Japan responds to *gaiatsu* is explained by theories of interdependence or transnational relations. They suggest that growing economic interdependence, defined as 'situations characterized by recip-rocal effects among countries or among actors in different countries' has a deep impact on economic policymaking.[5] Japan responds to US pressure to open its markets not only because the US has been a powerful hegemon but also because Japanese policymakers and business leaders fear that the US might close its markets to Japanese exports if Japan does not respond. Japan has a large stake in keeping US markets open due to Japan's heavy dependence – about 30 per cent of the total value of Japanese exports – on the US for export markets.

In sum, international system-level factors explain why Japan has few choices except to respond when pressured to open its markets. Thus, this level of analysis tells us that Japan cannot further close its markets. It also tells us that Japan has to make changes to satisfy US interests. Hegemonic pressure determines the direction in which Japan must change its po-licies. However, the speed with which Japan will make such changes in various issue areas remains to be explained.

The state

Given the historical and ideological celebration of small government, American political scientists paid little attention to the autonomous func-tions of the state.[6] However, in the late 1970s, this trend was challenged by the emergence of a number of writings using state-centred approa-ches.[7] In the field of foreign policy, while the state as an arena for policymaking was never forgotten,[8] it was only in the late 1970s that the state was considered to be an autonomous actor insulated from pressure groups.[9]

To be sure, the initial development of the state-centred approach in American political science was dominated by the concept of the US as a 'weak state'. Although the American state was gradually assigned a larger role independent of sectoral pressure, it was still considered to have lower capacity to attain goals than strong states such as France and Japan.[10]

This distinction between strong and weak states was rather misleading for a number of reasons. First, as Stephan Haggard points out, a state's ability to impose its own interest upon policy outcomes is not constant over time nor across issue areas.[11] Furthermore, a state may be insulated from sectoral pressure ('strong state') but nonetheless, as in the case of Japan's market liberalization, it may produce a policy outcome that is no different from the outcome of a weak state. Finally, the distinction makes it difficult to compare the capacities for policymaking and policy implementation over various issues of states that belong to opposite categories.

Although the strong state–weak state distinction has such faults as an analytical tool, the idea that Japan is a 'strong state' has been widely accepted in Japanese political science since the *Nihon Seiji Gakkai* (The Japanese Political Science Association) published a series of articles on the state-centred argument.[12] The state-centred approach to Japanese policymaking was often called the 'ruling triad' or elitist model.[13] This model is somewhat like a sophisticated version of the popular 'Japan, Inc.' stereotype, employing imagery which portrays the Japanese state as 'a unitary, interest-maximizing, rational actor'.[14] The elitist model depicts a Japanese state in which power is concentrated in the hands of the state bureaucracy, the LDP, and big business. The Japanese state is thought to pursue economic growth, supported by a consensus among these three actors.

In this model, the Japanese state makes economic policies and imposes them upon society. The underlying assumption of the elitist model was that the state bureaucracy presides on the top of the power triangle supported by the two other powerful actors, the LDP and big business. However, the policymaking of state ministries other than MITI, and to a far lesser extent, the Ministry of Finance, received next to no attention. This is because throughout the postwar period until the 1970s, MITI played an important role in obtaining what was considered Japan's overriding national interest, that is, rapid economic recovery and industrial growth. Needless to say, Chalmers Johnson's contention that Japan was a 'developmental state' led by MITI gained great influence in the study of Japan's policymaking.[15]

While the Diet, which is constitutionally the highest authority of Japanese state power, remained passive and the bureaucracy continued to be the main source of policymaking, some claim that by the mid-1970s, LDP politicians have gained increasing expertise and thus influence in policymaking.[16] Therefore, the relevant question is to what extent the LDP intervenes in policymaking and what is left for the bureaucracy to handle exclusively. On this point, Daniel Okimoto presents a useful issue typology based on the functional divisions of the state bureaucracy.[17] He contends that each issue and ministry in charge of the issue possesses a different degree of politicization depending on the type of political exchange between interest groups and the LDP. This typology helps to clarify the division of labour between the LDP and the bureaucracy. Moreover, it demonstrates that sectors under certain ministries such as MITI and the Ministry of Finance are less politicized than those under other ministries such as the Ministry of Agriculture, Forestry, and Fisheries.

However, Okimoto's view is only a snap-shot of political relationships. It is a mistake to assume that the type of relationship between an interest group and the LDP is constant over time (for example, the relationship between the LDP and rice producers seems to be becoming less politicized today than it was under the LDP's rule). Therefore, Okimoto's study only provides a framework within which further study on ministries is needed.

In addition, the usefulness of the entire body of literature on the LDP's policymaking ability has been drastically reduced since the LDP's monopoly on power was broken in July 1993. Even if the LDP regains power, as it did in June 1994, it will not be able to resurrect the ties it maintained with private sector interest groups before it left the government. Because the revision of the political funding law, which passed the Diet in January 1994, will place a strict limit on corporate contributions to both political parties and individual politicians (with the further provision that corporate contributions will be banned in five years), it is unlikely that the LDP politicians will try to lobby for increased public expenditures or favourable legislation for industries such as construction and transportation in exchange for financial contributions.

Interest groups

Society-level explanations based on pluralism maintain that policy outputs are the result of competition among groups or individuals for political and economic benefits.[18] In this political framework, the state *per se* does not play an active role and is alleged to play the role of a referee. In other words, a state does not have much autonomy from sectoral pressure.

Studies on interest groups are important for understanding social input into policymaking, but exclusive focus on private actors will overlook important factors that affect the policymaking process. Even in the US, where the state is often considered weak and offers what David B. Truman called 'multiplicity of points of access', the state has evolved into something more complicated than just an arena for bargaining among interest groups.[19] The US Congress may still offer points of access to sectoral interests, but there are other institutions more insulated from sectoral pressure.[20] For instance, foreign economic policy is formulated not only by the Congress but also by other government institutions such as the President, executive branch agencies, and departments such as the Departments of Treasury, State and Commerce. These institutions usually demonstrate some degree of insulation from the private sector. These varying degrees of insulation from sectoral pressure suggest that the interest group approach is still valid within a certain arena of policy-making, such as the Congress, but we may have to use other approaches to institutions less vulnerable to sectoral pressure.[21] By focusing on institutions and actors in the American state which are more insulated from sectoral pressure, we are better able to answer paradoxes such as why the US continued to reduce trade barriers after the Reciprocal Trade Agreements Act of 1934.[22]

While American political scientists began to pay more attention to the state in the 1970s, the opposite trend was seen in Japan. Some scholars unsatisfied with the elitist model focused on the activities of interest groups in Japan, thereby introducing a 'pluralistic' approach to Japan's policymaking.[23] This development was in part accelerated by the increasing visibility of interest group activities in Japan in the 1960s.[24] For instance, both Muramatsu Michio and Ōtake Hideo analysed how the different actors in the private sector influence the political process in Japan.

However, the application of American-style approaches based on interest group politics to Japan's policymaking appears to be subject to inherent limits, due to the nature of the Japanese state and its relationship with society. Most importantly, it is undeniable that the bureaucracy plays a central role in policy formation due to two main factors: its strictly meritocratic recruitment and its information gathering ability. Although it is debatable whether the entrance exam for career bureaucrats accurately tests ability to perform the roles expected of the bureaucracy by society, the policy of using entrance exams and excluding political appointees (except for the minister and one or two political vice-ministers for each ministry), gives ministries a high degree of autonomy from political pressure. In addition, due to the long history of close interaction between the ministries and the private sector, the Japanese bureaucracy vastly surpasses politicians in its ability to collect information on private firms, the economy, and the likely effects of policy changes.

An additional limit placed on private firms to compete freely for favourable policy outcomes is that the activities of firms in the Japanese private sector is severely limited to 'compartmentalized competition'.[25] Under this system, there is little room for private actors in different sectors to compete for policy influence, although different sectors each have their own free market competition. A main reason is that the bureaucracy has created divisions in the economy, by assigning each ministry (and more precisely each bureau of a ministry) specific industries to oversee, and these divisions have survived over time. Hence, a genuinely pluralist policy process is unlikely, because opposing interests across different sectors do not normally come into conflict with each other and compete for influence in policymaking.[26]

A GAP IN THE EXISTING LITERATURE

If the interest group approach faces certain constraints due to the peculiar nature of the state and society relationship in Japan, a state-centred approach that does not incorporate variations of policymaking patterns among different institutions is not sufficient to explain Japan's economic policy formation. Thus, among existing theories, the institutionalist argument is the most suitable for analysing patterns of policymaking.

The 'new' institutional approach originally conceptualized by James B. March and Johan P. Olsen places its focus on the state as a set of autonomous political institutions.[27] It de-emphasizes the role of economic and social conditions played in decision-making but leans more toward the 'design of political institutions'.[28] Institutional design, or structure, refers to both 'the organizational characteristics' of groups and to the rules and norms that guide the relationships between actors'.[29] This approach enables us to see capacities and resources of various organizations that comprise the state and thus will be useful for understanding the determinants of policy outcomes on various issues.[30]

The major weakness of this approach is that institutional structure itself does not necessarily determine the ultimate content of policies. In addition to structure and the interest calculations proposed by rational-choice theorists, the ideas held by policymakers encourage them to propose and shape the ultimate content of policies.[31] This is particularly true for Japanese bureaucrats, whose historical mandate has been social, economic and political reforms in order to attain an equal footing with the West, a goal which has often been indifferent to particular interests in society. Thus, ideas serve as a strong complementary factor in determining outcomes of foreign economic policy when they are incorporated into the institutionalist argument.[32] Moreover, in order to incorporate the merits of society-level explanations, a broader conception of institutional structure, which describes the structural relationship between state and society, will be useful in analysing how societal interests are represented in the policymaking of a state.

A MINISTRY-CENTRED APPROACH

Although more and more attention has been paid to the policymaking ability of the LDP, the Japanese state bureaucracy is still central to policy-making. This is even more the case now that the LDP's monopoly on power has been broken, with parties with much less governing experience coming into power. Without a strong political leadership and a political reform to weaken the power of the bureaucracy, it is unlikely that the bureaucracy will lose its capacity to conduct comparatively autonomous policymaking.

Despite the importance of the individual ministries, the theories that focus on the bureaucracy rely mainly on the tradition of the elitist model and assume that the bureaucracy is a unitary actor. To be sure, recent works that focus on the state bureaucracy have gone well beyond the elitist model to incorporate the ways that the state relates to the private sector, as seen in Okimoto's concept of Japan as a 'network state' and Richard Samuel's idea of 'reciprocal consent'.[33] However, as the elitist model assumed MITI as the leading actor, few studies have been conducted on ministries other than MITI and the Ministry of Finance as the central actors in Japan's policymaking.

It is undeniable that Japan's many important export industries still remain under the formal jurisdiction of MITI. Nevertheless, other ministries deserve more attention for two reasons. One reason is that MITI will lose some of its importance in the economy as many industries which formerly benefited from MITI's industrial policy reach maturity and service industries overtake manufacturing industries. MITI may find new sectors to nurture but as Japan's style of state-led industrialization has come under international criticism, MITI may not be able to implement the explicit industrial policy it did in the past. Next reason is that, given that Japan's trading partners are frustrated with closed Japanese markets, a wide range of sectors will be placed on the agenda of international economic negotiations. Therefore, ministries other than MITI which have jurisdictions over these sectors will be drawn to the front line of international disputes. In sum, in addition to the renewed study of MITI, an account of policymaking patterns of ministries other than MITI is needed.

The central question asked in this book is how various Japanese ministries respond to *gaiatsu* to liberalize markets. Under what circumstances do they fail to be responsive? In determining the degree of responsiveness, do ministries or the private sector play a greater role? What determines the importance of the roles played by the ministries and the private sector? Can we see any differences in the decision-making styles of the different ministries? If the private sector is important in shaping policy outcomes, how do the interests and preferences of the private sector become reflected in the decision-making process?

I construct a new approach in order to answer these questions. This approach is specifically designed to analyse cases where the degree of politicization is relatively low. When there is little political intervention, the ministries take the responsibility of policymaking; hence their contribution can be clearly analysed. In order to understand the varying degrees of Japan's responsiveness, I will try to focus on the capacity of each ministry and the types of relationship that the ministries maintain with the private sector.

The main argument of this book is that the greater the capacity of a ministry, the higher the Japanese responsiveness to demands for market liberalization. The determinants of the capacity of a state ministry are two-fold. First, the capacity of a ministry is restricted by the structure of the state bureaucracy which is composed of different ministries and agencies competing with one another for enhanced status and power. Moreover, the degree to which the goal of market liberalization conflicts with each ministry's institutional goals or interests and range of policy instruments available to each ministry affects the capacity of a ministry. Second, the capacity of a ministry is also affected by the ministry's relationship with the private sector.

The elements of the capacity of ministries

The primary explanatory variable in this book is the capacity of state ministries to make decisions on economic policies. In cases of market liberalization, state capacity simply means the ability of a ministry to remove formal trade barriers or regulations.[34] The capacity of a ministry is composed of three elements. The most important element is the ministry's autonomy, defined as freedom from intervention by other state actors. Another element is the policy instruments possessed by the ministry. Policy instruments are measures such as foreign exchange controls, tariffs, quotas, export subsidies and the like 'which policymakers can command in the pursuit of their objectives'.[35] The final element is the institutional objectives of the ministry also influence its capacity. Institutional objectives are usually assigned to a ministry at the time of its establishment as mandates that a ministry is supposed to pursue. However, objectives can change over time depending on the available resources of the ministry and the growth of industries under its jurisdiction. The problem for market liberalization emerges when institutional objectives generate interests, such as protection of the domestic market for the sake of growth or maintenance of employment, which conflict with market liberalization.

Capacity is not strictly the structure of a state if structure is defined as parts that comprise a whole that do not change in a short period of time. One element of capacity, namely, the autonomy of a ministry, changes depending on the issue discussed and the ministry's relationship with the private sector. Autonomy is not constant because a ministry can lose its autonomy if an issue that involves overlapping jurisdiction emerges. A ministry can also regain its autonomy once the issue is resolved.

While two elements of capacity, institutional objectives and policy instruments, are more stable than autonomy, they too change over time. For instance, a ministry may acquire new policy instruments due to increased intervention into an industry in the form of regulations, subsidies or credit allocation. However, given the recent rise in the private sector's demand for deregulation, it is likely that many ministries will lose many of their policy instruments. A ministry may decide to deviate from its original institutional objective, as in the case of the Ministry of Posts and Telecommunications in response to the diversification and development of industries under its jurisdiction. Therefore, capacity can best be characterized as a mixture of structural and variable factors, which varies over time and with respect to different issues. It is a concept designed to facilitate the analysis of market liberalization, rather than a concept to increase our understanding of the nature of the state *per se*.

Autonomy

The autonomy of a ministry is defined as the degree to which a ministry can make decisions on its own without intervention by actors external to the ministry. Autonomy is the most important element of the capacity of a ministry; even if a ministry possesses a wide range of policy instruments and has strong interests in market liberalization, fighting with intervening actors can drain resources and prevent market liberalization.

A ministry's autonomy is limited by other ministries' intervention in its decision-making. There are two general types of issues subject to inter-ministry conflict: newly emerging issues and issues with historically overlapping jurisdictions. Inter-ministry conflict, regardless of the type, delays resolution of international negotiations because the officials of the ministry formally in charge of the negotiation have to engage not only in drafting a palatable offer list but also in fending off intervention and conflict with other ministries.

The first form of inter-ministry conflict occurs when the issue is fairly new, complicated, and the jurisdiction is not established. A typical case is value added networks (VANs), where the terminal equipment belongs to the jurisdiction of MITI but the circuit lines that connect the equipment belong to the jurisdiction of MPT.[36] Because the scope of a ministry's jurisdiction is closely linked to the prestige and power of the ministry, each ministry tries hard not to lose battles over new issue areas for which no clear jurisdiction is defined. For this reason, ministries with plausible functional relations to the issue at stake tend to intervene in the decision-making process of the ministry officially in charge, often attempting to bring the issue under their own control.

The other form of inter-ministry conflict occurs when more than one ministry has legal jurisdiction. Whereas the former type of inter-ministry conflict occurs when the jurisdiction of the issue has not been decided, in this case, there is often no question asked about which ministries have authority. A typical example of this type of conflict occurs when one ministry has jurisdiction over details of regulation, whereas the Ministry of Finance (MOF) takes care of the budgetary aspects of the issue. In such cases, the MOF has the responsibility to intervene. The MOF can exert a decisive influence on the decision-making process if it does not assent to the prospect of greater expenditure or reduced income (which is quite likely from a regulatory change at least in the short run), because of its broad authority and power against other ministries. Therefore, if an issue involves the MOF's interest, the ministry in charge of the substantive issue must take care not to aggravate MOF officials. This effort takes time as well as the energy of the officials in charge of the international negotiation. Furthermore, because there is no guarantee that the MOF will agree on changes in the budget, the involvement of the MOF reduces the predictability of the trade representatives' decision-making process. Such constraints on a ministry's autonomy will cause serious delay at best and impasse at worst in an international negotiation.

Institutional objectives

The degree to which a ministry can pursue market liberalization is also restricted by the extent to which the prospective effect of a market liberalization policy conflicts with its own institutional objectives or interests. Although a ministry cannot reverse or completely ignore Cabinet decisions to liberalize markets, each ministry's institutional objectives, or interests other than market liberalization, may inhibit a ministry from moving promptly to implement the decision.

The institutional objectives, or functions assigned to a ministry, usually derive from the historical context that required the establishment of a specific ministry. Objectives are normally assigned by establishment law or other laws that stipulate the purpose of the ministry's administration. For instance, article four of the Establishment Law of the Ministry of Health and Welfare (MHW) states that 'the mandate of the ministry is to improve social welfare, social security and public health. The responsibility of the ministry lies in national health care and regulation of pharmaceutical affairs and illegal drugs.' Regarding pharmaceuticals manufacturing, the MHW's function is 'to regulate matters pertaining to drugs, quasi-drugs,

29

cosmetics and medical devices so as to ensure their quality, efficacy and safety'.[37] (Note that a ministry can have more than one institutional goal. Presumably, the number of goals within a ministry would reflect the number of bureaus performing various tasks.)

The manner in which an institutional objective interacts with market liberalization issues, however, is not predetermined. The same institutional objective can generate both the ministry's interest in supporting some market liberalizations and interest in refusing other proposed market liberalizations. Which interest the ministry acts upon depends on the nature of the issue being discussed. In pharmaceuticals, for instance, streamlining of regulation promotes market liberalization and achieves drug production at lower cost without risking the safety of production. On the other hand, allowing the automatic transfer of *shōnin* (an official approval to import or manufacture drugs in Japan), as the US requested in the MOSS talks, would have conflicted with the ministry's interest in the safe production of drugs. In sum, institutional objectives which conflict with market liberalization can pose a major obstacle to resolution depending on the seriousness of this conflict.

Policy instruments

A ministry needs effective policy instruments to pursue market liberalization. Policy instruments normally signify tools *applied* by a state to attain policy objectives. Therefore, traditional instruments have included 'licenses, tariffs, quotas, exchange controls, and export insurances' as well as a 'whole range of monetary and fiscal policies'.[38] The underlying assumption here is that these instruments must be *applied* by the state, not withdrawn. However, in the context of market liberalization, the purpose is to undo previous state involvement in the economy.[39] Therefore, 'policy instrument' in cases of market liberalization does not mean the number of options a ministry maintains to control markets, but means the type of pre-existing trade barriers, such as import control by tariffs and quotas, to be lifted. The implication is that without such trade barriers, a ministry might lack policy instruments.

There are two broad types of government-created trade barriers that hinder the access of foreign firms into the Japanese market. The first type of barriers are narrowly defined trade barriers, such as tariffs and import quotas, that discriminate against the entrance of foreign products or services into a market. Another type is market regulation. Normally, market regulations do not constitute entry barriers because they are applied to domestic as well as foreign products and firms. For instance, product standards must be met by all manufacturers. It would appear that the costs in meeting these regulations is the same for all firms.

However, regulation can become a market barrier for several reasons.

First, if a regulation requires imported products to meet a level of quality easily attained by domestic manufacturers but not by foreign manufacturers, it could work as a market barrier. A good example from the MOSS talks is the vertical strength requirements for containerboard boxes. Japanese box manufacturers make products only for Japanese users who must stack boxes high due to a lack of floor space, and do not have to make the costly adjustments of product design required of foreign makers wishing to export to Japan. In addition, a regulation could become a market barrier when the code of a regulation is so complicated that domestic manufacturers have the advantage of more knowledge, especially when such regulations are created and expanded by *shingikai*, councils with which ministers' consult in legislation process, with only Japanese members. Furthermore, if a product has to be tested and approved by an organization and the organization is granted much room for discretionary decision-making, discrimination against foreign products could occur.

There are other types of barriers, though. Non-governmental market barriers are barriers to market entrance not created by the state but caused by the behaviour of the private sector. Because undoing market barriers of this type involves mainly the effort of the private sector, the government has very few policy instruments to liberalize the market. The access of foreign merchants to such markets can remain low even after reduction of governmental market barriers. The primary example of this type of market barrier is vertical *keiretsu* that closely links manufacturers, wholesalers, and retailers. Because this type of obstacle to market access derives mainly from the historical evolution of the private sector and not from governmental initiative, government solutions are likely to be of only limited effectiveness.

Relationship with the private sector

In addition to the three elements of ministerial capacity, a ministry's relationship with the private sector affects the capacity of a ministry to open markets. There are at least four possible forms of ministry–private sector interaction: promotive, post-promotive, restructuring, and regulatory.[40] (Of course, in reality, these relationships are not mutually exclusive and an industry can maintain more than one type of relationship with the state.) The type of relationship between ministry and industry is determined by the nature of technological change in the industry, its growth rate, and the nature of the goods it provides.

A promotive relationship exists when an industry uses or creates dynamic technology and is perceived to have good prospects for rapid growth. If the technological innovation is dynamic, constant investment in basic and applied sciences is needed. The high risk that accompanies massive R&D for technological innovation, plus the conviction that technological innovation always contains some element of a public good, give strong rationale for ministries such as MITI to intervene in the private sector and promote technological change.[41] A ministry adopts favourable treatment of the sector through export subsidies, capital allocation, tariffs on imports, etc. The best examples of promotive relationships include MITI and strategically chosen industries such as steel in the 1950s and 1960s and automobiles and electronics for later periods.

A post-promotive relationship tends to develop when an industry which formerly had a promotive relationship reaches a growth plateau and technological stability, as seen in industries such as automobiles and household electronics. A promotive relationship will shift to a post-promotive relationship, mainly due to rising pressure from the private sector. Firms in an industry which has become competitive will be less dependent on the government for their growth, and see fewer reasons to tolerate bureaucratic intervention which may conflict with the firms' individual production and marketing strategies. These firms will, therefore, begin to demand arms-length relationships with the ministry with which the industry previously maintained a promotive relationship. For example, firms may demand that the ministry reduce control by relaxing conditions for *kyoninkaken*, or granting of approval.

When an industry declines, it can enter into a restructuring relationship with the state. Following the law of diminishing rates of returns, an industry reaches a point where expansion of productive capacity does not raise productivity. While such an industry is likely to face financial difficulty, it needs money to scrap excess productive capacity, relocate employees, or diversify. State intervention is often intended to help an industry to a 'softlanding' through provision of subsidies, credit, and technical expertise.

Finally, a regulatory relationship is a relationship between a ministry and an industry which provides public goods. In this sense, the meaning of regulation in Japan differs from what is generally used in the context of state–market relationships in the US. While regulation in the US often means governmental intervention to maximize the functioning of the market mechanism, with respect to Japan, the term more often means state intervention in the market in order to secure goals which may not be attained by free capitalist competition (often called 'market failures'). (Of course, this type of regulation is not absent from the US.) Typically, a regulatory relationship is most likely to appear in sectors that provide public goods (or negative externalities in case of problems such as pollution).

However, the nature of the output from a sector may not be the only determinant of whether it is considered a public good. While in some nations, goods such as clean air and water are accepted as public goods without question, in Japan, it appears that the goods included in the 'public goods' category seem to vary over time. Although this study does not intend to discuss definitions of 'public good' in detail, it is important to point out that within the context of Japanese political economy, the notion of 'publicness' is often influenced by the competitiveness of the private sector.

Telecommunications is a case in point. When Japanese telecommunications service and equipment production were relatively uncompetitive against their foreign rivals, the sector was seen as providing the public good of a reliable telephone network to all in Japan. The Nippon Telegraph and Telephone Corporation, or NTT, was the government telephone monopoly. However, once the telecommunication business became technologically advanced, such that even new companies could easily provide reliable service under market competition, and the industry began to encompass lucrative businesses such as Value Added Networks (VANs), the government saw telecommunications less as a public good and more as an ordinary business. This change in perception led to the privatization of NTT in 1985.

To be sure, even industries that do not produce products with the nature of public goods – thus the industry's relationship with ministries is not theoretically of the regulatory type – are extensively regulated in Japan. There are three reasons why Japanese markets are tightly regulated. The first reason is that courts do not function to protect consumers against defective products. It is only recently that the Japanese government began considering introduction of a Product Liability bill to ease plaintiffs' burden of proof. Under the current civil code, consumers must prove a producer's liability arising from negligence. Because it is technically difficult for consumers to explain the production process which may have produced defective products, Japanese consumers are discouraged from bringing cases of defective products to courts. Thus, in cases when a defective product causes injury, ministries are often made responsible for not taking precautions against such incidents. As a result, many regulations are created by the bureaucracy to pre-empt being blamed for allowing defective products in the market.

Another reason for extensive regulation is that many ministry officials have a strong sense of paternalism that justifies tight regulation of the Japanese economy. For instance, this sense of paternalism was seen in the case of liberalization of telecommunications equipment. The MPT hesitated in relaxing technical standards for telephones because it assumed that its role was to protect consumers (from making possibly bad choices). At an informal session of the MOSS telecommunication talks, an MPT official said:

due to the long history [of state monopoly], consumers have high expectations for [the quality of] telephones, and thus we need to set technical standards to ensure quality of communication and prevention of cross-talk [in addition to the 'no harm to the network' standard used in the United States]. These technical standards are not intended to exclude foreign countries, and please understand Japan's ideas (*kangaekata*) for consumer protection[42] [translation mine].

Furthermore, while an increasing number of officials in many ministries, including MITI, no longer believe in stiff formal protection of industries, the ideas of free market competition and minimum roles of ministries in the Japanese economy have not become dominant ideas. It appears that a traditional sense of pride among bureaucrats that they know better than businessmen and politicians accounts for the reluctance of bureaucrats to embrace free market ideals. A recent survey taken by the *Nihon Keizai Shimbun* indicated that a majority of senior bureaucrats think they must make policies, not politicians. Among 147 career bureaucrats who answered the questionnaire, close to 70 per cent supported the statement that bureaucrats must make policies instead of politicians (because politicians are unreliable).[43]

The same point was well illustrated in the controversy over rises in fees for public services in the spring of 1994.[44] The government had planned to raise fees on a variety of goods and services. Several top business leaders opposed the rises in a highly public, unusual way, arguing that the weak state of corporate profits did not permit the rises, and that the public sector should adopt belt-tightening measures, as the private sector had done throughout the recession.[45] The Hata cabinet sided with business, and the rises were postponed. Bureaucratic dissatisfaction with the decision was intense. An official of the Ministry of Transport criticized the decision as 'pandering (*ninkitori*) by a minority government'. A Ministry of Construction official remarked that 'it would be a lie if I said that I am not upset'.[46] These statements reflect the underlying assumption held by bureaucrats that such decisions must be made by bureaucrats, even if the decisions conflict with the interests of business and politicians.

Ministries can be divided into two large categories based on the dominant type of the relationship they maintain with the private sector: *kisei kanchō*, or regulator ministries, and *seisaku kanchō*, or policy-oriented ministries. On the one hand, ministries such as the ministries of Health and Welfare, Construction, and Transportation are *kisei kanchō*, maintaining mostly regulatory relationships with the private sector. On the other hand, ministries such as MITI and the Ministry of Finance, are *seisaku kanchō*, which have historically maintained promotive relationships with the private sector.

The relationships between ministries and the private sector are fluid, however. The rate of technological change may slow, leading a ministry which previously maintained a promotive relationship with an industry to shift its relationship to a post-promotive one. If the growth of the industry further slows to the point that it needs restructuring, again, the relationship may change to a restructuring one. In addition, as stated earlier, the definition of a public good which constitutes the grounds for a regulatory relationship can change. What is considered as a public good can be changed into a private good (and possibly, vice versa).[47] If the definition of the nature of the goods involved in an industry changes, presumably for political and technological reasons as well as competitiveness, the regulatory relationship between the sector and the ministry may become irrelevant. In this event, a ministry may try to shift its relationship from a regulatory one to another kind. Moreover, there is also a question of prestige. Because MITI, a powerful symbol of *seisaku kanchō*, has become a highly prestigious ministry, attaining the *seisaku kanchō* label has become an objective itself. Thus many ministries are attempting to shift to promotive relationships with the private sector.

These ministry–private sector relationships can affect the capacity of a ministry in several ways (Table 2.1). First of all, a ministry with a post-promotive relationship with the private sector has the least amount of decision-making autonomy. This is because in post-promotive relationships, the private sector has already become competitive and needs no help from the government. Private firms often have a strong voice in policymaking, or the ability to resist adoption or implementation of government policies. For instance, in 1980, despite a US request, MITI

Table 2.1 Types of relationship and the obstacles they pose for market liberalization

Type of relationship	Primary obstacle	Secondary obstacles	
	Level of autonomy	Interests other than liberalization	Policy instruments
Post-promotive	Low	Few	None other than remaining formal trade barriers
Promotive		Sectoral growth	Favourable treatment of the sector (e.g. capital allocation, tax breaks)
Restructuring		Industrial adjustment	Withdrawal of measures to facilitate adjustment
Regulatory	High	Public goods	Deregulation

could not successfully persuade Japanese automakers to manufacture in the US as a measure to suppress Japanese auto exports to the US.[49] The failure of MITI to persuade the private sector was partially due to the fact that within a post-promotive relationship, the ministry could not achieve its goal without the active cooperation of the sector.

The strong influence of the private sector on decision-making is also seen in promotive relationships, but to a lesser degree. In promotive relationships, a ministry tries to nurture the growth of an industry through utilization of various policy instruments such as tariffs, quotas, subsidies, etc. At the same time, the growth of an industry ultimately depends on private sector initiatives; therefore a ministry needs to cooperate with the private sector and cannot decide on issues autonomously.[48]

On the other end of the scale, regulatory relationships often give wide autonomy to ministries. Because a ministry has a good excuse to extend its authority under the guise of regulating a public good, the ministry is likely to be able to ignore most complaints and appeals from the private sector. A typical case is the relationship between pharmaceutical manufacturers and the Ministry of Health and Welfare. Because the ministry has extensive discretion deriving from its mandate as a guardian of the lives and well-being of the public, firms raise very few complaints or appeals to ministry decisions. The unchallenged autonomy enjoyed by ministries which mainly maintain regulatory relationships with the private sector sometimes derives from a ministry's historical origin. Ministries such as the MHW and Ministries of Construction and Labour were created out of the prewar *Naimushō*, or Home Ministry, which was responsible for tightly policing Japanese society.[50] Thus, the private sector has historically feared the authority of these ministries and has not opposed or intruded into their decision-making.

Restructuring relationships generally entail greater autonomy, as compared to post-promotive and promotive relationships, and lesser autonomy than regulatory relationships. Because a restructured sector is usually financially troubled, it is more dependent on governmental help for credit allocation or even coordination of output among individual firms. A market liberalization of this sector may further harm the industry, which is already likely to be suffering from problems such as excess productive capacity and heavy debt. However, if a ministry decides to accept some market liberalization, the industry has no choice but to accept it for fear that the government will withdraw help completely. Nonetheless, in contrast to the regulatory relationships, the autonomy of the ministry is restricted because the success of effective restructuring also depends on the efforts made by the private sector.

Ministries' interests in market liberalization also tend to correlate with the type of relationship with the private sector. For example, industries with a post-promotive relationship are typically competitive in world markets, so ministries are less likely to oppose market liberalization. Moreover, given the fear of retaliation by trading partners, most ministries are willing to open the markets. As for a promotive relationship, a ministry may hold an interest that is perceived to conflict with market liberalization, namely, nurturing sectoral growth. For the ministries with restructuring relationships with the private sector, their interest in shielding the industries while they implement adjustment may conflict with market liberalization. Finally, in a regulatory relationship, a ministry may oppose market liberalization if the proposed measure harms the quality of public good produced by a ministry's intervention in the private sector.

In addition to autonomy and interest in market liberalization, the type of relationship indicates the range of policy instruments available to ministries. In cases of regulatory relationships, ministries can eliminate regulations in order to expand access to the market. As for promotive relationships, ministries could end any of the means utilized to promote the growth of the sector, such as protective tariffs, and favourable government procurement programmes. Regarding restructuring relationships, again, ministries could withdraw the measure used to restructure and strengthen the sector, such as credit allocation. A problem arises when a ministry has a post-promotive relationship. In a post-promotive relationship, by definition, the measures applied to promote the growth of the sector are no longer in use. If some barriers still exist, the ministry can withdraw them to achieve market liberalization easily. But once these barriers are all gone, ministries possess very few policy instruments. Thus, combined with the competitive strength of the industry, which may discourage a larger market share for foreign firms, the ministry's lack of policy instruments will result in lack of progress in negotiations.

EXPLAINING CASES

In the following chapters, I will use the aforementioned framework in order to explain Japan's foreign economic policymaking. To be sure, the framework presented here does not exclude other approaches. In particular, the international systems-level explanation offers answers to the question *why* Japan responds to *gaiatsu*. However, the theoretical framework offered in this book tries to explain *how* Japan responds. In the following three chapters, instead of offering a rigorous testing of a theory which is not appropriate because of the limited number of cases, I will lay out actual examples of Japan's efforts to open markets with the goal of underscoring the importance of different patterns of policymaking in various ministries.

3

GAIATSU AND THE MOSS TALKS

Scholars of Japanese foreign policy traditionally have seen *gaiatsu*, or foreign pressure, as the major source of policy change.[1] According to this view, the Japanese government often used *gaiatsu* to justify unpopular policy changes. However, some studies recently demonstrated little or no relationship between the presence of *gaiatsu* and Japan's policy initiatives.[2] It may be true that there are policy changes that did not require *gaiatsu*.[3] However, the majority of changes in Japan's trade policy such as voluntary export restraints (VERs) for steel and automobiles, NTT procurement, semiconductor import agreement, etc., were induced by *gaiatsu*. Thus, the effects of *gaiatsu* should not be ignored.

This chapter aims at demonstrating the effect of *gaiatsu* in causing policy changes toward the direction desired by the US. At the same time, it underscores that there is no simple relationship between the presence of *gaiatsu* and Japanese responses. More specially, I will demonstrate that there is no linear relationship between the amount of pressure applied to the Japanese government and the achievement of market liberalization by examining the cases of the MOSS talks. The implication is that we need to look at domestic factors as the major source for determining Japan's trade policy formation.

EFFECTS OF *GAIATSU*

In this section, we will look at the general effect of *gaiatsu* on Japanese policy formation. Leonard Schoppa indicated that *gaiatsu* has the effect of 'alternative specification'. According to Schoppa, *gaiatsu* works to bring about positive outcomes, for example, if 'the Americans ... were able to help pull specific alternatives out of the policy primeval soup and attach them to the already recognized problem of land price explosion'.[4] As Schoppa points out, it is highly likely that specification of a problem and a solution may not work if the issue has never been recognized as a problem, while the strategy is effective if the Japanese are already looking for solutions to a problem that appeared on their policy agenda.

The findings of the MOSS talks indicate that *gaiatsu* is also effective in making ministries aware of certain problems that are faced by firms operating in Japan, both Japanese and foreign, which have never appeared on the policy agenda. The question of how an issue appears on a government's policy agenda is beyond the scope of this book. However, a few patterns of agenda formation can be mentioned here. In the ideal form of democracy, legislators bring issues on to the national policy agenda because their constituents lobby or vote for solutions to problems. If the bureaucracy serves as the main actor in policymaking, as in Japan, then there are two potential sources for ministry officials to derive ideas for new issues. As Chalmers Johnson's 'developmental state' model suggests, officials can autonomously set their own agenda.[5] In addition, officials can recognize problems through daily contact with the private sector, either directly or indirectly through elected legislators.

In ministries such as MITI, which had close contacts with the private sector, officials generally recognize problems faced by domestic industries. However, in ministries such as the MPT and MHW, which have regulatory relationships with most of the industries under their jurisdiction, ministry officials are often slow to recognize problems. Although some of these domestic industries grew over time and existing regulations became obsolete or obstacles to growth, no firm dares to make claims for change.

Under such circumstances, *gaiatsu* worked to bring specific issues to the attention of ministry officials. *Gaiatsu*-induced agenda formation was seen in the cases of pharmaceuticals and telecommunications of the MOSS talks. In these industries, domestic producers wanted current regulations relaxed. For instance, Japanese pharmaceuticals manufacturers wanted the Ministry of Health and Welfare to simplify most of the procedural requirements for such changes as change of address of factories and offices or minor changes of products for a long time before the MOSS talks. According to Japanese telecommunications equipment manufacturers, overprotective requirements for product quality (that is, consumer protection from defective products) such as noise control and high quality voice transmission, could be simplified.

However, because of the regulatory relationships these industries held with their respective ministries, they rarely claimed that there were problems. The regulatory relationships gave these ministries overwhelming discretionary power over whether or not to allow new products to be marketed. When facing these ministries, which could determine the life or death of new products, or even of a manufacturer, few companies ever voiced dissent to the ministries. Coupled with the enormous work load for the officials in the ministry, which left little room for policy change and hence encouraged bureaucratic inertia, the Japanese manufacturers had to wait until *gaiatsu* was exerted if they wanted anything to be changed.[6]

EFFECTIVE AGENDA-SETTING

All things being equal, some agendas more effectively solicit quick responses from the Japanese government than others. The first and most important element for effective agenda setting is to create a concrete list of request items that saves the time and energy of ministry officials, which otherwise would have been spent guessing American objectives in trade talks. As I. M. Destler and Hideo Sato found out in their study of various US–Japanese trade talks in the late 1970s, the US government often makes demands on the Japanese government without specifying the issues of their concern.[7] The lack of issue specification is still common in recent US–Japan trade negotiations. For instance, it appeared that the US – intentionally or unintentionally – did not specify its requests until the last stages of the Framework talks, which broke off without resolution in February 1994.

The case of pharmaceuticals discussed in the MOSS talks is a primary example of successful agenda-setting. Unlike other issues, the US was able to present a concrete list of requests at the first high-level meeting (see Appendix I). These requests consisted of problems faced by both domestic and foreign firms when doing business in Japan.

Effective agenda-setting was made possible by the long history of American companies' presence in the Japanese market. Unlike many high-technology sectors, in which foreign firms have yet to establish their business in Japan, foreign pharmaceuticals companies have a time-honoured business experience in the Japanese market. Prior to the Second World War, foreign pharmaceutical companies exported drugs to Japan. Then, in the postwar period, they either sold licences to local manufacturers or engaged in joint ventures with local manufacturers. More recently, in the late 1970s and 1980s, foreign companies began producing drugs in Japan after making direct investments in plants in Japan, which was allowed after the capital deregulation that began in 1975.

Although there was no formal arena for American manufacturers to discuss problems with Japanese manufacturers, the business experience of the American manufacturers helped the US negotiators from the Treasury Department, who did not possess expertise in pharmaceuticals, to formulate realistic requests that mainly involved problems common to both American and Japanese manufacturers.

By the same token, the US was able to strictly circumscribe the issue of

40

pharmaceuticals into that of streamlining the procedures and rules regarding the marketing of drugs. In other words, the US was able to avoid highly politicized issues, that is, the overhauling of the *yakka* (literally 'drug prices')[8]system, which is a pricing system determined by the MHW for reimbursement under the National Health Insurance system.[9] The *yakka* system seemed to have been causing as much trouble for domestic as foreign manufacturers. Due to this careful agenda setting, the decision was made solely by MHW officials and did not involve political intervention. Given the political strength of the *Nihon Ishikai*, or the Japan Medical Association, which has vested interests in maintaining the *yakka* system because it brings large profits to medical doctors, the US could have met strong domestic opposition to policy change if it had asked to change the system.[10]

However, there were two exceptions on the well-defined pharmaceuticals agenda. The example of kit products is a case in point. A kit is a product that 'combine[s] medicines with their delivery systems in single packages'.[11] The resolution of the issue of kit products was delayed because it was not at all clear what the US wanted to discuss. Reflecting the fact that the US negotiators from the Treasury Department were not experts in the field of pharmaceuticals, when the US asked Japan to streamline the procedures to introduce such products to the Japanese market, both the MHW officials and presumably the Treasury Department officials who represented the US government did not know what the US pharmaceutical industry meant by 'kit products'. After an extensive study on kit products marketed in the US in order to define the product to be discussed, the MHW officials categorized several types of kit products. As a result of this search for a clear definition of the item to be discussed, most time was spent reaching mutual understanding of the product itself throughout the talks.[12]

In addition, the resolution for cases of *shōnin* (manufacturing or import approval) was delayed because neither Japanese nor US officials could identify the nature of the problem.[13] Unlike the case of kit products, the case of *shōnin* transfer involved both issue identification and resolution. Due to a lack of familiarity with the issue by both the US and Japanese governments, the MHW's original response offered at the end of April 1985 did not fully resolve the issue.

In this first response, transfer of *shōnin* was accepted if 'the MHW could confirm that the firm which would succeed the *shōnin* would produce products with the same ingredients'.[14] However, the negotiators later discovered that the real problem lay in cases of 'unfriendly' transfer, when the succeeding manufacturer could not obtain full information and data from the former manufacturer. Thus, the Japanese response on transfer of *shōnin* turned out to be quite unsatisfactory to the US because the MHW's original provision was only possible when the transfer was 'friendly' and there was no problem of obtaining necessary information and data from the previous manufacturer. Thus, the MHW's offer of a resolution to the issue was delayed due to changing perception of the issue at hand, or faulty issue identification.

To be sure, in addition to the problem of issue identification, there was a difference between the way US and Japanese government officials approached the legal aspects of *shōnin* transfer. US officials viewed the issue of approval as part of a proprietary right to be transferred through private contracts. In an interview, Don Abelson of the USTR stated that 'proprietary innovations are the essence of drug manufacturing'. In other words, in the drug industry, the software is the proprietary innovation and the hardware is the marketing. Thus, the main objective of the US government was to protect the property rights of American manufacturers by making *shōnin* transfer easier, so that innovators of drugs could manufacture by themselves in Japan.

In the meantime, MHW officials argued that in Japan, *shōnin* is treated as a matter of public law which is independent of private relationships. They contended that 'the Pharmaceutical Affairs Law, a public law for drug regulation, has no concern with private business relationships or proprietary rights governed by private laws and leaves private disputes for the Patent Law, the Civil Law, etc. Therefore, the *shōnin* does not interfere with patents or proprietary rights'.[15] Thus, the ministry insisted, the transfer must be reprocessed by the government and it would not accept an automatic transfer based on a change in private contracts.

The cases of kit products and *shōnin* transfer were two major exceptions to the well-defined pharmaceuticals agenda. While all of the issues on pharmaceuticals agenda were resolved without much delay, these two issues (and the issue of price-listing, which will be discussed later) consumed a lot of time to reach agreements. Indeed, the MOSS talks are replete with ambiguous lists of requests which considerably reduced Japan's responsiveness.

Another example of a failure to present a good negotiation agenda is the case of electronics talks. First of all, no clear definition existed for the term 'electronics'. Thus, the US could not present relevant requests needed to solicit meaningful concessions from Japan. Then, for more than two months after the MOSS talks began, the US failed to clarify its requests. Moreover, as the US finally presented requests to Japan, most of the requests turned out to be items already implemented, leaving little to discuss. The only substantial issue in the request package was elimination of tariffs on computer parts.[16] But at the time of the MOSS talks, the level of tariffs on computers was already low (Table 3.1) so that the change in tariffs would not have made much difference in terms of US computer exports to Japan.

The reason why the US could not come up with a concrete list of

Table 3.1 Tariffs on computers before the MOSS talks (per cent)

Item	Japan	US
CPUs	4.9	4.3
Peripherals	6.0	4.0
Computer parts	4.2–4.9	4.3

Sources: Japan Tariff Association, *Customs Tariff Schedules of Japan* 1985, *Asahi Shimbun*, 27 April 1985

requests as in the other talks was because the real concern of the US was the semiconductor trade, not overall electronics trade. Semiconductors trade patterns showed the possibility of high trade barriers in Japan, because Japanese firms had dominated the Japanese market while US firms had dominated markets in the US and Europe. Because the MOSS approach did not allow the US to pick up one product, as opposed to a sector, and deal with trade problems specific to the product, the talks on semiconductors needed a different negotiation framework. Once the US began consultations with Japan on semiconductors following the US Semiconductor Industry Association (SIA)'s filing of a Section 301 case in June 1985, the urgency of the issue shifted the attention of negotiators away from the MOSS electronics talks. These talks ended abruptly without any formal conclusion.[17]

The obvious reason why the US requested changes that were already in effect was that the US negotiators lacked good knowledge of the Japanese electronics market. Therefore, the US could not pinpoint the problems that caused insufficient growth of US exports. However, the more substantive reason was that telecommunications, which was the main topic of US–Japan discussions over high technology trade prior to the MOSS talks, was separated from the electronics talks.[18] As a result, the US negotiators lost serious interest in electronics talks.

That most of the US requests made in mid-March were already in effect also means that there were not many formal trade barriers in the electronics market. By formal trade barrier, I mean discrimination against foreign firms regarding market entry *as a result of government policy* to limit competition. The only barrier that existed at the time of the MOSS talks was tariffs, which were eliminated by August 1985. Even before the decision to eliminate the tariffs, though, the level was not high (Table 3.1). Therefore, the MOSS approach, whose objective was to seek the elimination of formal trade barriers, was destined to fail.

Why, then, did the US put the issue of electronics on the MOSS agenda? Most likely, US policymakers felt that there was a 'trade imbalance' which did not reflect the competitiveness of the American electronics industry.

There is no agreement as to what 'trade imbalance' means among policy-makers and even economists. There are several ways to show such an imbalance. The simplest way is to calculate the difference between the value of US exports to Japan and Japanese exports to the US. Alternatively, growth (measured in percentage) of US exports worldwide can be compared to growth of US exports to Japan.[19] Some compare the ratio of total US exports to Japan to total US worldwide exports and the ratio of total US electronics exports to Japan to US worldwide electronics exports (see Table 1.1).

While trade figures are often used to support one's policy preferences, and a set of trade figures do not prove the existence of trade barriers, simple calculation, that is, the crudest measurement, showed an 'imbalance' that was large enough to raise US policymakers' suspicion: Japan imported only $1 billion worth of electronics from the US while exporting $5 billion worth to the US in 1984.[20] These figures seemed contradictory, given that US exports held a 30 per cent share in the world electronics market, while the Japanese share was 20 per cent.[21] Presumably, the suspicion about the trade barriers to the Japanese market, combined with the prospective size of the Japanese electronics market,[22] encouraged the US trade negotiators to put the issue on the MOSS agenda.

However, the inconsistency between the decision to adopt the MOSS format and the absence of governmental trade barriers needs to be explained. What motivated the US administration to negotiate electronics under the MOSS format? In an interview, a former USTR official explained that the answer lay in the internal politics of the US administration. Congress and the private sector had been pressuring the administration to do something about electronics. Despite the fact that the US Congress and the private sector were not too enthusiastic about the MOSS scheme, a faction supporting sectoral discussions emerged within the US administration in 1984. This faction consisted of the Departments of Treasury and State, the Office of Management and Budget (OMB), and the Council of Economic Advisors (CEA). This group wanted a trade negotiation to eliminate all governmental trade barriers modelled after the successful Yen–Dollar Agreement of 1984. Pitted against this faction were the administrative branches emphasizing the importance of results, namely, visible growth of US exports, and not the elimination of trade barriers. This faction consisted of the USTR and the Department of Commerce, or more precisely, US Trade Representative William Brock and Secretary of Commerce Malcolm Baldridge. As a result of bargaining, the former faction won and the MOSS format was adopted. Once the MOSS scheme was adopted, it was necessary to choose sectors to be targeted.

Hence, the negotiation format was chosen before the sector was decided, quite the reverse of what had to be done: choose an issue and find the way to cope with it. The internal politics of the US administration thus generated inconsistency. The US chose an issue which could not be solved by removing governmental barriers.

After several discussions on electronics, the MOSS negotiators came to realize that the real problem in the Japanese electronics market was not traditional trade barriers but 'commercial practices' in the distribution system, as referred to by the interim report of the MOSS talks.[23] This 'commercial practice' does not mean some sort of *dangō*, or bid-rigging, seen in other industries. It is rather a special distribution network developed by Japanese computer manufacturers.

Before small business computers began to be produced on a mass scale, sales of computers were simply done through the manufacturers themselves or through computer dealers capitalized by these manufacturers. However, when small business computers became more popular in the mid-1970s, the Japanese computer distribution system became rather complex, as some 300 dealers which were specialized to develop software to meet end users' needs suddenly emerged.[24] Large manufacturers owned many of these dealers, although there were some independent dealers of computer hardware. By developing a large distribution network, successful manufacturers such as NEC and Fujitsu expanded their market share by meeting the specific demands of users. They also kept up their business by establishing reliable maintenance systems.[25] Under such a system, it was extremely difficult for foreign firms to break into the established distribution network unless they possessed thorough knowledge of users' peculiar needs as well as the trustworthiness to convince buyers that they would provide a reliable maintenance system.

Because the realization of the commercial practices came rather late, and also because the nature of the problem did not necessarily fit the purpose of the MOSS talks, it was not thoroughly discussed at that time. But this problem remained one of the largest obstacles for foreign exporters, and it was formally addressed in the Structural Impediments Initiative (SII) talks that began in the fall of 1989. The effectiveness of the SII talks is yet to be seen. However, at the very least, the format of the negotiation to overhaul the structure of the Japanese (and the US) economy was better suited to the issue of the distribution system than was the MOSS scheme.

NON-LINEAR RELATIONSHIP BETWEEN *GAIATSU* AND RESULTS

The four cases of the MOSS talks indicate that there is no direct, linear relationship between the amount of pressure applied to the Japanese government and market opening (Table 3.2). Very strong pressure was applied in the cases of telecommunications equipment and forest products. Relatively less pressure was applied in the case of pharmaceuticals and electronics. However, the degree of achievement was high in the cases of telecommunications and pharmaceuticals, while talks on forest products and electronics produced smaller achievement.

A case of high pressure and high achievement: telecommunications

The case of telecommunications was obviously a top priority for the US because of the urgency set forth by the new telecommunications system which was to take effect on 1 April 1985, only three months after the Reagan–Nakasone meeting on 2 January. The new telecommunications system was designed to privatize then publicly owned Nippon Telegraph and Telephone Corporation (NTT), and at the same time, to liberalize the telecommunications market so private companies could begin telecommunications businesses.

The deadline worked to make telecommunications a top priority and successfully served as a vehicle for applying pressure on the Japanese government. The evidence indicates that the US strongly pressed for quick resolution during the first phase of the talks on wired telecommunications. For instance, at the first high-level meeting on telecommunications held on 29 January, Deputy US Trade Representative Michael Smith stated that the talks on telecommunications were the most important among the four sectors in the MOSS talks and that the success of the telecommunications talks would be a 'litmus test'. In the same meeting, both the US and Japanese negotiators acknowledged that 1 April marked a deadline for the telecommunications negotiation.[26] A US Department of Commerce document notes that 'these issues [of telecommunications terminal equipment and network services] were put on the "fast-track" because they were tied to Japanese legislation that would become effective on 1 April'.[27] Also, when US Trade Representative William Brock visited Tokyo from 10 to 12 February, he stated that because telecommunications was the 'symbolic' issue among the MOSS talks, it must be solved first. That the US negotiators placed the highest priority on telecommunications (and forest products, in a different fashion) was conveyed through the US Embassy in

Table 3.2 Amount of pressure and achievement

Cases	Amount of pressure	Achievement
Telecommunications	High	High
Forest products	High	Low
Pharmaceuticals	Low	High
Electronics	Low	Low

Tokyo so that the Japanese side was fully aware of the relative importance of the issue.[28]

The US not only referred repeatedly to the 1 April deadline in order to solicit a quick response from the Japanese government, but also used various forms of pressure. For example, toward the end of February, frustrated with the slow progress of the talks on telecommunications, Secretary of Commerce Malcolm Baldridge announced that unless Japan presented concrete plans, he would postpone Undersecretary of Commerce Lionel Olmer's visit to Japan scheduled for the first week of March.[29]

The second phase of the talks on wireless telecommunications began in June 1985. In contrast to the first phase, the second phase lacked an explicit deadline, which slowed the process of the talks somewhat at the beginning. This was apparent when the US and Japan spent the summer after the first phase exchanging information on the radio systems of Japan and the US, rather than negotiating on specific requests.

However, the relaxed mood of the second phase of the talks disappeared quickly when calls for retaliatory action emerged in the Congress. The protectionism in the Congress that arose in early 1985 was intensified during the second phase of the telecommunications talks. As early as 5 March 1985, the Electronic Industries Association (EIA) began appealing to the USTR for application of 'Section 301' of the Trade Act to telecommunications exports from Japan and other developed countries.[30] The US legislators' frustration was aggravated when the US bilateral trade deficit with Japan for 1984 reached the unprecedented level of 34 billion US dollars.[31] By the end of March the Senate adopted a non-binding resolution calling for increased market access in Japan, which was sponsored jointly by Senators John H. Danforth (R) and David L. Boren (D).[32] Even after the first phase of the talks was concluded at the end of March, the move toward adopting retaliatory bills continued within the Congress. By October, the Congress began considering retaliatory legislation ('Telecommunications Trade Bill of 1985') that was to limit Japanese exports of telecommunications equipment to the US.[33] In a letter to Foreign Minister Abe Shintarō dated 21 November, Secretary of State George Shultz warned that the 'pressures for protectionist actions will increase even as we enter the new year'.[34]

The Japanese negotiators were extremely alarmed by the protectionist movement within the US Congress. Deputy Minister for Foreign Affairs Teshima Reishi showed strong concern over the surge of protectionism against Japanese exports and emphasized the necessity of resolving the remaining issues at the MOSS meeting on 21 August in Hawaii.[35] Japanese negotiators engaged in the telecommunications talks were particularly concerned when the telecommunications sector was specifically targeted by the Congress toward the end of the year. As several MPT officials acknowledged, the credible threat of retaliation from the US Congress against flooding Japanese exports, telecommunications equipment in particular, throughout 1985 prompted the MPT to work harder toward resolution. Movement toward adoption of protectionist bills, as one official noted, increased the sense of urgency among the MPT officials.

The achievement of the talks on telecommunications seems to correlate with the high pressure exerted on the Japanese government. As for wired telecommunications (first phase), Japan agreed to all of the US requests by the end of March 1985. As for wireless telecommunications (second phase), all requests were met by early January 1986 (excepting only partial resolution of a few issues such as technical standards for radio transmitters and third-party radio services). There is no doubt that the credible threat was a major concern among the Japanese officials. For instance, the fact that Vice-Minister of Posts and Telecommunications Koyama Moriya and the US government decided on the visit of Special Assistant to the President Gaston J. Sigur, Jr. on the last day of March 1985 to publicize the achievement of the telecommunications talks indicated the serious concern of the Japanese as well as the US negotiators about flaming protectionism in the US Congress. Also, in December, writing to Undersecretary of Commerce for International Trade Bruce Smart, Koyama warned that their efforts made in the MOSS talks 'will be negated' should protectionist bills such as 'the Telecommunications Trade Bill of 1985' pass the US Congress.[36]

A case of high pressure and modest achievement: forest products

Although *gaiatsu* has almost always been necessary for Japan to start dealing with a new issue, the amount of pressure that the US exercises and the extent to which Japan opens its markets have not been related linearly. This is exemplified by the fact that during the MOSS talks, Japan failed to eliminate tariffs on forest products, even though the US had strong interests in the liberalization of the forest products market and applied much pressure.[37]

It was clear that the US considered forest products to be the most important issue, along with telecommunications. In an interview with *Sekai Shūhō*, Undersecretary of Commerce Lionel H. Olmer said forest products were among the items of highest concern to the US.[38] Also, past US–Japan trade negotiations indicated that tariff reductions on wood products have been 'at the top of the US government tariff request list for over two years'.[39]

The US government took every opportunity to express its concern over tariffs on forest products and met strong opposition from the Japanese every time. For instance, at a foreign ministers' meeting which was held parallel to the 2 January 1985 Nakasone–Reagan meeting which initiated

48

the MOSS talks, the US demanded that Japan reduce tariffs on forest products and Foreign Minister Abe Shintarō firmly refused it. Also, when the leaders of the LDP met with US Ambassador Michael Mansfield on 17 January, LDP Secretary-General Kanemaru Shin told the Ambassador that the reduction of tariffs on forest products is 'difficult because maintenance of the forestry industry is extremely important to national security as well as for the purpose of anti-flood and anti-erosion'.[40] Responding to the repeated demand to reduce tariffs on forest products at a meeting with US Vice-President George Bush, Vice-President of the LDP Nikaidō Susumu said 'there is a strong opposition [to the reduction of the tariffs] within Japan and the issue is so politicized that it is difficult to [accept your request and] implement the reduction'.[41] Again, on 28 January, Foreign Minister Abe repeated the virtual refusal of the reduction of tariffs at a meeting with US undersecretary level delegates.[42]

In spite of the strong pressure to reduce tariffs on forest products that was exercised from the very beginning of the MOSS talks, the Japanese government did not even express the possibility of tariff reduction until it announced the seventh External Economic Measures package on 9 April. In this package, however, Japan simply stated that the tariff reductions would be made 'approximately from the third year'.[43] Not only was the interpretation of this phrase left ambiguous, but also, the size of the reduction was not specified. The US had to wait until the very last day of the MOSS talks to hear Japan's plan. On 8 January 1986, at the informal meeting held after the plenary meeting, Japan finally offered a concrete schedule of tariff reduction. To the disappointment of the US officials, the offer was far from total elimination of tariffs (see Table 3.3).

To be sure, it is not true that *gaiatsu* had no effect on the evolution and outcome of the talks. Pressure from the US was necessary to put the issue on the bilateral negotiation agenda. In response to the pressure, Prime Minister Nakasone decided to consider a compensation programme to prepare for tariff cuts, even though Japan's response to proposed tariff elimination was absolute refusal at the beginning. Thus, persistent

Table 3.3 Forest product tariff reductions schedule (percentage)

Item	January 1986	April 1987	April 1988
Plywood	15.0–20.0	12.5–17.5	10.0–15.0
Particleboard	12.0	8.0	
Fibreboard	5.2	3.5	
Laminated lumber	10.0	8.0	

Source: The Forestry Agency

pressure from the US accounts for the limited change. But the case of forest products, together with the case on pharmaceuticals, suggests that the amount of pressure exercised by the US and the degree of Japan's responsiveness do not have a linear relationship. This indicates that an examination of mechanisms which filter *gaiatsu* is needed.

A non-linear relationship between the amount of pressure and outcomes is also apparent in the talks over other issues discussed within the forest products talks. While the issue of tariffs on forest products received high pressure and produced a modest outcome, the other issues on forest products received relatively low pressure and produced fairly high achievement. The negotiation history of the talks on paper products, which were also included in the talks on forest products, indicates that the US did not apply much pressure. For instance, while forest products had always been regarded as one of the priority US issues, the Japanese government was not informed that paper products were also included in the talks until the end of January. Moreover, in the negotiation process, discussion of tariffs on forest products always came first and paper products were discussed as a matter of secondary importance. Nonetheless, Japan was quick to reduce tariffs on paper products. In addition, Japan solved the issues of standards and approval without much problem. Partly because of their unimportance compared to tariffs, and partly because of their highly technical nature, these issues were rarely discussed by the US and Japanese high-level negotiators. The issue was handed down to the experts' meetings. By mid-December, virtually all issues on standards were resolved.[44]

A case of low pressure and high achievement: pharmaceuticals

What is intriguing about the talks on pharmaceuticals is the clear lack of pressure, but the effective resolution of the issues. Although President Reagan explicitly named pharmaceuticals as one of the sectors to be discussed for increased market access at the Reagan–Nakasone meeting of 2 January 1985, the US interest in the sector was never emphasized throughout the MOSS talks. Good evidence of low interest on the US side is that the US took a long time to appoint its representative for the negotiation.[45] It was not until March 12 – almost two months after the first meetings for telecommunications and forest products were held – that the talks on pharmaceuticals were opened.[46]

The reason why the US did not exert much pressure on the Japanese government was clear; there was no trade 'imbalance' between the US and Japan. In fact, until 1985, Japanese pharmaceutical exports to the US had never been very large (Table 3.4). As a result, there was no rise of protectionism within the US against pharmaceuticals exports from Japan in contrast to the cases of telecommunications and electronics.

50

Table 3.4 US–Japan pharmaceuticals trade before the MOSS talks
(million US dollars)

	1982	1983	1984	1985
US exports to Japan	450	526	534	567
Japanese exports to the US	n/a	103	92	98

Source: Compiled with data from OECD, *Foreign Trade by Commodities*, 1982–85

The real reasons that the US was interested in the pharmaceuticals market in Japan were twofold. First, there was potential for increased US sales.[47] Moreover, sales of products produced with the latest technology in the Japanese market were viewed as of critical importance to US companies. Although the US pharmaceuticals industry was still the most competitive in the world market, there was fear among US manufacturers that Japan would catch up with the US soon and would become the world's leader in terms of innovation, as had already happened in many other key industries. Therefore, the US manufacturers wanted procedures streamlined and simplified in order to introduce new drugs in Japan before the new technology to produce them diffused to Japanese manufacturers.[48]

Despite the low degree of *gaiatsu*, the Japanese government succeeded in reaching resolutions to the requests effectively. Except for transfer of *shōnin*, the first set of requests presented on 12 March was resolved by 25 April. As for the second set of requests presented on 20 August, all except for kit products and regular price listing were resolved by November.

A case of low pressure and low achievement: electronics

In the talks on electronics, the US applied little pressure on the Japanese government. The relaxed atmosphere of the early stage of the negotiation was characterized by MITI Councillor Wakasugi Kazuo as 'proceeding with a good atmosphere'.[49] Several pieces of evidence show that the US did not pay much attention to the electronics issue. The first evidence is that the first meeting was not held until mid-March, two and a half months after the Nakasone–Reagan meeting. Moreover, as mentioned earlier, the definition of 'electronics' was unclear. Furthermore, the list of requests the US finally presented on 18 March did not have much substance. Most of the requests were resolved by the time the MOSS talks began (except for the tariffs on computer parts).

In August 1985, the rise of protectionism in the US Congress did force

Japanese negotiators to reveal the decisions on computer tariff reductions that they had made much earlier.[50] However, by September, both the lack of interest on the side of the US and the resulting lack of pressure on the Japanese government led the talks to end without much achievement. Although the largest obstacles to the electronics trade were not tariffs but exclusive commercial practices (which MOSS negotiators came to realize later in the talks), the talks on electronics failed to deal with the issue effectively. These talks ended suddenly without much achievement other than the reduction of tariffs – unilateral reduction of tariffs on Central Processing Units (CPUs) and peripherals in addition to mutual reduction of tariffs on computer parts – once the US Semiconductor Industry Association (SIA) filed an 'unfair trade' complaint to the USTR and requested an investigation on Japan's semiconductor trade, thereby highlighting the issue of semiconductors.[51]

CONCLUSION

Although extrapolation of the findings in the MOSS talks must be done carefully because of the limited number of cases, the cases we have seen in this chapter signify some rules related to the effect of *gaiatsu* on Japan's responses. The first rule is that because of the international structure, US pressure will produce changes to the direction desired by the US government. However, as we have seen in the four cases of the MOSS talks, the amount of pressure applied to the Japanese government and the degree of achievement do not correlate. As seen in the case of forest products, strong pressure does not always lead to positive outcomes. Conversely, MOSS pharmaceutical talks suggest that talks that lack explicit pressure do not always lead to lack of achievement.

Another rule is, if the pressuring party has clear negotiation agendas, *gaiatsu* works to give clear indicators to the opponent. This 'indicator effect' is seen in three cases of the MOSS talks, namely, telecommunications, pharmaceuticals, and forest products. However, as in the electronics talks, if the negotiating partner fails to provide a meaningful set of requests, the Japanese government will lose its direction and as a result, will not respond effectively.

In addition, the cases of the MOSS talks give mixed evidence for the idea that *gaiatsu* does not matter much and the Japanese government liberalizes its market only when the liberalization is already underway due to domestic factors.[52] As regards telecommunications, it is true that there already existed a significant trend toward liberalization in the Japanese telecommunications market by the time the MOSS talks took place. The clearest example is, of course, the legislation to privatize NTT and liberalize the telecommunications services and equipment markets which passed in the previous year. As the GAO's review of the MOSS talks states,

52

'the *timing* and trade environment were ripe for these [telecommunications] MOSS negotiations' (emphasis mine).[53] By contrast, the pharmaceuticals market, which was significantly deregulated as a result of the MOSS talks, was far from liberalized when the MOSS talks began.

Finally, the MOSS talks indicate that there is weak linkage between heavy dependence of Japanese exports on the US market and the effectiveness of pressure in the form of protectionist threats. The evidence discussed above indicates that *gaiatsu* was effective in the telecommunications talks because Japanese telecommunications equipment manufacturers depended heavily on the US market for exports and as a result, they were highly sensitive to the rising threat of protectionism in the US. By contrast, the case of electronics suggests that the Japanese government will fail to be responsive even if the industry at issue is heavily dependent on the US market, if there is no list of meaningful requests. The reason for uneven responses may derive from varying capacity of ministries in charge of negotiations.

If the proposition 'if heavy market dependence, then *gaiatsu* is effective' is wrong, neither is the obverse of the proposition – namely, if low market dependence, then *gaiatsu* is less effective – necessarily true. In the case of the pharmaceuticals, which did not exhibit heavy dependency on the US market, *gaiatsu* was not expected to have much effect. Nevertheless, the Japanese government resolved most of the issues.

These cases suggest that *gaiatsu* works only under particular conditions. The cases indicate that the Japanese government may decide to give limited concession under maximum pressure or open its markets with minimum pressure. While we cannot deny the effectiveness of *gaiatsu* in soliciting an undefined 'reaction' from the Japanese state, the above cases suggest that there is a need to explore conditions under which the Japanese government can effectively respond to *gaiatsu*.

4

THE THREE ELEMENTS
OF THE CAPACITY
OF MINISTRIES

In the last chapter, we saw that *gaiatsu* causes changes in Japanese economic policies. However, this book casts doubt upon an automatic link between *gaiatsu* and Japan's responses. As Kent E. Calder has pointed out, Japan responds to international pressure 'erratically, unsystematically and often incompletely'.[1] Thus, the questions we must ask are how and under what conditions *gaiatsu* works to cause these changes.

In Chapter 2, we saw that the capacity of ministries offers a hint to understanding Japan's varying responses to *gaiatsu*. Based on this theoretical framework, we will examine how the capacity of ministries actually affects Japan's foreign economic policymaking through the cases of the MOSS talks.

This chapter will deal with the three elements of ministerial capacity, that is, autonomy, policy instruments, and institutional objectives. The focus will be the capacity of the four ministries that were the central decision-making bodies in the MOSS talks. The goal is to underscore the importance of ministerial capacity in achieving market liberalization. At the same time, I will point out that the lack of any one of the elements of ministerial capacity can lead to slow change of policy or no change at all.

AUTONOMY OF MINISTRIES

As stated earlier, autonomy is the most important element of the capacity of a ministry because fighting with intervening actors consumes resources which otherwise would have been used to resolve pending market liberalization problems. Overall, two cases that demonstrated high achievement – pharmaceuticals and telecommunications – showed that the ministries in charge had high autonomy. On the other hand, the cases with little

54

achievement – forest products and electronics – indicate that the ministries in charge had relatively low autonomy.

However, the ministries that were in charge of pharmaceuticals and telecommunications were not without problems regarding their autonomy. In this section, we will examine issues within the pharmaceuticals and telecommunications talks that ran up against the problem of ministerial autonomy. (Because the autonomy of the Forestry Agency and MITI was challenged by their relationship with the private sector, not by other ministries, we will come back to the cases of forest products and electronics in the next chapter.)

Pharmaceuticals and telecommunications represent two types of inter-ministry conflicts. The first type was seen in the case of pharmaceuticals; the MHW faced the MOF's intervention due to the fact that the issue involved historically overlapping jurisdictions. Another type was seen in the case of telecommunications; the MPT faced MITI's intervention because the telecommunications sector was a newly emerging sector that involved cutting-edge technology. In cases of newly emerging sectors that involve complicated technology, jurisdiction is difficult to establish under a single ministry. As a result, more than one ministry will try to put the issue under its control.

The MHW vs. the MOF

Generally speaking, the MHW could respond to most of the US requests on pharmaceuticals because the issue of pharmaceuticals was subject to a relatively low level of inter-ministry conflict. Unlike other high-technology issues where the sector itself had emerged only recently, causing ministerial conflict over a new sphere of influence, the pharmaceuticals sector is clearly under the jurisdiction of the MHW. Thus, the US requests involving little inter-ministerial conflict, such as testing and test data, change of address application procedures, and transparency of decision-making reached resolution without much delay.

However, where the National Health Insurance system was involved and if the issue involved the prospect of increased expenditure from the national budget, the Ministry of Finance (MOF) was likely to intervene in the policymaking process. Therefore, because regular price listing, that is, addition of prices of new drugs to the *yakka* list, was related to increased reimbursement from the national account, the US request naturally drew the interference of the MOF into the MHW's decision-making process. This caused the MHW to delay its offer of a resolution, because it had trouble persuading the MOF to accept the change.

Although officials from MOF did not represent the Japanese government at the pharmaceuticals talks, and thus lacked a formal position in the policymaking process, implicit pressure from the MOF against any change in the system of price listing was felt among the MHW officials.[2] The reasons for this resistance were twofold. First, regular price listing meant more frequent listing of expensive new drugs, which would cause pressure to expand national health insurance expenditures. The MOF, which compiles the national budget, is likely to resist increased expenditures regardless of the purpose. Moreover, regular price listing would reduce the power of the MOF over the MHW. When price listing was irregular, the MHW officials had to ask for a 'special favour' from the MOF every time a new drug was to be listed. However, if the listing were to be regularized, such case-by-case exercises of authority would no longer be necessary, thus diminishing the imbalance of power between the MHW and the MOF. Thus, while negotiating with the US, the MHW had to deal with the reluctant MOF, which delayed the resolution of the issue.

The MPT vs. MITI

The MPT eventually succeeded in resolving most of the US requests on telecommunications. However, much to the frustration of the US officials, some issues took a long time to resolve. One of these issues was type two telecommunications business, or Value-Added-Networks (VANs).[3] (The other two difficult issues, technical standards and third-party radio service, will be discussed later.) The US demanded that the approval procedures be relaxed, but the MPT procrastinated in meeting the demand until the very end of the first stage of the talks. To be sure, the delay was not due to domestic private sector opposition. The reason why the MPT took time to reach resolution was because the MPT's autonomy was seriously challenged by MITI.

Telecommunications is a primary example of a new industry that invited intense inter-ministry struggle over its jurisdiction. Because telecommunications involved roughly two pre-existing domains ruled by the MPT and MITI, with the former administering the telephone network and the latter in charge of terminal equipment, particularly computers, to be connected to the network, these ministries naturally insisted on their jurisdiction. In addition, the growing importance of telecommunications in the Japanese and world economy drew these ministries into life-and-death 'VAN wars' to assert their control.[4] Therefore, from the point of view of Japanese ministries, control over telecommunications was vital if the ministry was to maintain an influential role *vis-à-vis* the private sector.

However, the VAN wars were almost over by the time the MOSS talks began. The MPT had succeeded in drafting and then passing the Telecommunications Business Law, making it clear in Kasumigaseki (location of the ministries and agencies) that the MPT would oversee the newly liberalized telecommunications businesses. Although a representative or two from MITI were present at the telecommunications discussions throughout the MOSS talks, they played a role no larger than that of officials from the Ministry of Foreign Affairs, which played the role of coordinator.

The outcome of the VAN wars determined that the MPT had the authority to take charge of telecommunications in general. But the fact that the formal war was over did not mean that MITI was happy with the way it was settled. When the MOSS talks began, MITI launched a clandestine attack on the MPT to reduce its discretionary power. Although MITI lacked legitimacy in engaging itself in the MOSS talks on telecommunications, its efforts compromised the MPT's autonomy.

MITI made use of the fact that it shared an interest in the liberalization of the market with the US.[5] This was possible when the US revealed that it was not satisfied with the provision made in the Telecommunications Business Law regarding VANs. The new law stipulated that special type two telecommunications business, or 'large-scale' VANs, was subject to a registration requirement, which was stricter than the simple notification requirement for smaller-scale general type-two telecommunications business. Because the US foresaw a large market share once American firms with strong competitiveness and expertise were admitted to the market, it wanted to reduce the risk of exposing US suppliers to the MPT's discretion, which might work as a non-tariff barrier. The US repeatedly requested reduction in the scope of the MPT to exercise its discretionary power.

This US interest in blocking the MPT's effort to expand its discretionary power converged with MITI's interest to limit the MPT's control over the emerging information industry. From MITI's point of view, the registration requirement for special type-two telecommunications business represented MPT's desire for expanded jurisdiction. Thus, as an MPT official complained in an interview, MITI tried to influence the course of the talks by utilizing various measures, such as stacking deliberation councils with members who would represent MITI's views, and leaks to journalists and to the US negotiators, even though MITI was not an official representative in the MOSS telecommunications talks. MITI is also said to have leaked crucial information to the US through providing an internal MITI-supervised trade report called *Progress Report 1984* which was compiled by a group of trade specialists (the US–Japan Trade Study Group) which was supervised by JETRO (an organization affiliated with MITI).[6]

The MPT's frustration caused by MITI's intervention in the decision-making process was also seen when Koyama, at a press conference, angrily claimed that an American negotiator said that MITI told the American negotiators to complain to the MPT that 'the provision for the general type-two telecommunications business only allowed 500 circuits and did not have much room for serious business'. According to Koyama,

MITI also informed the Americans that 'the supplementary decision made by the Diet over the distinction between special and general type two telecommunications business could be easily neglected'. Based on MITI's advice, Americans demanded that the stricter registration requirement for the special type-two telecommunications business be relaxed.[7]

MITI's clandestine effort put the MPT on the defensive and made it difficult to accept the US requests. To agree with the US demand to revise the law was difficult not only because revision would take place before the law's implementation (scheduled for 1 April 1985), but also because the MPT would lose face against MITI, which had grudgingly accepted the MPT-drafted law. The MPT had to keep a hard-line attitude until it succeeded in putting a lid on MITI's complaints. However, faced with the strong US interest as well as continuous intervention by MITI, the MPT offered a compromise. The MPT offered a flexible interpretation of criteria – 500 circuits 1200 bits per second (BPS) – used to categorize special and general type-two telecommunications to allow high-speed VANs to be categorized as general type-two telecommunications business. In this interpretation, even if the information exchange was a high-speed exchange which transmitted more than 1200 BPS, if the exchange used only one circuit, it would be counted as one circuit. This compromise enabled VANs that were large scale but nonetheless used fewer than 500 circuits to be categorized as general type-two telecommunications. At the same time, the MPT avoided loss of face because the compromise avoided change in the basic framework of the new law which required registration for the special type-two telecommunications business.[8]

This compromise finally satisfied MITI and the MPT regained its autonomy without losing face against MITI. MPT, which finally overcame MITI's intervention at the end of March, decided on automatic approval of applications for special type-two telecommunication business within fifteen days.[9] (The 'automatic approval' meant the virtual elimination of the registration requirement.)

POLICY INSTRUMENTS

The four cases of the MOSS talks indicate that a range of policy instruments was necessary in order to carry out market liberalization. The liberalization of the pharmaceuticals market was made easy by the MHW's vast policy instruments. The case of telecommunications shows that the MPT had a variety of policy instruments, such as regulation of type-two telecommunications business. The difference between the MPT's policy instruments and the MHW's policy instruments was that the MPT had just acquired its instruments the year before, by passing new laws, which had not yet been implemented by the time of the MOSS talks. The policy instruments could be used for two opposing goals. If the MPT continued to possess the instruments, the telecommunications market would be highly regulated, and thus closed. If the MPT decided to give in to the US demands and relax some of the regulations, the market would be more open.

The two remaining cases of the MOSS talks indicate that policy instruments are necessary, but not sufficient conditions for successful market liberalization. The case of electronics indicates that MITI had few policy instruments in its relation to the electronics sector; thus, MITI failed to offer meaningful concessions. As for the talks on forest products, while the Forestry Agency had policy instruments to utilize, politicization of the issue presented the Agency from making tariff cuts as large as those demanded by the US government.

The MHW and the pharmaceutical sector

The MHW's policy instruments with respect to the pharmaceuticals industry were quite extensive. The reason why the MHW had a vast range of instruments as regards market liberalization was because the pharmaceuticals market was tightly regulated at the time of the MOSS talks. Seen from the American perspective, the tight regulation had to be undone to reduce the cost of production for American firms in Japan.

The tight regulation of the pharmaceuticals market was in part derived from the function of the MHW. The MHW functions as a doorkeeper to the pharmaceuticals market in Japan by utilizing *shōnin*,[10] or manufacturing or import approval, and *kyoka*,[11] or a licence to manufacture or import. Through these two instruments, the MHW reserves all authority to decide which drugs should enter the market. Over time, the MHW made the procedures for granting *shōnin* and *kyoka* unreasonably complex, as an attempt to avoid recurrence of serious side-effects of drugs such as thalidomide that occurred in the late 1960s and early 1970s.[12] The US asked Japan to streamline the excessively complex regulation system to reduce the large costs incurred by foreign manufacturers due to complicated procedures and quality control.

In addition to *shōnin* and *kyoka*, price listing is also an important policy instrument of the MHW. By determining *yakka*, or the official price of a drug, the MHW affects a manufacturer's profitability. Although the criteria for determining the price for a new drug seem objective – new innovation in the world, higher effectiveness, or low profitability (at least one of these must be met to be priced higher than an existing drug with similar effectiveness, pharmacological action, and chemical structure) – there is much room for

59

discretion by MHW officials. By interpreting these three criteria, the MHW can always give low prices to newly approved drugs.

The MPT and the telecommunications sector

Possible availability of policy instruments was important in determining the MPT's capacity to offer meaningful market liberalization. Prior to NTT's privatization, the MPT had few policy instruments to affect the activity of the private sector. In 1981, the MPT granted only 147 approvals for various businesses, which was far fewer than many other ministries and agencies (Table 4.1). This was mainly because NTT was the *de facto* 'ministry' in charge of development of the network, and the MPT played a role of 'liaison between NTT and the Diet'.[13] As a monopsonistic buyer, although NTT itself did not manufacture Customer Premises Equipment (CPE, or 'interconnect equipment' in the US), it had an effective 'policy instrument' to affect the private sector by determining which firms would enter and succeed in the telecommunications equipment market. Because of its lack of policy orientation and expertise in comparison to NTT, the MPT was a nominal supervisor of NTT, nicknamed the *Kasumigaseki shutchōjo*, or 'Kasumigaseki branch office', of NTT.

However, the power of NTT was about to be reduced at the time of the

Table 4.1 Number of approval grants in 1981

Approving agent	Number of approvals
Prime Minister's Office (except for the following three agencies)	187
National Police Agency	190
Science & Technology Agency	155
Environment Agency	115
Ministry of Justice	151
Ministry of Foreign Affairs	46
Ministry of Finance	971
Ministry of Education	246
Ministry of Health and Welfare	874
Ministry of Agriculture, Forestry and Fisheries	1,446
MITI	2,080
Ministry of Transport	2,203
MPT	147
Ministry of Labour	530
Ministry of Construction	620
Ministry of Home Affairs	84
Total	10,045

Source: Kawakita Takao, *Tsūsan Yūsei Senso*, p. 102, originally compiled by the Management & Coordination Agency, Prime Minister's Office

MOSS talks by its 1 April 1985 privatization. The consequence of this decline of NTT's power was an increased number of policy instruments for the MPT to affect the telecommunications market. In the new Telecommunications Business Law, the MPT had acquired effective instruments to determine which companies and what products would enter the telecommunications market. For instance, the MPT could establish several entrance barriers for telecommunications service and equipment suppliers, through registration requirements for special type-two telecommunications business, and a large number of technical standards.

The object of the MOSS talks was to reduce the number of such policy instruments the MPT had acquired. The new policy instruments allowed the MPT to put telecommunications business under tight regulation. However, the US wanted the telecommunications market to be as open as possible and thus demanded that the MPT's new policy instruments be reduced.

MITI and the electronics sector

MITI did not have effective policy instruments as regards the electronics market, other than eliminating remaining tariffs. Thus, MITI was unable to make meaningful offers to the US. To be sure, this is not to say that MITI has become a helpless ministry without policy instruments to control the private sector, as is often claimed. The truth is, MITI remains one of the most powerful ministries in terms of the number of *kyoninkaken*, or approval grants, it holds. As we see in Table 4.1, in 1981, the number of *kyoninkaken* held by MITI was second only to the Ministry of Transport. Today, the number of *kyoninkaken* held by MITI is highest among all the ministries and agencies, while the number has been reduced over time.[14]

If *kyoninkaken* were the primary policy instruments for MITI to *regulate* the private sector, then policy instruments such as tariffs and quotas were the means for MITI to *promote* the growth of domestic industries during the high-growth period. These instruments were applied to industries specified by MITI as strategically important to the national economy such as steel, automobiles, and computers. However, with the maturation of these industries and the results of several rounds of multilateral trade negotiations, explicit measures to promote domestic industries (which also protected domestic firms from foreign competition) largely disappeared over the last two decades. Therefore, while not losing all of its policy instruments to control the private sector, MITI has few instruments to employ as regards market liberalization of mature industries such as electronics.

The FA and the forest products sector

In the case of forest products, the FA had a number of policy instruments. First of all, tariffs could be reduced (Table 4.2). And then, as in the case of pharmaceuticals and telecommunications, regulations related to standards and approval could be relaxed. Although the case of electronics indicates that a ministry must have effective policy instruments to pursue market liberalization, the case of forest products demonstrates that even if a ministry has effective instruments, the negotiation may not produce much fruit if the issue is highly politicized.

INSTITUTIONAL OBJECTIVES

The second element of the capacity of a ministry is a ministry's institutional objective, and the interests which derive from the objective. So far, we have assumed that the ministries desired market liberalization but sometimes could not proceed due to their constrained autonomy and/or lack of policy instruments to carry out market liberalization. In this section, we will relax that assumption and think about the cases when ministries cannot promote market liberalization because their interests clash with market liberalization.

The Japanese government shares the basic principle of free trade with other industrialized nations, and thus the principle of open markets at home. To be sure, this was not necessarily the case in the early postwar period. At that time, the Japanese government's sole economic objective was to recover from the war-stricken economy and to catch up with the West. Many markets were closed, in perceived advancement of this objective. However, with the successful growth of the economy and the continued participation in the rounds of multilateral trade talks under the sponsorship of the GATT, protectionism lost legitimacy in the Japanese government.

Overall agreement with free trade principles is not synonymous with an agreement in practice, however. Officials interviewed at every ministry in charge of the MOSS talks agreed with the principle of market liberalization. However, when it came to details of their policy, ministries

Table 4.2 Comparison of tariffs on forest products (1985, per cent)

Item	US	EC	Japan
Softwood plywood	20.0	10.0	15.0
Particleboard	4.5–5.5	10.0	12.0
Fibreboard	3.0	10.0	5.2

Sources: MAFF and Japan Plywood Manufacturer's Association

showed reluctance to change their policy. The reason why these ministries could not agree to change their policy was primarily because they had interests other than market liberalization that derive from the objectives or functions of the ministries.

The Ministry of Health and Welfare

The Establishment Law of the MHW mandates the ministry 'to improve and promote social welfare, social security, and public health', as its institutional objective. In order to meet this mandate, the ministry is empowered to regulate 'pharmaceutical affairs and narcotics' (article four). The MHW's interest regarding the pharmaceutical industry based on this institutional objective is to provide safe and low-priced drugs to the Japanese public. Therefore, it is quite clear that what observers often assume of Japanese government ministries, that is, that they attempt to foster the Japanese industries under their jurisdiction into internationally competitive ones, is less applicable for the MHW than for ministries such as MITI.[15] Thus, even though the Japanese pharmaceuticals industry was not as competitive as its American counterpart, the MHW did not have much interest in blocking the expansion of both US exports and manufacturing in Japan. As long as the US demands in the MOSS talks met the interest of the MHW to provide safe and low-priced drugs in Japan – which most of the US requests did – the MHW had no objections to market liberalization.

The MHW was not established with, and has not acquired an institutional objective of promoting the growth of the pharmaceuticals industry. The origin of the MHW indicates that the ministry was not intended to be one of the economic ministries to promote Japan's economic growth. During the prewar period, while the main responsibility of health control was shouldered by Naimushō1 (the Home Ministry), other ministries also held jurisdictions over welfare and health control. Then, in 1938, the MHW was established with the main purpose of improving the war fighting capacity of Japan. The new MHW consisted of some bureaus separated from *Naimushō* with some officials relocated from the Ministries of Education and Communications (the current Ministry of Posts and Telecommunications).[16]

In addition, in the period after the Second World War, there is little evidence that the MHW adopted an aggressive industrial policy. Under the US Occupation, the MHW dropped its primary purpose of establishment, that is, to strengthen Japanese health in order to fight war. The MHW instead made efforts to enhance medication and the health level of the Japanese public, facing the society devastated by lack of sanitation, low standards of living, and contagious disease.[17] However, although the Japanese pharmaceutical industry was completely destroyed at this time, the MHW made no explicit effort to shield domestic industry from foreign competition. For instance, regulation of drugs was rather loose so that foreign competitors with innovative drugs faced lower entry barriers than they did at the time of the MOSS talks.[18]

To be sure, while MHW officials stress the importance of providing the best medication for the Japanese people, concern for market stability also exists to some extent. One official stated that 'the market has to be reorganized because there are too many manufacturers, but we need to give them time', implying a need for gradual adjustment of the industry. This point is reflected in the MHW's decision-making process on the issue of *shōnin* transfer. The MHW saw deprivation of *shōnin* from small manufacturers as disruptive to the market. But this type of concern for the survival of domestic manufacturers should not be confused with industrial policies aimed at strengthening the competitiveness of Japanese manufacturers.

Most current regulations have been created not because the Japanese government wanted to protect industry from foreign competitors. As we have seen in the previous section, the complex features of current regulations were developed as a reaction to some tragic incidents caused by loose regulation, such as SMON disease and thalidomide babies. Although the regulatory system was created through ad hoc reaction to external events, as one MHW official complained, no active effort has been made to streamline current regulations, which are often irrational and inconsistent.

Thus, the MHW's lack of interest in industrial growth as well as its interest in promoting inexpensive and safe drug production helped attain resolutions in the MOSS talks on pharmaceuticals. However, the issue of *shōnin* transfer remained unresolved because of the conflict between the MHW's interest in 'safe' drug production and the proposed deregulation. The Japanese government never offered what the US repeatedly requested, namely, automatic transfer of *shōnin* in cases of 'unfriendly' transfer (see pp. 41–2, Chapter 3), but merely simplified the procedures when the proprietary right of licence to produce a drug is transferred from one manufacturer to another.[19]

The problem of *shōnin* transfer derived from the historical evolution of the pharmaceutical industry in Japan. Foreign firms entered the market in Japan in various ways, such as importation through Japanese wholesalers, importation and direct marketing, or licensing of manufacture to Japanese firms. Because direct investment was restricted prior to 1975, the only way for a foreign firm to do business in Japan was either to have local distributors import its products or to cooperate with local manufacturers through licensing. Since 1975, the restrictions on direct investment have been relaxed and a growing number of foreign firms have established businesses on their own. However, the MHW regulations lagged behind the change in business practice and required renewed application for *kyoka* and *shōnin* in the event a licensing company decided to begin manufacturing in Japan. From the American point of view, the contractual relationship regulated by the civil code conflicted with the relationship between the firms and the government which is regulated by the system of drug approval.

The MHW officials declined to accept automatic transfer of *shōnin* because they thought that without a thorough MHW investigation, the safe production maintained by the former licensee could not be guaranteed. Thus, the MHW officials insisted that when a change in contractual relationship occurred, new approval was needed to secure complete transfer of the information and data needed by the new manufacturer. The MHW said that it would not grant a *shōnin* unless it could 'confirm that the manufacturer or importer has full knowledge and information on efficacy, safety, and quality control of the product and is able to do its business under all obligations imposed by the Pharmaceutical Affairs Law (PAL)'.[20]

To be sure, the MHW considered protecting smaller manufacturers, because the ministry envisaged possible damage caused to them by simplified transfer of *shōnin*. Because many small Japanese companies relied heavily on production of a single kind of drug through licensing, an increased number of *shōnin* transfers would vitally affect the fate of such manufacturers. However, this concern for domestic manufacturers did not receive continuous attention throughout the talks and was not an element of a well-planned industrial policy. At the least, by August the concern for small manufacturers was significantly downplayed.[21] By that time, Japan decided to accept easier transfer of *shōnin*, which meant increased deprivation of licences from former (Japanese) licensees.

The Ministry of Posts and Telecommunications

As in the case of the MHW, the Ministry of Posts and Telecommunications agreed with market liberalization in principle, but some issues were not resolved easily because the ministry had other interests. During the period leading to the MOSS talks, the MPT displayed strong interest in reducing entry barriers to the Japanese telecommunications markets. This interest emerged as a result of growing domestic demand for an improved system to match the development of technology and the diversified needs of the business community as well as individual users. The decision to privatize NTT and open the market in order to let private firms participate in common carrier services as well as VANs in April 1985 signified the MPT's effort to meet this growing demand. This decision also included the liberalization of CPEs so that users could attach any kind of terminal equipment bought independently of the supplier of the network.

The MPT's need for further liberalization of the market intensified when exasperated US legislators began to move toward adopting protectionist bills against Japanese exports, telecommunications equipment in particular. For instance, by the end of March 1985, the US Senate adopted a non-binding resolution sponsored jointly by Senators John H. Danforth and David L. Boren calling for increased market access in Japan.[22] Several MPT officials expressed their belief that because Japanese suppliers relied heavily on the US export market, the MPT had to try hard to forestall the US from adopting such protectionist bills against telecommunications equipment exports.[23]

The MPT had interests other than market liberalization, however. Most importantly, the MPT's institutional objective regarding telecommunications was to regulate the industry in order to secure a reliable telecommunications network. This objective is evident in the MPT's reply to the US request to relax technical standards for terminal equipment:

> With regard to technical standards for approval, much depends on one's thinking concerning 'harm to the network' [the proposed US criterion for CPEs]. There exist approximately 60 million telephones currently in use in Japan. Should sub-standard telephones with respect to sound volume, noise, [and] cross-talk be connected to the telephone network, that would result in deterioration of the network function and in nuisance to other users of the networks. Decade-long efforts have been made in Japan so that such things will not happen, and we would like to maintain the fruit of these efforts in the next generation.[24]

This institutional objective generated interests that conflicted with liberalization. The *Yomiuri Shimbun* put the case well suggesting that 'the US–Japan conflict exemplified by the case of VAN business emerged with the backdrop in which there was a difference in tradition and political culture regarding bureaucratic control. There is a big difference between Japan, where administration has played a large role even in the sphere of consumer protection, and the US, where the concept of consumer responsibility has been developed.'[25] According to the MPT, a US negotiator stated at the negotiation table that 'we came from different philosophical backgrounds. In the US governmental intervention is deemed unnecessary in principle. In Japan, there is a philosophy that governmental intervention facilitates the operation of the system.'[26]

In the US, private firms freely carried out their business and the FCC played the role of a 'night watchman'. The US request was that Japan adopt a system similar to that of the US where market forces determine the fate of firms. Consumers were expected to choose products at their own risk and if they ended up buying defective products, courts were supposed to solve the problem. The Japanese insisted that given that telephone service had been a government-sponsored business since its initiation in 1890, Japanese consumers were not well trained to choose equipment to suit their needs.

Because the MPT's institutional objective to provide a reliable telecommunications network generated interests to protect consumers from possibly defective products, some issues such as technical standards for wired telecommunications and receivers for radio telecommunications faced delayed resolution. The MPT responded to the US that criteria in addition to 'no harm to the network' (which is used in the US), such as 'no nuisance to other users' must be included to maintain the quality of phones, given the long history of users' expectations for high quality telephones provided by NTT.[27]

If consumer protection was the MPT's interest that was perceived to clash with market liberalization, MPT had another interest: to expand its jurisdiction to incorporate fast growing sectors. While the MPT's historical institutional objective was to regulate the telecommunications industry in order to provide a reliable network, the ministry was contemplating remodelling itself into a ministry with a new institutional objective to promote industrial growth, by making use of the opportunity presented by NTT's privatization.[28] In other words, instead of relating to the private sector with regulatory relationships, the MPT planned to begin relating to certain industries with promotive relationships, in the manner MITI historically related to strategic industries. In so doing, the MPT would gain higher status as a *seisaku kanchō*, or policy-oriented ministry, as opposed to a *kisei kanchō*, or regulatory ministry with lower prestige. The MPT's plan to adopt a new institutional objective generated interests to keep certain industries – fast growing high-technology industries – under tight regulation so that the ministry would be able to influence the future of these industries.

The conflict between the MPT's interest in keeping some industries under its control and market liberalization is seen in the case of technical standards for distributing radio frequencies for transmitters. Because the sector of radio telecommunications contained industries of future growth such as cellular phones and cordless phones, the MPT could not let go of its ambition to become a *seisaku kanchō* after its dream had been significantly crushed in the first stage of talks on wired telecommunications. The MPT insisted that the technical standards used in the US, 'interference control' and 'spectrum availability', were not sufficient and that the latter had to be modified as 'efficient use of spectrum'. (While the FCC's role was to regulate the market as little as possible but to exercise its authority to invalidate licences when the need arose, the MPT concern went beyond the regulation of the market and involved the growth of the market.) As a result, the US demand to reduce the technical standards for radio telecommunications (transmitters) was only partially successful in the sense that it persuaded the MPT to discard unnecessary criteria. But because Japan clung to 'efficient use of frequencies' as opposed to the US-proposed 'availability of frequencies', the US did not achieve its original goal on the issue.

The case of third-party radio service is an even more explicit case that shows the MPT's effort to form a compromise between the two interests: the interest in complying with the US requests and liberalizing the market and the interest in preserving as much power as possible to establish a promotive relationship with the private sector. The outcome was a strange mixture of these two. The MPT gave a licence to a US firm (thus partially liberalizing the market, because prior to the MOSS no private firms, domestic or foreign, were allowed into the market), but continued to regulate the rest of the market by not letting any other firms begin similar businesses.

The US asked Japan to offer market access similar to that enjoyed by foreign (Japanese) firms in the US regarding third-party radio services. Third-party radio services offer a system called a trunked system consisting of relay stations and users (dispatchers and mobile stations).[29] A relay station sends messages to other stations in a region too far away to be communicated with simply by private radio communication between a dispatcher and a mobile station. Also, this system can simultaneously relay messages sent by various sets of dispatchers and mobile stations so that cross talk can be avoided. The US claimed that although in the US third-party radio systems were operated freely, in Japan, the service was restricted to the operation of the non-profit organization called the Mobile Radio Center.[30] In mid-October, the US requested market access comparable to that enjoyed by Japanese companies in the US but the issue was not solved until the last day of the talks, 8 January 1986.

Japan's inability to offer a solution to liberalize third-party radio services must not be confused with the MPT's overt refusal to consider such measures. In fact, the MPT fully intended to accommodate the US interest in liberalization even prior to the MOSS talks. An MPT official stated that before the MOSS talks, when Motorola began to appeal to the MPT that the Japanese system should be changed to allow private firms to begin third-party radio services, the MPT started to investigate the possibility of liberalization.[31] At the time of the MOSS talks, according to this official, the MPT had already decided to let private firms open service. To support this point, once the US officially requested the liberalization, Japan quickly (about a month from the request) promised to revise the law, which is very unusual for the Japanese government given its reluctance to change laws.[32]

Why, then, did Japan wait until 8 January of the next year to offer a resolution satisfactory to the US? The MPT's official account of this delay was that the issue was a legal problem. The MPT had a serious problem of classifying the business into the Japanese legal framework. The MPT explained that the Telecommunications Business Law did not have a category of telecommunications services that combined the nature of a common carrier, such as telephone networks (which are open to the public), and private telecommunications, such as an intra-firm VAN.[33]

The MPT was extremely reluctant to revise the law before its implementation, just as it was in the case of the registration requirement for type two telecommunications business. However, after a long consideration and examination of the telecommunications laws, the MPT changed a section in article five of the Radio Law, which prohibited licensing to foreign firms, in order to grant licences as 'private' radio services to foreign firms wanting to begin third-party radio services. Interestingly, because the MPT officials hastily prepared this resolution, the final outcome was a patchwork of provisions with contradictions. An obscure classification of foreign firms as nominal 'maintenance agents' of local systems was made in order to let foreign firms pass legal loopholes. With this provision, a foreign firm could virtually operate a third-party radio service; at the same time, it would not be categorized as a licensee. Thus, the MPT's parallel effort to revise article five of the Radio Law was rendered meaningless.[34]

A more interesting reason for the delay in liberalization was the conflict with the MPT's desire to maintain administrative control over the private sector. The MPT wanted to preserve its control by limiting the number of participants in the market.[35] However, the MPT also had to comply with the US request somehow because of the surging protectionist movement within the US Congress. By making use of an effective policy instrument – licensing in this case – the MPT successfully combined these two conflicting interests and finally came up with a resolution. The MPT succeeded in granting an exclusive licence to Nippon Motorola, a Japanese subsidiary of the US company Motorola and the only US firm interested in third-party radio service, while secretly persuading other Japanese manufacturers not to apply for licences.[36]

An MPT official offered another account for the above agreement with the US based on the MPT's perception of the industry's competitiveness. The official stated that the MPT feared that if third-party radio services are liberalized to let other firms, Japanese firms in particular, compete in the market, the US firm would lose market share. Although Motorola was one of the suppliers for the Mobile Radio Center, Matsushita possessed the predominant share (one-third) as an equipment supplier at the time of the MOSS talks, indicating the strength of domestic suppliers. In the opinion of some MPT officials, Motorola, a competitive supplier of telecommunications equipment with one trillion yen worldwide sales, could not compete with Japanese manufacturers in their 'home ground' because of their strong distribution networks.[37] Therefore, to reduce trade friction with the US, a protected market had to be created for a US firm.

The Forestry Agency

Given the interest of the Ministry of Agriculture, Forestry, and Fisheries (MAFF) in protecting Japanese agriculture, the interest of the Forestry Agency in market liberalization was not obvious.[38] MAFF's institutional objective is to 'promote national economic growth through improvement and development of agriculture, forestry, and fishery industries, promotion of welfare for workers in these industries, and stable provision of national foodstuff'.[39] However, agriculture had lost its weight in the Japanese economy over time since this institutional objective was stipulated in the MAFF's establishment law in 1949. Thus, the overall objective of promotion of national economic growth through improvement of agriculture had become unrealistic. Instead, due to the political importance of the agricultural sector, combined with the low international competitiveness of Japanese agriculture, 'promotion of welfare for workers' has gained much more attention, and thus MAFF's overriding institutional interest became 'to protect farming villages and to develop the basis for Japanese agriculture'.[40]

However, the interest in protection of agriculture had gradually changed by the late 1970s when Japan faced strong *gaiatsu* to liberalize its agricultural trade. For instance, during the US–Japanese negotiations over oranges (1977–78), an agricultural negotiator from the MAFF is known to have said that 'agriculture cannot exist in isolation from the Japanese economy as a whole', implying that Japan could not simply refuse the US demands.[41] In their analysis of import liberalization of beef and oranges, Hideo Sato and Timothy Curran note that 'because Japan was so heavily dependent on the United States for supplies of many important agricultural products, the ministry (MAFF) could not afford to ignore US demands completely'.[42] More recently, the Minister of Agriculture, Forestry, and Fisheries, Tanabu Masami, was quoted as saying 'we made this decision [to end drift fishing] because we have to give consideration to Japan's position in international society', suggesting that an economic power such as Japan cannot keep protecting its domestic fishermen (or farmers) in light of strong international pressure.[43]

Indeed, the MAFF on the whole had mixed interests, as Minister of Agriculture Sato's statements exemplify. On the one hand, consistent with the interest in protecting agriculture from being damaged by increasing foreign competition, he showed firm opposition to tariff reduction.[44] On the other hand, Sato told plywood manufacturers, in mid-January 1985, that he needed to review measures, such as cutting production costs, to rationalize the industry.[45] These measures are needed because 'the government cannot ignore the US requests and forever maintain the current level of tariffs'.[46]

In addition to the MAFF's general tendency to gradually abandon protectionist policies, the Forestry Agency had reasons of its own to agree with market liberalization of forest products. The Forestry Agency was aware that the forest products industry needed restructuring. This is why some said that the programme of subsidies the Japanese government adopted during the MOSS talks to compensate industries affected by tariff reduction was a *watari ni fune* (literally, a boat presented to you when you need to cross a river, meaning a timely offer).[47] In the case of the MOSS talks, because allocation of subsidies needed for revitalization of the forest products industry was closely linked to accepting some tariff reduction, the Forestry Agency's interest in revitalization also included to a degree an acquiescence, if not interest, in accepting market liberalization.

In fact, the Forestry Agency demonstrated its interest in market liberalization in issues such as reduction of tariffs on particleboard and laminated timber. Because the manufacturers of these products did not rally with interest groups from upstream industries, such as tree growers and timber producers, to oppose tariff cuts, the agency was free to pursue its interest in market liberalization and decide the tariff reduction.[48] Therefore, although the offer of tariff reduction on particleboard was not presented until late because it was linked to other tariffs, the agency reduced tariffs from 12 to 8 per cent. This rate is not only lower than tariffs on other products but also, unlike the case of plywood, the tariff reduction was not staged. Tariffs were to be reduced in one step down to 8 per cent in April 1987. For laminated lumber, the agency voluntarily reduced the tariffs from 20 to 15 per cent suddenly over the year-end administrative recess of 1985 (see Table 4.3).

Furthermore, the quick resolution of the issue of technical standards,[49] such as granting more active roles to foreign testing organizations, indicates that the agency was interested in a more open market. The Forestry Agency's quick response was possible for two reasons. As in the case of particleboard and laminated lumber, the agency's autonomy was secured due to the fact that the issue was handed down to the experts

Table 4.3 Forest product tariff reductions

Item	January 1986	April 1987	April 1988
Plywood	15.0–20.0	12.5–17.5	10.0–15.0
Particleboard	12.0	8.0	n.a.
Fibreboard	5.2	3.5	n.a.
Laminated lumber	20.0	15.0	n.a.

Source: The Forestry Agency

group isolated from sectoral pressure. Also, because the issue of product standards was logically unrelated to the upstream industries, there was no way for the upstream industry to oppose the proposed liberalization.

MITI

MITI's interest in market liberalization was relatively stronger than any other ministry, except for the Ministry of Foreign Affairs. With the increased competitiveness of Japanese industries, MITI had acquired an interest in market liberalization, although its institutional objective still remained the same: Japan's industrial growth. MITI acquired this interest through hard experiences of several threats and actual retaliation by the US. Today, most Japanese officials, MITI officials in particular, recognize the need to open Japanese markets in order to continue exporting to the world markets.

However, while agreeing on the general principle of market liberalization, oftentimes MITI is hesitant in liberalizing the market when it comes to specific industries. This is because MITI still retains its institutional objective of industrial growth and to meet this goal, MITI officials still feel a need to intervene in the Japanese economy. Thus, for some technologically dynamic industries such as computer software and supercomputers, MITI is reluctant to withdraw its prior involvement (even when the involvement's effects on growth are dubious). Regarding sunset industries such as aluminium, glass, or paper, however, MITI is becoming more willing to give up protection and adopt market liberalization. Although MITI had been historically involved in the structural adjustment of these types of industries, the increasing international pressure of market liberalization and MITI's willingness to protect export markets for growing high-tech industries against retaliatory measures are forcing MITI to withdraw prior commitments to declining industries.

The reason why MITI has been trying to develop an interest in market liberalization lies in the sectoral growth of industries under its jurisdiction. Originally, MITI adopted heavy protection of Japanese industries to pre-empt direct exposure of Japanese firms to competition with foreign firms. However, the eventual growth of several key industries in Japan, which signified the perceived effectiveness of industrial policies, rendered these policies unnecessary. At the same time, MITI's strategy shifted from protection of key industries to liberalizing the markets. MITI, whose institutional objective was Japan's industrial growth, realized that given the private sector's strength and dependence on overseas markets, it was better to open its own market in order to avoid retaliatory closure of trading partners' markets. By the mid-1970s, MITI maintained that protectionism could no longer be used as its main strategy. For instance, as regards import liberalization of the computer industry, MITI began to reduce tariffs in 1973 and by 1983, the level of tariffs on Central Process-ing Units (CPUs) was 4.9 per cent.[50] Therefore, at the time of the MOSS talks, although MITI showed resistance to US requests for unilateral elimination of tariffs, MITI was ready to go along with the US demand.

However, the case of mainframe computers indicated that MITI's in-stitutional objective of industrial growth had not yet changed. The Jap-anese mainframe industry was not competitive in the world market, and thus it maintained a promotive relationship with MITI, whereas the rest of the computer industry (save supercomputers and next-generation com-puters) maintained post-promotive relationships. The perceived strategic importance of the industry gave incentives for MITI to nurture indigenous mainframe manufacturers. At the same time, Japanese industry still wan-ted some form of protection by MITI.[51] Therefore, MITI had less interest in reducing protection of mainframe computers. However, because MITI realized that crucial importance of avoiding US retaliation in order to secure overseas markets, MITI decided to reduce tariffs even for main-frame computers. The reason for some delay in offering the final plan for tariff reduction was that MITI needed to spend some time persuading the manufacturers of mainframe computers that the change was necessary.[52]

CONCLUSION

Japan's trading partners can learn a number of lessons from the MOSS talks. Given an issue, the first important task of a policymaker is to identify which ministry (or ministries) claims jurisdiction. If the issue involves cutting-edge high-tech industry or changes to the national budget, there is a high likelihood that the ministry that has the mandate to deal with trade negotiations will first have to deal with other ministries. Trade negotia-tions of this kind may take a long time because negotiation partners must wait until the ministry comes to some accord with other ministries.

In addition, before bringing the issue up on the negotiation agenda, thorough study of the nature of trade barriers must be done. Although Clinton administration officials may disagree, a lack of policy instruments on the side of the Japanese government will likely result in a lack of achievement. Unlike the case of reducing tariffs, a ministry may not have effective policy instruments if the barriers to the Japanese market are caused by private sector practices.

Finally, it is important to know what kind of institutional objectives the ministry in charge has as regards the issue. It is wrong to assume that every ministry is inclined to protect the industry under its jurisdiction. However, it is equally important to know the complex nature of the interests deriving from a ministry's institutional objectives. Oftentimes, these interests pose serious obstacles to resolution if they strongly conflict with market liberalization.

73

5

RELATIONSHIPS WITH THE PRIVATE SECTOR

In addition to the three elements of ministerial capacity, ministries' relationships with the private sector will have a large impact on the course of Japan's economic policy formation. The talks on electronics and forest products were adversely affected by relationships between the ministries and the private sector. However, the manner in which the relationship affected the two issues was different. In the case of electronics, the post-promotive relationship between MITI and the electronics sector gave more power to the private sector, making it difficult for MITI to offer meaningful resolution. In the case of forest products, by contrast, the involvement of politically influential upstream industries, not the Forestry Agency's relationship with the forest products sector, complicated the issue.

TYPES OF RELATIONSHIP AND SHARED INTERESTS

The MOSS cases indicate that a relative lack of sectoral pressure was important in giving high autonomy to the ministries. In all of the MOSS talks except for electronics, ministries were relatively free from opposition to market liberalization from firms in the directly affected sectors. The reasons are two-fold. The first reason is that all of these ministries held regulatory relationships which discouraged petitioning. Another reason is that firms in the private sector shared interests in market liberalization with the ministries.

Types of relationship

As noted earlier, the Ministry of Health and Welfare's main interest deriving from its institutional objective is the provision of safe and low-priced drugs to the Japanese public. While securing the latter interest, that is low-priced drugs, has been as important as ensuring the safety of drugs, several drug-related accidents such as thalidomide babies and SMON disease related to defective medicines made the ministry focus strongly on the safety of drugs. Thus, at the time of the MOSS talks, the MHW had evolved to hold mainly regulatory relationships with the pharmaceuticals industry.

In the regulatory relationship maintained by the MHW and the pharmaceutical industry, the life and death of a drug or a firm is in the hands of the MHW. By withholding *shōnin* or *kyoka*, the MHW can virtually determine the fate of a manufacturer. Because drug manufacturers invest considerable amounts of time and money in developing new drugs it is crucial for manufacturers that the newly developed drug be approved. (It is said that the time for innovation, from conception to commercialization, ranges from 10 to 16 years. The cost involved for such an innovation is at least 8 billion yen.)[1] As a result, the pharmaceutical industry historically did not oppose the MHW's decisions, but accepted them silently.

The same is true for the relationship between the Ministry of Posts and Telecommunications and the telecommunications industry. The MPT maintained a regulatory relationship with the industry and again, private companies were usually not willing to express dissent against the ministry's policy. However, due to the presence of the monopoly public corporation, Nippon Telegraph and Telephone Corporation (NTT), until April 1985 there was a slight difference in the manner in which the MPT interacted with the wired communications sector.

Before the privatization of NTT, the MPT maintained an indirect regulatory relationship with the private sector through the operation of NTT. Article four, section twenty-two, paragraph two of the MPT Establishment Law, revised in 1982, stipulates that the MPT 'supervises' NTT as well as Kokusai Denshin Denwa Co. Ltd., the international carrier. NTT collaborated with the 'NTT family' of equipment manufacturers (NEC, Hitachi, Oki, Fujitsu, and specialized smaller manufacturers),[2] thereby helping industrial growth (NTT also checked the technical standards of equipment). Thus, for wired communications in general, before the privatization of NTT, the MPT did not have much to do with the private sector other than the 'regulation and supervision' (article four, section twenty-two, paragraph three) needed to provide a reliable telephone network.

The MPT had a more explicit regulatory relationship with the wireless (radio) telecommunications sector. Before the rise of cellular phones and pagers, which motivated the MPT to adopt a more active role in promoting industrial growth, the Radio Department of the MPT engaged itself mostly in licensing, approval of equipment, and allocating frequencies to users (article four, section twenty-two, paragraphs five, six, eight, and eleven). The goal of the regulation was to maintain an orderly environment for radio communication.

The relationship between the Forestry Agency and the forest products sector can be described as a mixture of regulation and restructuring, which still left the agency with a relatively high degree of autonomous decision-making authority. The Forestry Agency's main function toward the industry was to regulate the quality of products to be marketed to meet the Japanese Agricultural Standards (JAS). The Agency also had maintained a restructuring relationship with the industry since the early 1980s. The Agency began vigorous restructuring of the industry when the decline of the forest products industry was accelerated by a sudden increase of imports from Indonesia. The Agency implemented several series of emergency remedies, such as the 1982–83 and 1984–85 projects, to rationalize production.[3] Being dependent on both the Agency's decisions on product marketability and the Agency's willingness to help restructure the industry, the private sector was inclined to comply with the Agency's decisions.

MITI had a post-promotive relationship with the computer industry in contrast to the previous three cases. Historically, MITI held either promotive or post-promotive relationships with industries of strategic importance such as automobiles and computers. Post-promotive relationships grow out of promotive relationships. In a promotive relationship a ministry has to cooperate and in part depend on initiatives taken by the private sector, thus reducing the ministry's autonomy. This characteristic of promotive relationships is magnified in the case of a post-promotive relationship. When an industry becomes mature and sufficiently competitive, the former promotive relationship transforms into a different kind in which the industry does not depend on governmental assistance. Therefore, in this relationship, the private sector gains more influence over the ministry's decision-making. Conversely, the ministry loses much of its influence over the industry.

By the time of the MOSS talks, the computer industry (excluding cutting-edge computers such as mainframe computers, supercomputers and next-generation computers) was strong enough to withstand competition with foreign firms, it did not oppose MITI's proposed liberalization of the Japanese market. But if the remaining trade issues are beyond institutional trade barriers and are related to individual firms' decisions, as in the case of procurement of semiconductor chips, private firms tend to resist MITI's requests. Because MITI's main policy tool was administrative guidance, whose effectiveness derives not from law but from the private sector's willingness to abide by MITI's directions, the reluctance of private firms largely reduced MITI's ability to attain increased access for foreign firms.

Shared interests

Thus, for the ministries which held regulatory relationships in three of the four cases of the MOSS talks, dissent from the private sector was rare. However, officials also felt that it was important not to adopt policies that were drastically against the perceived interests of the private sector.

Therefore, to some extent, it was important that the private sector shared the interest in market liberalization, in order for the ministries to offer positive answers to the US requests.

In the case of pharmaceuticals, the most important aspect of interest sharing was that the talks carefully avoided involvement of politically powerful groups. The most important such group was the *Nihon Ishikai*, or the Japan Medical Association. The JMA had strong 'reciprocal patronage' ties with the LDP, whereby the JMA provided funding and votes in exchange for favourable legislation.[4] By avoiding issues such as overhauling the *yakka* system itself, in which the JMA had strong vested interests, and focusing on more technical issues, the pharmaceuticals talks successfully contained the possible intervention by politicians.[5]

Thus, only the manufacturers of pharmaceuticals were directly affected by the talks. In general, the pharmaceutical manufacturers shared the interest in a more deregulated and open market. However, the interests of pharmaceutical manufacturers were divided into at least two groups regarding some American requests. Large manufacturers who were members of the Japan Pharmaceuticals Manufacturers Association (JPMA) mainly shared interests with the American manufacturers. Because large companies with high R&D expenses were likely to be innovative, they were interested in streamlining the approval process for new drugs and eliminating unreasonable test data requirements to introduce new drugs to the Japanese market. Thus, large firms agreed with the core requests of the MOSS negotiations. (A representative of an American company in Japan stated that because international pressure is an important factor in causing policy change, JPMA almost 'used' the shared interest to cause desired changes in Japanese policy.[6])

Also, as an executive from JPMA said, large manufacturers were aware of the need to 'go abroad' (to export or to manufacture overseas).[7] The urge to initiate overseas business was due mainly to two factors. The first factor was obviously the prospect of increased competitiveness deriving from high R&D expenditures by Japanese manufacturers (10.71 per cent of the total value of sales in 1985).[8] Yet another factor was the peculiar Japanese market system, namely the *yakka* system where profits keep falling, which made many Japanese pharmaceuticals companies adopt a strategy of international expansion. Under the *yakka* system, because doctors and hospitals earn profits from the spread caused by the difference between the market price and the official price (*yakka*), heavy competition to lower prices among producers occurs. To reflect the falling market prices, MHW reviews the *yakka* occasionally. The setting of new prices causes another round of competition among the producers to lower their prices. In addition to this mechanism which puts downward pressure on drug prices, the Japanese government adopted a policy to reduce overall medication costs in the early 1980s. As a result, the *yakka* has been reviewed every year, which further pushes down drug prices. Given the need to expand overseas operations, Japanese manufacturers began to be interested in harmonization of regulations, as did other Western world-class manufacturers. The Japanese manufacturers also recognized the necessity to open the Japanese market, for fear that otherwise foreign governments would retaliate by closing their own markets.[9]

By contrast, the interests of smaller manufacturers differed somewhat from those of large manufacturers in a few issues, namely, transfer of *shōnin* and price listing for new drugs. As for the transfer of *shōnin*, because small manufacturers could not afford expensive R&D, they tended to rely on generic drugs or licence manufacturing of a single drug. For those relying on licence manufacturing, their market would be threatened if the originators of licences, which were often foreign firms, decided to manufacture in Japan.[10]

Regarding the listing of new drugs and their pricing, most Japanese manufacturers, innovative manufacturers in particular, wanted more regular and frequent listings.[11] In fact, until the MOSS talks, the listing of new drugs was a nightmare for drug manufacturers in Japan. Because the listing was irregular and infrequent (twice a year at most) manufacturers could not plan the production of new drugs. This system not only caused enormous inventory costs but also threatened innovative producers: while they waited for a new drug to be marketed, it was likely that others would start making drugs with similar effects, thus eliminating the competitive edge of the innovator.

However, manufacturers of generic drugs had mixed interests. On the one hand, makers of generic drugs profited under the current system; by not having frequent price listing of new drugs, generic drug makers had ample time to imitate new drugs. Moreover, these makers feared that more frequent listing of new drugs would result in far more new, competing products reaching the market. On the other hand, frequent listing of new drugs gave them more objects to imitate. However, despite the fact that the solution actually favoured innovative manufacturers, generic drug manufacturers made no objection to the MHW's decision to accept more regular and frequent listing.[12] This reticence was presumably due to two factors. The manufacturers that relied heavily on the sales of generic drugs could not object to the legitimacy of the more transparent system of regular and more frequent price listing. Also, the private sector was unable to oppose the MHW's decisions, due to the regulatory relationship.

In contrast to the divided interests among large and smaller pharmaceuticals manufacturers, telecommunications equipment manufacturers and telecommunications services firms shared interests in more open markets. For the equipment manufacturers, the reasons for supporting market liberalization were two-fold. Firstly, the rising competitiveness of

Japanese telecommunications equipment manufacturers made them confident against foreseeable competition with foreign suppliers. In addition, there was a growing sense of fear toward emerging protectionism in the US. As for telecommunications services, the US spoke for the interests of the Japanese firms which were interested in entering the telecommunications market after the 1 April liberalization, and which therefore wanted lower market barriers in markets such as VANs.

Telecommunications manufacturers possessed clear confidence with respect to foreign rivals. Yamamoto Takuma, President of Fujitsu and Chairperson of the Communications Industry Association of Japan (CIAJ), the largest association of telecommunications equipment manufacturers, repeatedly expressed the view of firms in the sector that 'the liberalization will serve as the basis for the further development of the sector'.[13] This confidence was based on high quality, price competitiveness and low production costs.[14] This confidence is convincing when one looks at the trade figures. Between 1982 and 1985 Japanese exports of telecommunications equipment increased steadily (Figure 5.1).

The export competitiveness of the sector was based on the technological lead of the Japanese manufacturers. Although technological advantage must be proven by comparisons of precise data, for the purpose of this section, it suffices to quote a research paper prepared for the US Department of Commerce in 1984. This paper stated that 'the technological level of Japanese manufacturers of telecommunications equipment now exceeds that of their US counterparts in mass produced hardware products such as communication cables, facsimile systems, and telephone

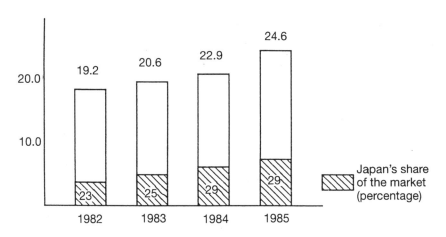

Figure 5.1 Growth of world telecommunications equipment export market and Japan's market share (billion US dollars).
Source: United Nations, *International Trade Statistics Yearbook*, 1986

sets. As a result of their technological competitiveness in these areas, Japanese manufacturers have been able to maintain a dominant position in their domestic market and to expand sales internationally.'[15]

The confidence in the competitiveness of the large firms in the sector, that is to say, the former members of the 'NTT family', was a crucial element for the private sector's promotion of the US cause. The former members of the NTT family were potential opponents of liberalization of the telecommunications equipment market because their exclusive supply-procurement relationship with NTT would be challenged. (On the other hand, the US interest to increase the market access of foreign telecommunications equipment suppliers coincided with the interest of Japanese suppliers such as Toshiba and Mitsubishi which had been excluded from NTT procurement.) But the request to further liberalize the telecommunications market made by CIAJ, in which former NTT family members were still dominant, suggests that the family members did not specifically oppose a more open market.[16]

The interest in further liberalization was not only supported by the manufacturers' confidence in their products' competitiveness but also by their fear of protectionism in the US. This was particularly true for firms such as Toyō Tsūshinki and Nihon Musen, whose success depended on exports.[17] This feeling was expressed by an executive of a telecommunications equipment manufacturing company, who said 'if we did not increase imports, the US would "squeeze" us harder and it would be more difficult for our business'.[18]

Likewise, telecommunications services firms were either actively interested in liberalization, or did not oppose it. Although the Public Telecommunications Law of 1953 was revised in 1982 in order to allow VANs for medium and smaller enterprises, large-scale VANs (special type-two telecommunications service) were yet to be liberalized. When large-scale VANs were finally permitted on 1 April 1985, nine firms registered to join the market (see Table 5.1).

At the time of the MOSS talks, it was well-known that US firms were far advanced in terms of VAN technology. A section in the analysis of the Japanese telecommunications market presented to the Department of Commerce which noted Japan's technological lead in equipment manufacturing also said that '[the Japanese] continued to lag behind their counterparts in production of equipment and installation of systems which utilize sophisticated software technology, for example ... Value Added Network (VAN) systems'.[19]

The reason is quite simple given the fact that Japanese firms still lag behind US firms in software production. VAN is a service that connects terminal equipment. To be sure, in order to provide such a service, hardware is required to physically convert protocols, codes, and the speed of data transmission among different types of terminal equipment.

Table 5.1 The size of VAN carriers (the first nine companies to register in 1985)

Company	Capital (billion yen)
Intec	42.0
Fujitsū	194.0
The Japan Research Institute	54.0
NEC	155.0
Hitachi Information Network	0.3
United Net	4.0
Japan ENS	7.1
Oki Network Service	0.9
Network Information and Communication	2.5

Source: *Jōhō Tsushin Nenkan* (Information Communications Almanac) 1991, Tokyo: Jōhō Tsushin Sōgō Kenkyū-jo, 1990

But the most important element of the VAN service is the software that enables these tasks. The US VAN firms had not only possessed expertise in VAN businesses since the early 1970s, but also had an advantage in the development of advanced software. Given the large difference in competitiveness, it seemed that the Japanese firms were vulnerable to competition from the US firms. These firms were expected to oppose the possible expansion of market share by US firms.

The new Japanese large-scale VAN firms did not oppose the US requests, however. They did not resist US demands for the further relaxation of regulations on the special type-two telecommunications business. There were two reasons for this lack of opposition. The first reason was that, new VAN firms were beginning to start international VANs. Except for Oki and Fujitsu, all VAN carriers which began VAN business in 1985 registered for international VAN licences (RPOA or Recognized Private Operating Agency, stipulated by the International Telecommunication Convention).[20] Thus, it was not in these firms' interests to object to the US request for VAN deregulation which could have complicated their prospective business with US counterparts.[21]

Moreover, as a representative of the Special Type II Telecommunications Carriers Association explained, the lack of opposition was because the sector was mainly composed of large firms with 'abundant capital, experienced management, and capacity for large R&D' (Table 5.1).

There are a number of reasons why the sector had only large firms. In the first place, the companies which planned to begin large-scale VAN services were mostly large ones, such as banking, insurance, and trading companies, which already had expertise in intra-firm VANs.[22] For instance, banks maintained intra-firm VANs to manage automatic teller machine networks. Furthermore, the other new entrants were ones which wanted

81

to make use of their advantage in equipment manufacturing and software development. These were mostly former members of the 'NTT family'.

The history of state involvement was the final but perhaps most important reason for large firms to be the only provider of VANs. NTT began VAN service in 1980 because of its self-imposed sense of 'national obligation' aimed at catching up with its US counterparts.[23] Because this service was not born out of users' demand, NTT had to provide the service at very low rates cross-subsidized by its profits on long-distance telephone services. When other firms were allowed to enter the market in 1985, they had to reduce their rates to compete with NTT. This artificially created low-price competition screened out small firms which could not subsidize loss-making VAN businesses with profits from other businesses. Therefore, at the time of the MOSS talks, Japanese firms were not so much concerned with prospective increased competition with US firms but were more worried about the price-setting ability of NTT.

As for third-party radio services, there was no market prior to the MOSS talks (as in the case of VAN business). The Mobile Radio Center, a semipublic nonprofit organization capitalized by the MPT, NTT, and sixteen telecommunications equipment manufacturers, provided the service. However, also as in the case of VANs, some Japanese firms were strongly interested in starting such businesses. Interested firms included Matsushita, NEC, Toshiba, and Mitsubishi, which together held a 60 per cent share of the equipment supplied to the Mobile Radio Center. These firms favoured liberalization for the same reason they supported liberalization of telecommunications equipment, that is, because they were confident in the competitiveness of their products.

As regards the forest products industry, the interests of the manufacturers shifted from one of opposition to market liberalization to support with the condition that ample compensation be offered. As we will see in the following section, the forest products sector did not initially share interests in market liberalization with the Forestry Agency and opposed reduction of tariffs. What the manufacturers of forest products feared most was a sudden increase of imports from Southeast Asian nations, Indonesia in particular, due to the reduced tariffs. At the same time, manufacturers were aware of the need to make the domestic industry more efficient. Thus, when the government moved towards reducing tariffs while promising to grant subsidies to promote industrial restructuring, the manufacturers decided to accept this option. Instead of asking to maintain the heavily protected market, they decided to strengthen their competitiveness and accept a more open market. Due to the government's decision to provide subsidies to the industry, forest products manufacturers had stopped lobbying for prevention of tariff reduction by the end of March 1985.

In general, the electronics sector (except for mainframe computer manufacturers) had no objections to removing *governmental* barriers. As we will see in the following section, however, the barriers to exports were due to exclusive commercial practices, not barriers to trade such as regulations, tariffs and quotas. The private sector's agreement on market liberalization did not mean that the MOSS electronics talks would be successful, however. The MOSS format, which aimed at removing government-created barriers, was not suitable for coping with the problems foreign firms faced in the Japanese electronics market.

WHY MITI FAILED TO BE RESPONSIVE IN THE MOSS TALKS

MITI's inability to offer much beyond elimination of tariffs on computers, which were already at low levels at the time of the MOSS talks, is perplexing for those who were impressed by MITI's ability to liberalize goods imports and capital inflows throughout the 1960s and 1970s. Why was it that MITI could not make significant offers regarding electronics, including semiconductors, when there were obvious export problems for foreign suppliers in the Japanese market?

The answer seems to be the loss of effectiveness of MITI's well-known 'administrative guidance'. Administrative guidance means, according to John O. Haley, 'a method or process for implementing bureaucratic policy involving legally voluntary – but not necessarily uncoerced – compliance with informal recommendations or directions by government officials'.[24] The important point here is that the effectiveness of administrative guidance is not due to its legal foundation. As well described in Chalmers Johnson's work, MITI failed to formalize its power by its failure to pass the Special Measures Law for Promotion of Designated Industries in 1963.[25] Administrative guidance worked during the high-growth period, primarily because the Japanese markets were regulated by laws that restricted the flow of capital and technology. Based on laws such as the Foreign Exchange and Trade Control Law, MITI acted as a gatekeeper of incoming capital, technology, foreign exchange, and raw materials which were badly needed by Japanese industries.[26] The threat of denial of access to such crucial input raised the effectiveness of MITI's administrative guidance.

However, the conditions favourable to the effectiveness of administrative guidance disappeared with the liberalization of Japanese markets over the last twenty years. Firms grew internationally competitive, such that many no longer rely on MITI's help. While MITI still maintains a public image that it is a powerful ministry, administrative guidance seems to work only under two conditions. One is when an industry relies on the government's protection of the market against foreign competition. The other is when firms and MITI share interests in adopting specific measures.

The electronics industry did not meet both conditions needed for

effective administrative guidance. In the first place, the electronics industry was competitive and did not rely on MITI's protection. In addition,
firms were not interested in making the market more open through
changes in commercial practices. Commercial practices such as close
relationships between manufacturers, retailers and users through
development of 'user-friendly' products that met users' specific demands
obstructed access of foreign manufacturers to the computer market (see
Chapter 3). While such practices are likely to be perceived as obstacles to
free trade by foreign manufacturers and governments, there was no
awareness among Japanese firms and government officials that practices
that are not necessarily designed to exclude rival companies but that
resulted in exclusive trading relationships must be changed.[27]

In sum, the four cases of the MOSS talks indicate two important
conclusions. First, it is important that all three elements of ministerial
capacity be met in order to ensure market liberalization. In addition, the
importance of shared interests between the private sector and a ministry
depends upon the type of relationship. In a regulatory or restructuring
relationship, shared ministry–private sector interests may not be too
important because private companies are usually afraid to object to
government decisions. Even in these relationships, accepting US requests
may be delayed because ministries must consider, if not protect, the
interests of domestic industries. In a post-promotive relationship, because
the private sector has more power in relation to the ministry, the private
sector's interest heavily affects policy outcomes. It is difficult to open the
market if the private sector opposes market opening measures.

So far we have looked at the usefulness of the theoretical framework
presented in Chapter 2 in explaining Japan's responses to the US demands in the MOSS talks. However, the case of forest products still
remains to be explained. The Forestry Agency held all three elements of
ministerial capacity. First, the Agency's autonomy was relatively high. The
Agency was the sole ministry in charge of the forest products sector,
except for paper and fibreboard overseen by MITI.[28] To guard against the
possible intervention of the MAFF, the Agency historically guarded its
autonomy through measures such as independent personnel management and continuous appointment of experts (as opposed to generalists)
as the director-general (i.e. head of the agency). These measures gave the
agency an identity separate from the MAFF.[29] There was an obvious policy
instrument, that is tariffs, to utilize to open the market. In addition, the
Agency's interest was gradually shifting toward market liberalization.
Furthermore, the Agency's relationship with the forest products manufacturers – a mixture of regulation and restructuring – posed little
problem for accepting tariff reductions. However, the talks on forest
products did not reach an agreement until the informal meeting after the
final meeting of the MOSS talks. Even at this meeting Japan refused to

eliminate tariffs as the US proposed. In the following section, we will look in detail at the causes for this failure to open the forest products market.

EXPLAINING AN EXCEPTIONAL CASE: FOREST PRODUCTS

The forest products talks suggest a limit to the theoretical framework offered in this book. So far, all cases were insulated from political pressure and thus ministries were the main actors for making decisions. By contrast, the case of forest products became increasingly politicized. Once politically active sectors are involved, and politicians begin to intervene, resolution will not be attained easily.

As we have seen in the previous chapter, the Forestry Agency had adequate capacity to meet the US demand to reduce tariffs on forest products. In addition, the agency maintained a mixture of restructuring and regulatory relationships that discouraged dissent from the private firms. One problem as regards its capacity arose from the fact that the Forestry Agency had to negotiate with the MOF over the size of compensation subsidies that was proposed by Prime Minister Nakasone as a precondition for reducing tariffs. This negotiation was a significant cause of the delay of resolution. However, the more important factor that constrained the Agency's capacity to fully respond to the US requests was the politicization of the issue.

In this section, we will see the process by which the issue was politicized. The politicization occurred in two stages. In the first stage, the

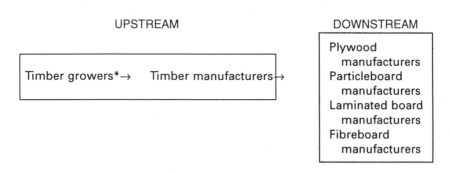

Note: *Timber growers are technically not agriculture workers. However, because they are often growers of other agricultural products, timber growers and agricultural workers are allied politically. In the forest product talks, agricultural workers joined lobbying with timber growers.

Figure 5.2 Distinction between upstream and downstream industries

85

actors directly affected by tariff reductions, namely, forest products manufacturers, lost interest in opposing the tariff reductions. In the next stage, the upstream industries (Figure 5.2), or forestry and manufacturers of low-value added forest products, such as lumber, got involved in lobbying. Then, I will discuss the effects of politicization on the negotiation outcome. Politicization prevented the US from gaining large tariff cuts, and also prevented domestic forest product manufacturers from defending their interests.

Fading opposition by the downstream manufacturers

In early January 1985, when it became clear to the private sector that forest products were going to be targeted in the MOSS talks, the alarmed plywood manufacturers actively lobbied the government against the tariff reductions.[30] Plywood manufacturers were well organized. The industry association, the Japan Plywood Manufacturer's Association (JPMA), consisted of 554 plywood manufacturers, divided into 8 local organizations. The sector even had a separate political lobbying organization called the *Nihon Gōhan Sangyō Seiji Renmei* (Political Federation of the Japan Plywood Industry). This organization initially lobbied actively in opposition to tariff reduction by jointly submitting petitions with the All-Japan Federation of Lumber Associations, the Japan Forestry Association, and the National Federation of Forest Owners' Associations to the Minister of Agriculture Satō Moriyoshi and other politicians.[31]

However, the petition and lobbying drive began to lose momentum once the government decided in April 1985 to accept tariff reduction to some degree and simultaneously to launch a compensation programme.[32] The plywood manufacturers, in spite of their opposition to tariff reduction, seem to have felt that tariff reduction was inevitable and decided to accept the subsidies for compensation. In an interview with the *Nihon Keizai Shimbun*, Fujinaka Akio, Chairperson of the JPMA, stated 'because the US has been severely complaining about tariffs on coniferous plywood [for a long time], I was prepared for the reduction of the tariffs'.[33]

What convinced the JPMA to accept tariff reduction was the offer of compensation. Initially, members of the LDP, from the *Nōrin zoku* (agricultural lobby) in particular, opposed tariff reductions.[34] However, Prime Minister Nakasone, who was strongly aware of the need to cooperate with the US, took initiatives to respond to US demands. As early as 8 March, Nakasone directed Minister of State Koomoto Toshio to investigate a compensation programme in the event of forest products market liberalization.[35] On 25 March, at the LDP–government joint meeting, Nakasone expressed the need for a compensation programme plus the need for tariff reduction. He said '[the issue of forest products] must make progress within approximately three years while making various compensations for the sector'.[36] Due to Nakasone's initiatives, by late March, leaders of the LDP began to agree on the need for a compensation programme (based on the assumption that tariffs would be reduced). On 29 March, at the LDP Research Commission on Forestry, it was agreed that first, a comprehensive programme to protect forest resources and to promote forestry must be implemented, after which the possibility of tariff reductions would be investigated.[37]

Thus, after the 29 March decision to offer compensation to the private sector, JPMA stopped lobbying against tariff reductions. Although it showed disappointment that the reduction of tariffs was accepted, it announced that it was grateful to those who formulated the programme to revitalize the industry.[38] JPMA arranged a meeting of all the plywood manufacturers on 17 April, and discussed what was needed to rescue the industry when the tariffs were actually reduced. The manufacturers decided on a two-track strategy; first, to demand that tariff reduction be minimal, second, to press for quick implementation of an adequate compensation programme.[39]

In addition to the shifting consensus among LDP leaders for accepting tariff reduction and adopting compensation, there were a number of reasons for the lack of momentum on the side of the downstream manufacturers. The first reason is that the downstream manufacturers were not worried about the reduced tariffs on softwood plywood and veneers, which were the main interests of the US. These makers thought that Japanese users were so quality-conscious that they would not use coniferous products, which have large knots, as much as hardwood products from warmer regions.[40]

Second, because American manufacturers had not invested in making products according to the Japanese standards typically used in Japanese house construction, the Japanese manufacturers knew that producing Japanese-size products was not cost-effective for US makers, so US exports would not increase rapidly.[41] Moreover, because the downstream manufacturers were aware of the rising trend in the US toward restricting exports of logs, they could not consistently oppose the tariff reductions through fear of losing a source of raw materials.[42]

The plywood manufacturers worried most about increased exports from Southeast Asia, mainly Indonesia. Indonesian plywood is made of hardwood, and as a result of technology cooperation with Japanese trading companies, its quality and standards met the needs of Japanese users.[43] After the government decided on the tariff reduction and compensation programme, the interest of the downstream industries changed from opposing the tariff reduction to acquiring significant amounts of financial support from the national account to dispose of surplus capacity.

Involvement of the upstream industries

The Japanese government's inability to reach resolution until the very last day of the MOSS negotiation was due to magnified sectoral opposition. Unlike the paper industry or fibreboard, which are linked to the domestic forestry business through the supply of raw materials, the upstream industry had few reasons to oppose reduction of tariffs on plywood. However, the close relations of the timber growers (upstream industry) to the ruling party and the fact that the manufacturing sector fell under the jurisdiction of the Forestry Agency encouraged the upstream industries to bandwagon on to the lobbying effort with the prospect that some compensation would be provided.

One of the interesting aspects of the issue of forest products was the number and variety of private actors that actively lobbied against the US requests. The MOSS talks on forest products dealt with processed products as opposed to raw materials such as logs.[44] However, sectoral opposition not only involved lobbying by finished products manufacturers but also by upstream industries, i.e., producers of logs. Farmers of completely unrelated products, such as rice, also took part in the opposition to the proposed tariff reduction.

As we have already seen, in January 1985, the four large upstream and downstream organizations lobbied Minister of Agriculture Satō for maintenance of current tariff rates (see Figure 5.2). The group included the JPMA, the All-Japan Federation of Lumber Associations, the Japan Forestry Association, and the National Federation of Forest Owners' Associations.[45] Then, again on 14 March 1985, the same group of organizations appealed to the MAFF and politicians.[46] Given that the US request for tariff reduction involved only manufactured products, not raw materials such as logs, the participation of the two latter organizations was rather unexpected.

As the government proceeded toward accepting the US request on tariff reduction in early April, opposition to market liberalization spread to include various agricultural organizations. In opposition to the External Economic Measures (EEM) package announced on 9 April, nineteen agricultural organizations, including dairy farming and stockbreeding, forestry, and fisheries put a half-page advertisement titled 'Sayonara Nihon' (Good-bye Japan) in major newspapers. The advertisement stated that the proposed market liberalization would destroy natural resources of forests and the ocean as well as reduce self-sufficiency of food.[47] Although this advertisement did not specifically mention forest products, it was clear that these organizations were opposed to the proposed tariff reductions on forest products because forest products were the only agriculture-related item listed in the EEM.

The lobbying against tariff reduction was led by the upstream industry, the National Federation of Forest Owners' Association in particular, although the downstream manufacturers did not invite the upstream ones to join them.[48] On the surface, the reasoning of the upstream sector for joining the opposition made sense. Upstream firms and workers emphasized the need for protecting the domestic industry to process their primary product, because many Japanese forests would reach the cutting period by the mid-1990s.[49] Most of the trees commercially planted in Japan were planted in the 1950s, because high demand for domestic wood products during the Second World War and the immediate postwar period exhausted the domestic supply of wood.[50] However, most informed opinion doubted this connection of the upstream to the problem of downstream manufacturers. The connection was questioned because 90 per cent of the wood used for plywood was imported; therefore, even if the domestic plywood manufacturers declined, it would have had very little direct impact on the domestic forestry industry.[51]

Why did the upstream and downstream industries form a coalition? The first answer is the fact that the upstream and downstream industries both fell under the jurisdiction of the Forestry Agency making it easier for the upstream to mobilize itself in support of the downstream's lobbying. In addition, the upstream industries, timber growers in particular, held a clientelistic relationship with the ruling party, and the MOSS talks presented firms and individual growers with an opportunity to demand benefits from the Japanese government. There are two additional reasons for the ostensibly unrelated agricultural sector to join the opposition to tariff reductions. First, because forestry does not require full-time labour, 70 per cent of private forest workers were also engaged in farming of other products.[52] Second, the farmers were willing to support the forestry sector because they felt a need to maintain 'a unified front' against market liberalization of agricultural products in general.[53]

The upstream sector originally cooperated with the downstream manufacturers in opposition to the tariff reductions. However, once the government decided to reduce tariffs, conflicts of interests between these two sectors became apparent. On the one hand, the downstream manufacturers 'legitimately' lobbied for the larger subsidies this sector was to receive in compensation for the damage suffered by expanded imports. On the other hand, the upstream sector vied for larger compensation to *itself* under the guise that the damage caused to the forest products industry would severely damage the upstream industry, or forestry.[54] Because the overall size of the *Gokanen Keikaku*, or five-year compensation plan, was already decided to not exceed 85 billion yen (the size was reduced to 50 billion yen during the final stage of the negotiation, Tables

Table 5.2 The *Gokanen Keikaku* proposal (billion yen)

Measure	National account	Loan
To increase the demand for wood	6	–
To strengthen the wood products industry	32	56
To revitalize forests and forestry (thinning, tendering, and other methods)	47	60
Total	85	116

Source: *Yomiuri Shimbun*, 14 June 1985

5.2 and 5.3) by June 1985, the lobbying by the upstream and the downstream sectors became more and more like a zero-sum game.

The upstream sector, combined with the agricultural sector, was destined to win this game against the downstream manufacturers. Not only were the upstream industry and the agricultural sector, in particular, well organized, with a nationwide network of agricultural cooperatives, but they also had strong ties to *Nōrin zoku* politicians. Because of the sheer number of workers engaged in the upstream sector (forestry (or upstream) industries employed 150,000 people and were able to form a loose coalition with 4.8 million farm workers – and thus votes – compared to the ones in downstream manufacturing where only 35,000 workers were employed), politicians tended to support the former when the game became zero-sum.[55] Although the upstream sector would not be directly affected by the tariff reduction, the need for preservation of forestry was often cited by politicians in conjunction with the problems of national security and environmental protection.[56]

Effects of politicization

Nakasone's initiative reconciled the increasing domestic opposition to tariff reduction and the US pressure to liberalize the market. As aforementioned, on 25 March, Nakasone, at the LDP–government joint meeting, announced that '[the issue of forest products] must make progress within approximately three years'. He also said that 'compensation for the sector would be made'.[58] However, Nakasone's leadership did not solve the problem but rather generated a more difficult problem of 'who gets what'. Logically the primary recipient of the compensation ought to have been forest products manufacturers. However, because the decision was made under pressure from the upstream industries, the LDP had to decide how much would be given to which sector.

The choice to decide which industries would receive the compensation

Table 5.3 The final draft of the *Gokanen Keikaku* (billion yen)

Measure	National account	Loan
To increase the demand for wood	5.0	–
To strengthen the wood products industry: of which[57]	10.0	60.0
development of technology	0.2	–
business conversion	1.3	12.8
disposal of surplus capacity	8.5	47.2
To revitalize forests and forestry (thinning, tendering, and other methods)	35.0	40.0
Total	50.0	100.0

Source: Nikkan Mokuzai Shimbun, 9 November 1985

initiated an intensive debate among LDP leaders. Secretary-General Kanemaru, representing the interests of *Nōrin zoku* politicians, used the rhetoric that the problem of tariffs on forest products was related to the maintenance of forests in Japan, and hence was a problem of national conservation. Kanemaru, in a speech delivered to the private sector, stated 'we cannot let the Japanese land turn into a desert', and insisted that upstream industries be included in the proposed compensation programme.[59] In contrast, Finance Minister Takeshita, representing the group which wanted to limit the size of the programme, emphasized the need to help the downstream industry.[60]

The battle between the two camps undermined Nakasone's initiative and delayed resolution of the issue. Takeshita and the MOF opposed an extended compensation programme, *Nōrin zoku* politicians backed by powerful LDP leaders such as Kanemaru and the LDP Policy Affairs Research Council (PARC) chairman Fujio Masayuki tried to give as much compensation as possible to their constituencies. The final settlement indicated that a majority of the LDP supported the Kanemaru camp and opted for stretching the scope of beneficiaries. In retrospect, this was a somewhat necessary conclusion from the perspective of the number of votes involved.

As a result of political bargaining within the LDP, the JPMA's effort to obtain large subsidies failed. Originally, the JPMA asked for 87 billion yen (1.5 billion yen to be spent on each of 58 plants, which was 40 per cent of the capacity to be closed down) but the JPMA was forced to revise its proposal to a more realistic plan later.[61] On 30 July, the MAFF and the MOF came to an agreement that the overall size of the five-year plan would be 50 billion yen.[62] In this agreement, compensation was even smaller than the plan suggested by the Forestry Agency earlier in June.[63] In the final draft of the *Gokanen Keikaku*, 10 billion yen was allocated to the finished products manufacturers and the rest went to the upstream industry (Table 5.3). Moreover, although forest products manufacturers lobbied actively for a large subsidy to dispose of surplus capacity after they realized that a tariff reduction was inevitable, the agency did not even consult with these manufacturers and decided suddenly that only loans, and not subsidies, would be available.[64]

In sum, by joining the sectoral opposition, the upstream industries not only won a large sum of the compensation but halted the negotiation over tariff reductions. Because the downstream industries were left with little compensation, the Forestry Agency could not respond to the US demand for elimination of tariffs but offered only small tariff cuts.[65]

6

CONCLUSION

What are the implications of the studies presented in the previous chapters? In the first half of this chapter, I would like to present two sets of implications on the nature of state and society relationships in Japan. The first set of implications is drawn directly from the cases we saw in the previous chapters, and can be summarized thus: 1 the Japanese state intervenes in its economy with a goal to open its markets; and 2 the proximity of relationship between ministries and the private sector varies from sector to sector and ministry to ministry. The second implication is somewhat indirect but nevertheless closely related to the findings of these cases. I maintain that in the long run, the power of the Japanese bureaucracy will decline (although the bureaucracy will stay powerful for a short period, until the current political turmoil subsides). In the second half of this chapter, a number of practical policy suggestions on managing US–Japanese trade problems are presented.

DIRECT IMPLICATIONS: A 'SNAPSHOT' VIEW

The first implication of this study on the relationship between state and society is that we need to modify our automatic association of state interventionism with mercantilism (which is usually contrasted with the liberal state and classical economics of the nineteenth century). Peter Katzenstein has labelled Japan's foreign economic policy 'neo-mercantilism' in contrast to liberalism represented by British and American foreign economic policies.[1] His reasoning for calling Japan neo-mercantilist was based on T.J. Pempel's observation that the ruling triad – big business, the LDP, and the bureaucracy – pursues collectively the objective of national economic growth.[2]

Even though this observation was made a while ago (1977), more recent authors have adhered to it (with some modifications).[3] However, major economic and political changes have taken place in the last twenty years. In these years, Japan became a world economic power and the LDP lost power. While it is still possible that the LDP will regain monopoly of power in the near term, it is very likely that old parties will be destroyed and new ones created in the next few years. In such an event, the ruling triad model and its variations for Japan's policymaking will lose considerable meaning.

What is of most importance here, however, is not the accuracy of the above model. What needs to be re-examined is the labelling of Japan as neo-mercantilist. It is true that in the two decades following the Second World War, the Japanese state actively intervened in the economy through measures such as credit allocation and import of technologies to encourage fast recovery and catch-up with the Western economies. For this period, Katzenstein was correct to label Japan neo-mercantilist. Japan's mercantilistic pursuit of economic growth was supported by the fact that MITI, which held industrial growth as its institutional objective, played a central role in Japan's economic policymaking. It was the main ministry in devising measures such as export subsidies and cartel formation to nurture industrial growth, at the same time heavily protecting the domestic market from foreign competition.

However, when Japan faced *gaiatsu* to modify its one-sided economic expansion in the 1970s, changes occurred in this pattern of foreign economic policymaking in two stages. In the first stage, in the 1970s, Japan no longer could pursue economic expansion at the expense of others. Japan's trading partners, the US in particular, demanded that Japan reduce its exports. Thus, Japan accepted voluntary export restrictions (VERs) in a number of industries such as steel and automobiles. At first glance, this act of export control itself seemed to have changed the image of a neo-mercantilist Japan. However, the motivation behind controlling exports was to subdue flare-ups of protectionism abroad, and thus to continue to secure export markets. Thus, until the 1980s. Japanese efforts to control exports were compatible with neo-mercantilist goals: to secure markets for Japanese exports.

In the following stage, Japan was pressured to open its markets to imports. During the 1980s, through the MOSS talks, the US government sought to open Japanese markets in various sectors which belonged to the jurisdiction of ministries formerly not involved in trade negotiations. As a result, Japan's economic policymaking began to involve far more ministries than MITI. The introduction of ministries other than MITI increased the number of economic goals Japan had to satisfy in trade negotiations. Ministries such as the MHW and the MPT had goals other than the economic growth of the industries under their jurisdiction. The MHW's primary goal as regards the pharmaceuticals industry was to ensure safe and cheap production of drugs, whether by Japanese or foreign makers.

The MPT's stated goal as regards telecommunications was orderly provision of services to customers, in addition to the goal of industrial growth supported by the ministry's desire to become a *seisaku kanchō* (which was sharpened by the privatization of NTT in 1985).

MITI's institutional objectives began to diversify in the 1980s, too. Because most of the industries under its jurisdiction had become competitive, single-minded pursuit of industrial growth began to look somewhat obsolete. To be sure, MITI retains its goal of industrial growth for emerging high-tech industries such as next-generation computers and so-called multi-media.[4] However, as we can see in MITI's slogan 'Import Now!', the preservation of the world free trade system through increased imports is receiving increasing priority as an institutional objective.

These changes signify that while the Japanese state actively implements policies that influence the openness of Japanese markets and remains interventionist, the purpose of intervention has shifted from single-minded pursuit of industrial growth to a more diversified one which includes expansion of imports. The MOSS cases show that Japanese ministries remain interventionist. However, some of these ministries intervened with the intention of making markets more open. Thus, the cases presented in this book suggest the need for renewing our dichotomy between intervention and liberalism: states may intervene in the market with purposes other than protecting national economic growth.

The MOSS talks showed that the ministries make policies based on various institutional objectives. This, in turn, indicates that the Japanese government can no longer sustain a single goal of industrial growth. An interesting question is whether this diversification of economic goals is supported by a change in public opinion. At the time of the MOSS talks, not much discussion on national goals took place and therefore it appeared that the Japanese public was either unaware of or unsure about the need for new national goals.

However, by the end of the 1980s, after gaining an international reputation as a world economic power, the Japanese people increasingly questioned the assumed national goal of economic growth. By then, the gap between Japan's GNP and the public's satisfaction with standards of living had become too obvious. When people began asking 'growth for what?', the legitimacy of economic growth as the national goal diminished. Prime Minister Miyazawa Kiichi, who entered office in November 1991, was the first national leader to set a clear goal of '*Seikatsu Taikoku*' (literally 'life superpower', but the meaning is closer to 'better quality of life for the people').[5]

This idea of improving quality of life seems to have become the linchpin of the succeeding governments. Indeed, the fact that these governments all espoused variations of this idea means that all major political parties and their leaders agree on the principle of the need to improve quality of life in Japan. The Hosokawa government upheld *Seikatsusha Jūshi*, or 'consumer oriented', policies. While Prime Minister Hosokawa's effort to introduce Welfare Tax resulted in an egregious failure, his government succeeded in submission of an important law to protect consumers, namely, the Product Liability Law of 1994, to the Diet. The Hata government lasted too briefly to produce effective policies based on the consumer-oriented principle but Hata explicitly stated the need for the 'construction of a more prosperous and secure society' in his first (and last) policy speech made in the Lower House of the Diet on 10 May 1994.[6] The Murayama government also maintains improvement of the quality of life as one of the main pillars of its policy programme which is embodied in its slogan *'Yasashii Seiji'* (caring politics).

Thus, the idea that the Japanese people need better quality of life is supported by not only the general public but also by all major political parties. Yet both political leaders and the general public have so far failed to reach any concrete conclusions about what Japanese society with a better quality of life should look like in the near future. For instance, there is no clear agreement as to how much of the government budget should be allocated to increasing social capital. Together with the lack of agreement on Japan's foreign policy among political leaders, diversification of economic goals has left Japan with no blueprint for the future.

The second direct implication of this study on the nature of Japan's state and society relationships is that the Japanese state relates to society through ties that vary in terms of their strength and length. In Chapter 1 we asked to what extent interest group competition accounts for policy output. The case studies we have seen offer some clues to modifying existing models. Most recent studies of Japan's capitalism seem to agree that the Japanese market can be characterized by what Murakami Yasusuke called 'compartmentalized competition'. The reason why the market is 'compartmentalized' is that the bureaucracy created divisions in the economy according to its jurisdictions. Thus, while contemporary scholars use various terms such as 'network state', 'bureaucratic-inclusionary pluralism' and 'compartmentalized pluralism' to describe the close relationship between the Japanese state and market (or society depending on whether the issue discussed is economic or political), market competition is largely limited by the 'compartmentalizing' role of the bureaucracy.[7]

What these models do not capture, however, is the varying degrees of bureaucratic involvement in each sector depending on the type of relationship between the sector and the ministry. A comparison of the relationship between the pharmaceutical industry and the MHW, and the relationship between the electronics industry and MITI, exemplifies this point. While there is cut-throat competition in both markets, the 'networks' formed between the ministry and the industry do not look the same. As for the pharmaceuticals industry and the MHW, the network seems heavily imbalanced in favour of the ministry, due to the regulatory nature of the relationship. The MHW's main concern is to regulate the pharmaceutical products market in order to secure safe drugs for the Japanese public. The need for manufacturers to adhere to the regulations in order to ensure marketing of their products, combined with the ministry's historical origin within the repressive Home Ministry, leave the manufacturers with little influence on the ministry's decision-making process. By contrast, the network between MITI and the electronics industry is much more balanced in favour of the private sector. As an effect of having a post-promotive relationship, MITI does not have tight control over the industry. As a result, MITI cannot make decisions that conflict with the manufacturers' perceived interests.

INDIRECT IMPLICATIONS: A LONG-TERM VIEW

The pattern of policymaking in the MOSS talks also offers clues to understanding long-term shifts of the power balance between politically influential actors. More specifically, the power of the bureaucracy in relation to the private sector and political leaders will be discussed here.

Is the power of the Japanese bureaucracy declining? Before answering this question, we must ask what kind of power the Japanese bureaucracy has had so far. As Chalmers Johnson's 'developmental state' model claimed, the Japanese bureaucracy, economic ministries in particular, played a central role in shaping the postwar Japanese economy. Through the control of capital and technology, the bureaucracy, in the 1950s and 1960s, had power over industries. In addition, as the ruling-triad model suggested, the bureaucracy has been at least as powerful as the ruling party.

Some claim that although the bureaucracy dominated the LDP since the party's creation in 1955, by the mid-1970s, the LDP had gained expertise in policymaking.[8] However, at a minimum, Kasumigaseki retained its power in relation to the LDP politicians due to its role as the exclusive think tank for the party. For instance, throughout the postwar period, the majority of laws which passed the Diet have been submitted by the cabinet and thus, drafted by the bureaucracy.[9] Even when laws were drafted by politicians, oftentimes, the bureaucrats helped them fill out the technical details.[10] Furthermore, bureaucrats helped ministers – visibly and invisibly – by providing answers to opposition party queries and defending draft laws in Diet committees and on the floor. These activities were all possible because the bureaucracy retained thorough knowledge of the national economy, while politicians tended to focus their attention on the needs of their local constituents. Thus, if the LDP relied heavily on the bureaucracy for technical knowledge and the drafting of laws, it is doubtful that the LDP increased its ability in policymaking independent of the bureaucracy. To be sure, on issues involving constituencies, such as rice market liberalization and the liberalization of markets 'related to' the forestry industry (as we have seen in the forest products negotiations), the bureaucracy had reduced control over policy outputs.

This book offers a qualified answer to the question whether the power of the bureaucracy over industries is in decline or not. The overall trend is that the bureaucracy has lost its tight control over the economy due to a series of market liberalization measures taken since the mid-1970s. Two major instruments for controlling the economy were examined in this book: formal trade barriers and regulations. As a result of a series of multilateral trade talks and bilateral trade talks such as the MOSS talks, both formal trade barriers and regulations are diminishing. While this is more so in the case of formal trade barriers and there are many regulations yet to be relaxed, generally speaking, the bureaucracy's power to control markets is in decline.

However, as we look at individual ministries and their relationships with various industries, the speed and degree to which each ministry has lost power over the private sector varies. As for the power between a ministry and an industry with regulatory relationships, *gaiatsu* to remove excessive regulations reduces the control of the ministry over the industry. Likewise, for a ministry that maintains a restructuring relationship with an industry, *gaiatsu* may work (if the issue is not politicized as in the case of forest products) to remove protective measures. In post-promotive relationships, the fact that the industry has matured signifies reduced dependence of the industry on the ministry, thereby reducing the power of the ministry.

Some cases show the continuing power of the bureaucracy, however. These are the cases in which industries hold promotive relationships with a ministry. Emerging industries such as next generation computers,[11] HDTV, biotechnology, and multi-media all tend to have promotive relationships with ministries. With the private sector's presumed need for large capital investment, R & D, and safeguard against risks, it is quite likely that ministries will remain heavily involved in the growth of these sectors.

It appears that the idea that a new technology needs guidance from a ministry (or ministries) to grow into a competitive industry still persists in the minds of some ministry officials, particularly in the economic ministries. For instance, MITI recently made a proposal to revise the copyright-protection law and establish a so-called Digital Information Center in order to provide manufacturers of multi-media easy access to copyright protected software.[12] As a consequence, it seems quite likely that ministries will continue their effort to create new promotive relationships. The constant emergence of promotive relationships between ministries and high-technology industries signify continued bureaucratic power in shaping the economy.

However, there is a high likelihood that for every new high-tech industry there will be more than one ministry to claim its jurisdiction. This means that the era when MITI dominated important industries is forever gone. In emerging industries, ministries engage in ministerial rivalry. As the cases of protection of software copyrights and telecommunications indicate, eventually one ministry will win the legal jurisdiction of a new industry.[13] The end result of a turf battle is that a ministry may be able to claim that a new industry is under its jurisdiction, but with considerable compromise on its control of the industry. Thus, even for a promotive relationship, a ministry's power in relation to a new industry will not be as strong as that held by MITI in the past. The result of a reduced ministerial grip on high-tech industries is increased influence of private sector decisions on the industrial structure. For instance, whether Japan's telecommunications will be based on wired telecommunications or satellite communications will be decided by business prospects for profits, not by the MPT's desire to increase its power within the bureaucracy.

As for the bureaucracy's power over politicians, there are short- and long-term trends. For a short period of time, the bureaucracy in general will remain powerful in relation to political leaders because of the current political crisis. The continuing power of the bureaucracy became apparent during the Hosokawa and the succeeding Hata governments, because they were a mosaic of various parties, both new and old, most of which had never had experience in government. The current government – an unlikely coalition of the SDPJ, LDP and Harbinger Party – gives even more room for the bureaucracy to manipulate political leaders because these parties, the SDPJ and LDP in particular, have fundamental disagreements about major policy issues such as defence and UN peace keeping operations. As a result, gridlock is likely.[14] Furthermore, the passage of political reform bills in March 1994, which may result in a major reshuffling of political parties, will lengthen the period of bureaucratic dominance.[15] The passage of these bills will naturally draw political leaders' attention to strategies for winning the next election, thereby increasing the autonomy of the bureaucracy.

These bills change the electoral system from the current multi-member districts (between two and six seats per district) to a system that combines single-member districts and proportional representation. This shift, the change from multi-member districts to single-member ones in particular, will accelerate the ongoing fission and fusion of political parties for two reasons. First, the two traditionally largest parties, the LDP and the SDPJ, will probably break up because in the new electoral system, the parties will have to determine only one candidate per district, at the same time withdrawing official endorsement from many who used to run in the same district. In addition, as we saw in the formation of the New Frontier Party, small parties will face an increasing need to cooperate with one another or create new parties, because 'winner-take-all' single-member districts work to favour larger parties with broader public appeal, organization, and funding.

In the long run, however, once the new political system stabilizes, it is likely that the power of the bureaucracy in relation to political leaders will decline as Japan faces problems that the bureaucracy cannot resolve effectively. Bureaucracy-centred policymaking will eventually face a number of such problems for several reasons. The first reason is that bureaucracy-led market liberalization has its limits. As we saw in the case of electronics, for instance, many barriers to imports are not created by the government. Trade conflict often occurs when a Japanese industry grows competitive in the world market, as the cases of automobiles and semiconductors suggest. However, these industries, because they tend to have post-promotive relationships with ministries, do not come under the control of ministries easily. Thus, various trade-restricting practices observed by private firms are hard to change.

In addition, as Japan increases its interdependence with the world economy, market liberalization limited to specific sectors will not be sufficient. Cross-sectoral adjustments such as change in the distribution network are needed in order for Japan to engage in mutually beneficial trading relationships with other countries. Unless the current bureaucracy is redesigned to form ministries that do not divide the national economy into jurisdictions based on industries, cross-sectoral adjustments are difficult to achieve by the action of the bureaucracy. Such redesigning of the ministries cannot be achieved without strong political initiative. Ministry officials are unlikely to reach an agreement on the new design of ministries, because ministerial restructuring requires merging bureaus within a ministry and/or ministries which in turn will both create new offices and eliminate current offices.

Finally, the bureaucracy is effective only when political leaders assign it a clear task. The bureaucracy-led policy formation worked during the postwar catch-up period because political leaders such as Yoshida Shigeru and Ikeda Hayato agreed on the national goal for economic growth. Because of this agreement, MITI's role was to help Japanese industries become world competitive. The political agreement assigned ministries of Transport and Construction such tasks as the establishment of industrial infrastructure in order to modernize the economy. However, the period of single-minded economic growth ended by the late 1980s. What Japan confronted was the question 'growth for what'? The bureaucracy cannot offer creative answers to this question. The reason is that the bureaucracy is not accountable and thus cannot effectively respond to changing

100

national preferences. It is the responsibility of political leaders to redefine Japan's national goals.

The rise of problems that are not effectively resolved by the bureaucracy does not automatically lead to increased political leadership. However, as a result of political reform, the introduction of single-member electoral districts in particular, political parties will become increasingly oriented towards generating policies that respond to the changing needs of voters. Under the current multi-member districts, policy differences among political parties were often lost because more than one candidate from the same party often ran in the same district. However, single-member districts eliminate this possibility. Thus, each candidate will have to highlight differences in his/her party's policy platforms and appeal to voters, which, in turn, requires policy platforms to reflect the preferences of voters. Such an emergence of policy-oriented political parties will mean increased political leadership, because political leaders will face an increasing need to implement policies they promised to the voters. Under such circumstances, the rise of new problems that require political initiatives will offer a great opportunity for politicians to further strengthen their leadership in relation to the bureaucracy.

POLICY SUGGESTIONS FOR THE US AND JAPANESE GOVERNMENTS

What lessons can the American and Japanese governments learn from the MOSS talks? What should the US government expect from future sector-specific trade talks? Should the US continue to apply pressure to achieve more open markets? Or should the US give up opening markets but aim at forcing Japan to give foreign firms or US companies a certain share of market while leaving the basic operation of Japanese markets intact? Is there any lesson the Japanese government can learn from its past trade negotiations with the US? What kind of trade strategies should Japan adopt in order to prevent future trade conflicts?

For the US government, the central issue is the choice between opening markets in Japan and a results-oriented trade strategy (with or without a pretence that it is still pursuing free trade policy).[16] To put my conclusion first, the US should, for political reasons, choose to maintain its strategy to pressure for opening of Japanese markets, at the same time making macro adjustments jointly with Japan.

Before we discuss the general trade strategy that the US government should adopt toward Japan, let us see what lessons the cases of the MOSS talks give us. First of all, the US government must not choose issues on which *gaiatsu* has poor prospects of success. Therefore, the most important first step is to examine the cases that are to be placed on the negotiation agenda and check if these cases meet the conditions under

101

which *gaiatsu* works. As the MOSS talks suggest, obstacles to market liberalization arise when one or more elements of capacity of a ministry are missing and/or the ministry has relatively low control over the private sector because the relationship is either promotive or post-promotive. Also, if the case is politicized due to the involvement of politically powerful interest groups as in the case of forest products, market liberalization is difficult to achieve even if strong *gaiatsu* is applied.

The negative effect of careless selection of cases with little prospect for *gaiatsu* to succeed might not be contained within these cases, but could have a broader impact on the future of US–Japan relations. The repeated use of *gaiatsu* on cases that failed to achieve resolution is likely to lead to increased confidence among members of the Japanese government that they withstood *gaiatsu*. A result of increased confidence is to view future (and the past) US demands as unreasonable and Japan as a victim of such demands. Once Japan establishes the view that Japan is a victim, there will be no market opening measures because in the minds of Japanese policymakers, the villain is not Japan but the US, i.e., the US government is pushing for expanded exports of products that have no international competitiveness.

However, it is rare that a ministry in charge of the case meets all the elements of ministerial capacity. Thus, we need to know which element poses the most difficult obstacle to market liberalization. Among the three elements of ministerial capacity, problems related to the lack of autonomy are the most likely to be resolved if pressure is placed on the Japanese government to determine which ministry has jurisdiction over the issue. In this process, the US government might be used by a ministry (ministries) or other political actors to tip the power balance between two opposing groups, as the cases of VANs and software copyright protection suggest.[17] And to help achieve favourable outcomes, the US may need to continue applying *gaiatsu*. But as the past cases suggest, this type of obstacle to market liberalization is not often left unresolved; *gaiatsu* can be an effective catalyst and opposing groups have a strong interest in resolving the issue of jurisdiction.

A case that involves institutional objectives that conflict with market liberalization is slightly more difficult to resolve than a case that involves missing ministerial autonomy. Many ministries, in efforts to meet a variety of institutional objectives, try to regulate markets under their jurisdiction. These regulations may prohibit entry of new firms, both Japanese and foreign, into the market.

As discussed in Chapter 2, ministries regulate the economy for reasons such as protection of public goods, lack of consumer protection, paternalism, and qualified acceptance of free market ideals. While the first two – protection of public goods, and lack of consumer protection – are changing, paternalism and only qualified acceptance of free market ideals still persist in the thinking of ministry officials. These two elements are difficult to change because reducing them would imply a smaller role for ministry officials. Thus, ministries tend not to accept market liberalization as a principle, and prefer that future sector-specific negotiations be done on a case-by-case basis. Trade negotiators, Americans in particular, who come from economies governed by the principle of free market competition may continue to be frustrated with such case-by-case market liberalization in Japan. However, talks such as the MOSS negotiations on telecommunications and pharmaceuticals indicate that trade negotiators, through effective agenda formation, can succeed in convincing ministry officials that excessive regulations hinder both foreign firms' access to the market and Japanese industrial growth through competition.

Cases for which ministries lack effective policy instruments pose particularly complicated problems for foreign governments. In the context of market liberalization, lack of effective policy instruments means lack of formal trade barriers and regulations in the given sector. This situation often arises in industries that maintain post-promotive relationships with their respective ministries (most likely MITI), as we have seen in the case of electronics. The responsible ministry cannot offer an effective resolution to the closed market for two reasons. First, the barriers to market access are often the result of commercial practices that exclude participation of new firms. Thus, the ministry has no formal barriers to eliminate. Furthermore, if the private sector is responsible for creating such barriers, under a post-promotive relationship, the ministry has very little power to influence private firms' decisions.

Keiretsu relationships are a typical example of commercial practices that hinder market access. For instance, a recent study on the automobiles trade indicated that the *keiretsu* system is one of the main reasons why auto dealers cannot increase sales of American cars.[18] *Keiretsu* refers to a loose conglomerate of firms linked by a bank (functioning as a core financial institution) as well as common product and labour markets. There are two types of *keiretsu* relationships. The first type of *keiretsu* relationships is horizontal *keiretsu* that centres around cross-share holdings by member firms. Because member firms are not exposed to the risk of takeovers, this type of *keiretsu* is thought to have the virtue of stabilizing management. In addition, there are vertical *keiretsu* relationships that bind small suppliers to large buyers or large suppliers to retail stores (e.g. car dealers). It is the second type of *keiretsu* that tends to close markets for non-member firms. While Japan's trading partners are increasingly frustrated with such business arrangements, it is difficult for the Japanese government to break *keiretsu* relationships because firms possess legal rights to choose their trading partners.

The fact that it is not easy for a single ministry to change the *keiretsu* system does not necessarily mean that there is no remedy to this problem, though. The remedy is to pressure political leaders, not the bureaucrats. To be sure, policies that aim at the total demolition of *keiretsu* might invite strong resentment among Japanese business. Potential or real opposition from business would mean political leaders are unwilling to accept such a change. However, a close examination of the nature of the problem offers keys to the US government to press for correction of specific problems.

For instance, the US government should pressure the Japanese government to revise the Anti-Monopoly Law, such that commercial practices that are not necessarily in violation of the current Anti-Monopoly Law but nonetheless promote exclusive trade relationships between dealers and manufacturers will be punished. In the case of automobiles trade, for example, the problem with Japanese auto dealers is not that they have exclusive contractual relationships with a manufacturer, which is potentially a violation of the Anti-Monopoly Law.[19] The dealers' unwillingness to sell foreign automobiles is mainly due to the fact that they receive commissions from a manufacturer if they achieve the annual goals that are set very close to the maximum number of cars a dealer can sell. Thus, an auto dealer is compelled to deal with the manufacturer's cars and has no incentive to deal with other cars. The US government, therefore, should pressure the Japanese government to correct commercial practices that may not be formally exclusive but have the effect of producing exclusive relationships.

Another way to change commercial practices that hinder access to Japanese markets is to increase the power and independence of the agency that is in charge of enforcing the Anti-Monopoly Law, namely, the Japan Fair Trade Commission (JFTC). The weak status of the Commission is mostly a result of pressure from both the bureaucracy (read MITI) and business during the high-growth period when MITI played a large role in Japan's economic policymaking.

There are a number of reasons why the JFTC is rather ineffectual. The primary reason is that it does not have its own enforcement authority, such as the right to conduct on-site investigations held by the police or prosecutors. Another is that the organization is heavily influenced by other ministries such as the MOF and MITI because the members of the Commission (the chair and three commission members) are usually appointed from these ministries (except for one member, who is a career officer in the Commission).[20]

Because powerful ministries such as MOF and MITI have a high stake in keeping the Commission as it is, if the US government exerted pressure on the bureaucracy to change the status of the Commission, it is unlikely that such pressure would produce much fruit. Changes in the Anti-Monopoly Law and the status of JFTC will only come from political leadership. However, political leaders have neither debated this issue thoroughly nor have they come to an agreement. Therefore, in order to place this issue on the Japanese government's policy agenda and accelerate the process of resolution to *keiretsu* and other issues that require increased market competition, the US government should pressure political leaders.

Unfortunately, in the short run, such political initiatives will not occur because of the current political turmoil. Therefore, for the time being, the US government should resort to other measures. Some recommended utilization of multilateral provisions such as the GATT article twenty-three, which stipulates punitive actions such as suspension of concessions in case a member country seriously violates GATT rules.[21] Continued use of multilateral – instead of unilateral – pressure may work, without stirring resentment against the US, to raise the awareness of Japanese manufacturers that to continue their business in the world market, exclusive trading relationships at home must be corrected.

In sum, if cases are carefully chosen with the thorough understanding of the nature of the obstacles to resolution, as the case involving *keiretsu* relationships demonstrated, pressure to open markets will work. This point proves that what some officials in the Clinton administration seem to believe – the sole remedy to market access problems in Japan is 'results-oriented' or managed trade – is wrong. Instead, US trade policymakers can continue their policy to open markets abroad by carefully designing the policy based on their past trade negotiation experiences with Japan.

In addition to these reasons why market opening measures work, there are three reasons why a results-oriented trade strategy should not be adopted. The first reason is the fact that there is a strong objection to managed trade among Japanese policymakers and business. If the US adopted this policy, it would likely cause resentment among Japanese political and business leaders, which in turn would endanger future US–Japan relations. Moreover, adoption of managed trade would not bear much fruit, because the Japanese government cannot force the private sector to buy more US-made products. In order to avoid a 'trade-war', the Japanese government may agree under pressure on a numerical target with the possible qualification that it is not an agreed share but merely a *doryoku mokuhyō* (preferred achievement). However, such an agreement is not likely to be successful: the Japanese government would not be able to guarantee the achievement of the share, and there is no clear logic why such an agreement would lead to more open markets.

Finally, and most importantly, it is of crucial importance that the US stick with free trade principles because they provide the US with legitimacy as the world's political leader. Recent debate over the effect of results-oriented trade policies seems to centre on their domestic economic effect, that is, whether they would increase US exports or not. However,

US political leaders must also consider the international political effect of such trade policies.

The question of whether US hegemony has declined or not is beyond the scope of this study. However, it is undeniable that the US still remains the most powerful leader in world politics. Why? What makes the US a legitimate leader? There are many answers to this question. As the US leadership in the Gulf war, US attempts to restore democracy in Haiti in September 1994, and the effort to halt a potential second Iraqi invasion of Kuwait in October 1994 demonstrated, overwhelming military power still counts as a resource for leadership. In addition, large markets are in a sense a form of potential power. As the MOSS talks indicated, large American markets provide incentives for US trading partners to accept US requests. However, it is not just the tangible military capability and the size of markets that make the world accept (with varying degrees of reluctance, perhaps) what the US government says and does.

I contend that the universal ideal of free trade the US upholds provides legitimacy to US leadership. If a government tries to improve its trade balance through either closing its markets to foreign products or pursuing results-oriented trade with its trading partners, it is unlikely that those trading partners will accept the country's claim that others are trying to exploit its economy. By contrast, if a government maintains free trade policy, it can legitimately demand reciprocity from other governments. If the US decided to adopt more 'results-oriented' trade policies, the US would lose its legitimacy as the guardian of world free trade, thereby reducing its political leverage over its trading partners.

It is in the interest of the US to maintain its global political leverage as the world faces post-Cold War turbulence. Whether the US should maintain its ability to influence world affairs must be debated elsewhere. However, the Clinton administration seems to keep a strong willingness to influence current world affairs despite the president's image that he focuses on domestic affairs. US interest in world affairs ranges from economic issues such as relationships with the European Union, APEC, and NAFTA, to security issues such as the maintenance of peace in the Middle East and the suspected development of nuclear weapons in North Korea. Not only is it crucial for the US to maintain its economic and military power resources, but it is also important that the world perceives US foreign policy as legitimate in order for the US to attain desired outcomes.

Two trade policies are preferable to a 'results-oriented' trade strategy. The US government should encourage the Japanese government to adopt a more aggressive macro-economic policy. According to IMF estimates, Japan's structural budget balance is expected to dip only briefly into deficit in Fiscal Year 1994 (April 1994–March 1995), and even then, this deficit would be the smallest among the G7 countries.[22] *If current policy continues and the government does not change its fiscal policy dras-tically*, the situation will continue at least through Fiscal Year 1995 and possibly until the late 1990s. From Japan's point of view, expansionary fiscal policy is needed not only to correct current trade problems between Japan and its trading partners but also for domestic reasons. Because Japan needs to prepare for the ageing of its citizenry in the form of an increased stock of social infrastructure, the Japanese government must opt for increased government expenditure in welfare-related public works.[23]

In addition, the US government should tailor its trade strategies to political changes in Japan. For several reasons, recent political changes will transform the nature of political intervention in trade negotiations. First, with the end of the LDP's monopoly on power, interest groups that were long involved in close, and sometimes clientelistic, relationships with the LDP will no longer be so powerful. Politically influential interest groups ranged from business associations to groups of farmers and small business owners. These groups have all lost the easy communication channels they maintained with the LDP.

In the new political age in which every political party – with the exception of the Communists – has a chance to become a ruling party, interest groups can no longer maintain an exclusive relationship with one party. For instance, Keidanren (Federation of Economic Organizations) can no longer maintain an exclusive tie with the LDP but must also support other conservative parties such as the New Frontier Party and Harbinger Party in case the LDP is driven out of power again. Long-time supporters of the SDPJ, labour unions for example, have also been reconsidering their policy of sole support for this party.

What is more relevant for market liberalization is that political change has weakened the power of interest groups such as agriculture and small business that represented sectors which are not internationally competi-tive and thus posed obstacles to market liberalization negotiations (as illustrated in the case of the MOSS forest product talks). The increased diversification of interest group–political party interaction and the result-ing weakening of the political power of these groups mean that political leaders may face decreased resistance from interest groups on tradition-ally politicized issues (which are mainly issues that involved less competi-tive sectors.)

Moreover, electoral reform – the introduction of proportional repre-sentation for 200 seats and replacement of multi-member districts with single-member districts for 300 seats in the Lower House – will force political parties to establish distinct identities based on policy platforms and ability to govern. Because most of the newly emerging political parties are centrist, projections of distinct policy platforms may not happen in the near future. In the meantime, politicians face an urgent

107

need to show their ability to govern. Since the early 1990s, governability has received much public attention as an important qualification for politicians, due to criticisms made by both the US government and the mass media.[24] These criticisms pointed out that the Japanese bureaucracy is an obstacle to policy changes, and political leadership is needed to overcome bureaucracy-centred policy formation. Thus, instead of intervening to protect the interests of local constituents, political leaders will intervene in the process of trade negotiations in order to resolve issues that cannot be left to ministerial initiatives, such as expanding government expenditures, and issues that cut across the jurisdictions of various ministries.

These political changes should favour US interests. Politicians' increased ability to govern in particular should strongly support US interests because the US government is more interested in increased exports of goods that are of strategic importance to the US economy, such as computers and telecommunications equipment and services, than exports of agricultural or low-value added products. While Japanese political leaders may struggle to take initiatives to increase imports of these products, market liberalization may not proceed as fast as the expectations of both US negotiators and Japan's political leaders because talks may face problems such as inter-ministerial rivalry. The US can accelerate the process of market liberalization by exerting pressure on Japanese political leaders to take initiatives. As we have seen in the case of wired telecommunications, setting specific deadlines will help raise the consciousness of Japan's policymakers – both political leaders and bureaucrats – that promotion of market liberalization must take place as quickly as possible.

The MOSS talks and the recent US–Japan trade negotiations indicate that there are a number of 'actions' the Japanese government must initiate to correct the one-sided accumulation of trade supplies. Now that formal trade barriers such as tariffs and quotas are almost gone, the Japanese government must remove two remaining government-created market barriers to promote the openness of Japanese markets. First, regulations that create obstacles to market access must be relaxed. In addition, procedures for government procurement should become more open to foreign suppliers. The government procures a variety of high-value added products, such as supercomputers and aircraft, increased exports of which would meet a key goal of US trade policy. Thus, it is important that the Japanese government does not exclude foreign suppliers.

Unfortunately, far more needs to be done than deregulation and increased government procurement. The following policy changes or 'actions' that need to be taken are all important, but they will not be realized as fast as we would like because these changes must be made through effective political leadership and the current political crisis may temporarily prevent the government from taking such actions.

The first policy change is, as discussed above, the implementation of expansionary macro-economic measures. This requires two stages of political initiatives. In the first stage, political leaders must agree among themselves on reversing the present bias toward tighter than necessary fiscal policy. In the next stage, political leaders must persuade the powerful Ministry of Finance, which often opposes spending increases or revenue cuts, to accept more expansionary fiscal policy.

That the initial stage – that is, an agreement among political leaders – is crucial for policy change is well-illustrated by the fate of plans for tax reform presented by the Hosokawa government and its successors. While the need for an extensive tax reform was continuously emphasized by the Hosokawa government, it failed to implement anything but a temporary income tax cut (20 per cent across the board) for the next fiscal year. After the short-lived Hata government, the SDPJ–LDP coalition government finally approved a new plan to reform the tax system. However, against expectations for drastic tax reform which would have a long-term effect on economic growth, the reform was done half-heartedly. Instead of overhauling the entire system, the reform only changed tax brackets for middle-income earners leaving taxation for higher income earners intact. One account stated that 'tax reform has greater *near-term implications for politics* than for the economy' [italics mine].[25]

Media reports suggested that MOF made explicit efforts to resist political leaders' effort to change the taxation system drastically and reduce income taxes.[26] However, as indicated by the Socialists' objection to the Hosokawa government's plan to introduce a large hike in consumption taxes, the real cause of the failure to introduce the change in fiscal policy was that political leaders could not agree on the direction of change. Thus, the Japanese government needs strong leadership that brings about agreement among political leaders and the MOF.

Another policy change must occur in the overall shape of public works. Not only should new public works meet the Japanese public's desire for higher standards of living; in addition, new public works should include redesigning of public facilities in order to provide an environment suited for the ageing society.[27] New public works for senior citizens and the handicapped must include obvious facilities such as escalators in the public transportation system, expanded sidewalks, and ramps for wheel chairs in public buildings. The government revised its ten-year public works plan on 7 October 1994, and allocated a large portion (over 60 per cent) of the plan – 630 trillion yen to be spent over the next ten years – to 'seikatsu kankyō, fukushi, bunka kinō' (the living environment, welfare, cultural functions) but the actual allocation used specifically for welfare purposes is not clear.[28] Moreover, the government has yet to announce a blueprint for the long-term transformation of the Japanese welfare system.

The comprehensive welfare programme requires reorganization of ministries according to new functions, not industries, for two reasons. As the MITI–MPT conflict over telecommunications policy in the early 1980s indicated, current ministerial divisions do not enable ministries to effectively cooperate with one another for tasks which cut across various ministerial jurisdictions. Thus, for example, a new Ministry of Welfare which incorporates functions currently performed by the ministries of Health and Welfare (Social Welfare and Children and Families Bureaus), Construction (City Bureau), and Transport (Railway and Road Transport Bureaus), should be created. This ministry would be able to coordinate the design of public facilities to improve quality of life and meet the needs of ordinary people, the elderly, the handicapped or ill, and small children.[29]

Another reason for the need to reorganize ministries is that the Japanese government must change its spending patterns to meet the increased requirement for social welfare. However, the current process of budget formation is not favourable to a radical change in Japan's budget allocation. In Japan, the national budget is based on requests made by each ministry. The budget formation process starts at the section-level of each ministry. Section demands are coordinated at the bureau level, and finally a ministry produces the ministry request which it submits to the MOF.[30] The MOF is in charge of assessment and coordination of each ministry's (often bureaus') requests and in drafting the overall budget proposal.

The allocation of Japan's general account budget since the early 1980s has not changed much, in part because of the so-called 'ceiling' set by the Ministry of Finance to limit the growth of government expenditures. Under this 'ceiling' policy, MOF has set a target of a certain percentage marginal growth (often zero per cent) for ministries' budget requests, constricting the ability of any ministry to increase its share.[31] While the ceiling policy is the direct reason why budget allocation has not changed much over the last ten years, the routine process of budget formation based on requests made by ministerial units – sections, bureaus, and ministries – and coordination that takes place at each level, certainly made it easier for the MOF to continue adhering to this ceiling policy. In other words, the budget formation process works to produce a 'balancing effect', in which no ministry's (bureau's or section's) budget increase will be much larger than that of other ministries. Thus, if the Japanese government were to spend a large sum of its budget for welfare-oriented public works, the Japanese government either has to abandon this 'ceiling' policy or change the ministerial (and bureau) configurations. (Because the abandonment of the 'ceiling' is most likely to lead to intense inter-ministerial rivalries, it is unlikely that the ceiling will be eliminated soon).

The final and probably most important policy change is related to this idea of ministerial reorganization. The involvement of ministries in industrial development has to be thoroughly questioned. The rise of internationally competitive Japanese firms over the last twenty years has demonstrated that they are capable of business initiatives. By contrast, the unclear success of the fifth generation computer and 'Technopolis' projects initiated by MITI, or the MPT-led development of analogue HDTV while digital HDTV is becoming the mainstream world standard indicate that there is a limit to ministerial initiatives on industrial development. It is time to reduce Japanese ministries' intervention in the private sector for the purpose of nurturing domestic industries.

However, the current design of the ministries – so-called *tatewari* or vertical division according to industries – encourages both close industry–ministry relationships and continued ministerial intervention in the private sector. On one hand, the vertical division of ministries based on industries nurtures close relationships between the bureaucracy and industries because it ensures a single channel for industrial leaders to access policymakers. On the other hand, such divisions will create incentives for inter-ministerial (or inter-bureaus) rivalries because of overlapping functions across various ministries and bureaus. These rivalries, in turn, will result in continued creation of ministry-initiated projects such as Multimedia. Ministries (or bureaus) involved in turf battles create such projects with the hope that they will increase their ministry's power in the form of expanded jurisdiction and/or budget allocations.

Thus, through political initiatives, ministries must be reorganized in order to reduce ministry involvement in industrial growth and effectiveness through reduced inter-ministerial conflicts. For instance, a Ministry of Trade could be created by merging trade policy-related bureaus such as the International Trade Policy Bureau of MITI, the Telecommunications Policy Bureau of the MPT, and the Economic Affairs Bureau of the Ministry of Foreign Affairs.

In addition to bureaucratic reform, another measure to reduce ministerial intervention in the private sector is to revise the Anti-Monopoly Law and give more power to the JFTC. The stricter implementation of the Law could accomplish two aims at once. First, as mentioned earlier, stricter implementation would facilitate the access of foreign firms into the Japanese markets. In addition, increased competition means more firms – both domestic and international – will be competing in Japanese markets. Given that the current close relationship between ministries and the private sector is made possible by the small number of firms in a given jurisdiction, the increased number of firms in a market will help reduce the grip of ministries over the private sector.

The most important question here is whether the Japanese government can actually make these changes. As I stated earlier, the political reform that is to take place in the next election will make political parties more sensitive to policy programmes and the issue of governability. Because of this need to offer new policy programmes that are appealing to voters along with the need to demonstrate governability, these changes are likely to occur in the long run. However, these changes, namely adoption of expansionary macro-economic measures, initiation of new types of public works, and reduction of ministerial intervention, all require political leadership. Given today's political instability in Japan, effective leadership may not emerge easily, and thus short-term change is unlikely.

The ongoing political turmoil tells us that the Japanese government may not be able to adopt these policies very soon because of a lack of effective leadership. It is true that the current reshuffling of political parties seems finally to be converging in three main camps – the conservatives (LDP/SDPJ coalition), the centrists (the New Frontier Party) and a third force consisting of groups defecting from the other two camps. While this process of convergence leads us to expect increased political stability, strong political leadership may not emerge quickly since neither of the new coalitions or parties has strong leadership.

The conservative group does not have a strong leader or leaders simply because the LDP – the only source of leadership – lost a large pool of next-generation leaders such as Ozawa Ichirō, Hata Tsutomu, Kakizawa Kōji, and Kaifu Toshiki, when groups of politicians split from the party since 1993. The old leaders such as Takeshita Noboru and Nakasone Yasuhiro are unlikely to re-emerge as leaders because they are associated with the LDP's past involvement in money politics and scandals. The Socialists, on the other hand, still do not have strong leaders because of the left-centrist split within the party.

The centrist party may also have problems with its leadership. It is true that the New Frontier Party drew a large number of politicians with high potential to become leaders of the party. However, the problem of *Kenryoku No Nijū Kōzō* (double-layered power), in which the actual holder of power does not become the official party leader, looms large in the process of choosing leaders. This problem was traditionally seen in the LDP where some leaders had enormous power without becoming the head of the party. This style of party governing was practised by the coalitions that ruled the government under Hosokawa and Hata. In these coalitions, Ozawa Ichirō had the most ability to influence politicians, and above all, to collect large amounts of funds. However, because there were members within the coalition who strongly disliked Ozawa-style leadership – reportedly secretive and authoritarian – and because of Ozawa's negative public image, the coalitions had to choose someone else such as Hosokawa and Hata as the formal head. So long as this problem continues

– and it seems to continue in the New Frontier Party because of Ozawa's continued centrality in the party management – this *Kenryokū No Nijū Kōzō* problem will weaken the coherence of the centrists.

The movement to create the third camp is emerging slowly. Therefore, it is totally unclear whether this will become a significant political force. While it is quite interesting to see what kind of political party will emerge eventually as regards its position on the political spectrum, given that the first two camps have attracted the majority of representatives, it is unlikely that the third party will become large enough to produce effective leadership in the near future.

CONCLUSION

The introduction to this book asked the question whether Japan is like 'us', i.e., if the Japanese government is both internationally responsible and internally accountable to its citizenry. The discussion and cases of market liberalization dealt with in this book cast light on this issue. The MOSS cases suggest that the bureaucracy was still the central actor in making Japan's foreign economic policies in the mid-1980s. The centrality of the bureaucracy certainly reduces Japan's chances of taking spontaneous initiatives internationally and limits accountability toward its citizens. The discussion in this chapter suggests that this centrality of the bureaucracy must be corrected through strong and effective political leadership, which is yet to emerge in Japanese politics.

It is true that the emergence of strong leadership will take some time and therefore thorough changes in Japanese politics and policymaking can only occur gradually. However, several current changes suggest that change in the Japanese political system is already underway. The first change is continued deregulation. Although deregulation in the MOSS talks was initiated by US demands, it is likely that even without *gaiatsu*, deregulation will continue because of intensified demands for deregulation from Japanese business. Deregulation will reduce the discretionary power of the ministries, at the same time increasing the competition among firms due to increased market participation. This, in turn, will weaken the grip of ministries over Japanese markets.

In addition, quality of life will be improved. Provision of the social infrastructure, as opposed to industrial infrastructure, that is needed for higher standards of living and the ageing society requires effective political leadership. A lack of effective leadership, despite an agreement among most political groups on the goal of improved quality of life, will certainly hinder drastic policy changes. However, the current trend toward deregulation will also help increase quality of life in Japan. As the deregulation of telecommunications rapidly increased the variety of telecommunications services available to consumers, as illustrated by the recent surge of portable phone and pager users, deregulation of various business such as postal services and banking could greatly improve quality of life in Japan.

Finally, accountability in the political system will increase. Public policies will reflect the preferences of Japanese voters more accurately than they did under the LDP's rule, due to two aspects of political reform. First, the reapportionment that has accompanied the new electoral system will give more weight to the policy preferences of urban voters, in line with demographic trends. In addition, parties that have concrete policy programmes should emerge. The reason is that voters will vote for parties, not for individual candidates, in the new electoral system. Thus, future elections will not be about the personal favours that politicians bring to their constituencies, but will be about political parties' 'actions'.

On the international front, Japan will remain 'reactive' for a while, although it is urgent that the Japanese government become more responsible in making foreign policies and taking spontaneous 'actions' before its trading partners exert pressure. Unfortunately, the current political changes delay the emergence of the strong political leadership needed for such actions. As a result, in the short-run, Japanese trade policy will continue to look the same: 'reaction' to *gaiatsu*.

This 'reaction' is second-best compared to 'action'. However, as this book suggests, the direction of change is clear; markets are becoming more open and deregulated. Furthermore, with the emergence of strong leaders, in the long-run, Japan will look more like 'us', and will begin to take actions. After all, however slow it may be, the Japanese state and society are changing, which is better than no change at all.

APPENDICES

Chronology of the talks on pharmaceuticals

2 January 1985   Reagan–Nakasone meeting

12 March   First high-level meeting

The US requests:

1 acceptance of foreign test data
2 speedy approval of in-vitro reagents
3 simplification of procedures for change in locus of manufacturing
4 adoption of notification requirement for minor product modifications
5 simplification of address change procedures
6 automatic transfer of *shōnin*
7 transparency
8 simplification of customs procedures

9 April   Japanese government announces the Seventh External Economic Measures package (the numbers below correspond to the numbers of the US requests made on 12 March)

1 Japan accepts foreign clinical data
7 representatives of foreign firms to hear instructions and give explanations for public regulatory bodies

25 April   Second high-level meeting

Japan responds to the other US requests (the

115

numbers below correspond to the numbers of the US requests made on 12 March

2 shorter time for approval of reagents
3 simpler application procedures when locus of manufacturing changes
4 streamlining of type of modifications that need only simple re-application procedure
5 simplification of procedures for address change
6 transfer of *shōnin* with strict conditions
8 simplification of import clearance procedures

22 June	Third high-level meeting Japan indicates cases for which foreign clinical test data are accepted
20 August	Fourth high-level meeting The US presents a new request package asking for:

1 new guidelines for kit approval and price listing
2 adoption of a 'time clock' for approval process
3 change of the health insurance reimbursement system
4 change of custom categorization of vitamins
5 deregulation of trade of blood products

1 October	Japan sets up a 'time clock' (request number 2 of the above requests)
November	Experts meeting. US and Japan reach agreement on blood products and vitamins (request numbers 4 and 5 of the 20 August requests)
11 December	Final high-level meeting Japan presents resolution to the remaining requests on kit products, health insurance reimbursement system, and *shōnin* transfer

APPENDIX II

Chronology of the talks on telecommunications

First Phase (2 January 1985–1 April 1985)

2 January	Reagan–Nakasone meeting
28 and 29 January	First high-level meeting US requests: 1 disclosure of ordinance drafts 2 elimination of distinction between the special and general type-two telecommunications businesses
End of January	US presents formal request package: 1 inclusion of NTT-leased equipment and PBX's in the new approval system 2 independence of JATE 3 enforcement of data checking 4 avoidance of redundant application for conformity seals 5 inclusion of equipment used by NTT under the new approval system 6 disclosure of ordinance drafts (give foreign suppliers opportunities to comment on technical standards) 7 single conformity seals (no seals from agencies other than the MPT) 8 reduction of technical standards to 'no harm to network'
2 February	MPT's response (numbers correspond to the above request numbers): 1 ,5 All the CPE must meet the new approval requirement 2 JATE is independent of suppliers and users 3 test data checking accepted 4 simplified application for re-application 6 no comment 7 single conformity seal will be implemented 8 no comment
Late February	Disclosure of ordinance drafts
6 March	MPT's response: 1 simplification of registration procedures for special type-two business

117

	2 simplify technical standards from current 53 to 30
	3 accept foreign firms to advisory councils (response to request number 6 of the US request package)
13 March	Second high-level meeting
	US presents a revised request package:
	1 elimination of registration requirements for special type-two telecommunications business
	2 elimination of arbitrary distinction between special and general type-two telecommunications
	3 participation of foreign experts in the Telecommunications Advisory Council (TAC)
	4 establishment of an appeals process
	5 test data checking
	6 reduction of technical standards to 'no harm to network' only
	7 establishment of a single approval agency
	8 give opportunities to foreign suppliers to comment on proposed administrative procedures
	9 prevention of cross-subsidization by NTT
	Japan's immediate response:
	Koyama refuses number 1. Regarding number 3, the MPT states no foreign representatives are accepted. However, Japanese representatives of foreign firms are made eligible
15 March	Japan's response (numbers correspond to the above US requests made on 13 March):
	3 the MPT will consult with foreign suppliers on technical standards
	7 JATE will check all the CPEs
	9 NTT will clarify its accounting procedures
	5 approval based on test data accepted
	8 establish an agency for appeals
	Regarding the issue of type-two telecommunications business (request number 1 and 2), Japan states that it will maintain the registration requirement but shorten the application process from 30 days to 20 days. Japan refuses to adopt the sole standard of 'no harm to network' (request number 6)

March	The MPT sends a 'side-letter' (unknown date) noting that high-speed circuits will be counted as one circuit
26 and 27 March	High-level meeting The US requests Japan to revise the law regarding the special type-two telecommunications business. Japan refuses
28 March	Koyama confirms the content of the 'side-letter'. Also, standards will be reviewed within 60 days. Regarding special type-two telecommunications business, Koyama says applications will be approved automatically in 15 days; if not, full reasons will be given in 30 days
31 March	Gaston J. Sigur and Lionel Olmer make an emergency visit to Japan
1 April	In response to the above visit, Koyama promises to start studying the technical standards 'immediately'

Second Phase (3 June 1985–8 January 1986)

3 June	Third high-level meeting The US requests: 1 reduction of technical standards 2 accept foreign testing organizations as approval agencies 3 adopt a cellular phone system used in the US Japanese response: cellular phone standards are under the process of revision, foreign testing organizations are accepted
23 September	Experts meeting US presents a request package: 1 expansion of CCTS 2 conversion of CCTS into type approval 3 acceptance of test data submitted by manufacturers 4 limit technical standards to 'interference control' and 'spectrum availability'

119

5 independence of MKKK
6 increased transparency

Japan's response (numbers correspond to the above requests):
1 to 3 refused
4 accept the need for revision
5 no complaints have been expressed by foreign suppliers
6 the MPT has already established an organization to draft standards and US firms are represented in this organization

14 and 15 October

Experts meeting
Japan promises (numbers correspond to US requests made on September 23):
1 to expand items covered by CCTS
4 to reduce standards to 'interference control' and 'efficient use of spectrum' for transmitters.
5 to eliminate representatives of suppliers from MKKK
2 Japan refuses to accept type-approval
3 acceptance of foreign test data given 'FCC chairman attests to US companies' reliability and status as US legal entities'

US presents second set of requests:
1 increased access to third-party services
2 single licence that permits construction and operation of radio station
3 elimination of examination for the qualification of radio operators and requirement of their presence at radio stations
4 removal of the fee for issuing licences*
5 public notification of allocation of radio frequencies

*US later drops this request after finding out that the fee is minimal

22 to 25 November

Experts meeting
Japan's response:
1 revision of the Radio Law to accept foreign firms in third-party services
2 accept type approval and foreign test data

            3 reduce technical standards for receivers from ten to five
            4 grant licence to those who have taken a short course
            5 circulate the allocation of frequency tables, notify public of future change in standards and create an agency to provide information

            The US agrees on the standard 'efficient use of spectrum' instead of 'spectrum availability'

8 January 1986   Koyama writes a letter to Bruce Smart noting that the MPT will accept the US request to expand access to third-party radio service market. Also, technical standards of receivers will be reduced from five to one

            Concluding meeting of the MOSS talks

APPENDIX III

Chronology of the talks on forest products

2 January 1985   Reagan–Nakasone meeting
            Tariffs on forest products discussed

28 and 29 January   The first MOSS meeting
            Undersecretary of Agriculture Amstutz states that the discussion of forest products includes particleboard and paper products. Japan refuses to reduce tariffs

25 February   High-level meeting
            Japan refuses to reduce tariffs

8 March   Nakasone directs State Minister Koomoto to investigate a compensation programme. Increased sectoral opposition

25 March   Nakasone states that progress be made within 'approximately three years'

29 March   The LDP agrees on implementation of a programme to compensate for tariff reduction

5 April   The LDP decides to accept tariff reduction

9 April	External Economic Measures Japan announces that tariff reductions will be made 'approximately from the third year'
13 and 14 May	High-level meeting The US requests: earlier implementation of tariff reductions, acceptance of voluntary testing, and elimination or drastic reduction of tariffs on paper products Japan refuses to accept requests on tariffs. The US and Japan agree to establish working groups regarding testing
25 June	Tariffs on paper products reduced 20 per cent across the board
9 and 10 July	High-level meeting The US requests earlier implementation of tariff reduction. Japan refuses. The US shows satisfaction with the tariff reduction on paper products. The US makes requests on testing and fire code
24 to 26 July	Experts meeting The US and Japan agree on testing, transparency, and technical standards
30 July	Announcement of the Action Programme Japanese government announces that the tariffs on forest products will be reduced in April 1987
21 August	General Plenary Meeting on MOSS The US requests earlier implementation of tariff reduction and elimination of tariffs
Early September	Japan offers staged reduction of tariffs on selected paper products
26 and 27 September	Experts meeting Japan presents new schedule for testing ponderosa and lodgepole pines, method to designate foreign organizations for testing, and plan to accept foreign representatives in the JAS committee

29 October	High-level meeting The US again requests earlier implementation and elimination of tariffs
8 November	The Forestry Agency submits a blueprint for *Gokanen Keikaku*
17 December	Experts meeting Japan and the US agree on procedures to: grant JAS standards for ponderosa and lodgepole pines, establish JAS for structural panels, and foreign institutions to grant JAS, and continue talks on fire and building codes and demonstration wood structure projects
20 December	The Forestry Agency presents a tentative outline of the tariff reductions (23 December, the Cabinet pass the supplementary budget plan of Fiscal Year 1985)
7 January 1986	High-level meeting No agreement on tariffs
8 January	Informal session The US relaxes its request on elimination of tariffs and an agreement on Japan's tariff reduction is reached

APPENDIX IV

Chronology of the talks on electronics

18 March 1985	US presents a package of nine requests regarding: 1 tariffs on computer parts 2 protection of semiconductor chip design 3 copyright protection 4 participation in JIS drafting process 5 acceptance of foreign test data 6 participation in government-sponsored R&D 7 relaxation of Foreign Exchange Law 8 customs procedures 9 patent applications Japan's response: counterproposal to eliminate tariffs mutually on CPUs, peripherals, and computer parts

123

27 March	The US Senate Budget Committee adopts a non-binding resolution calling for opening of Japanese markets
Mid-April	MITI decides to accept the US request for unilateral elimination of tariffs in addition to mutual reduction of tariffs on computer parts but decides not to convey the decision until August
26 April	Japan states its acceptance of requests 7 and 9 Also, Japan indicates that all the other requests had already been resolved before the MOSS talks US refuses Japan's counterproposal on tariffs
14 June	SIA files an 'unfair trade' complaint to the USTR
22 August	Japan officially accepts the US request to eliminate unilaterally tariffs on CPUs and peripherals in addition to mutual elimination of tariffs on computer parts
September	Talks on electronics 'disappear' from the MOSS agenda

NOTES

1 INTRODUCTION

1 Katayama Tetsu of the Socialist Party was the prime minister between June 1947 and February 1948.

2 For instance, T. Inoguchi, *Gendai Nihon Seiji Keizai no Kōzu*, Tokyo, Tōyō Keizai Shinpō-sha, 1983, chapter 1; articles by Masumi Junnosuke and others in Nihon Seiji Gakkai (ed.) *The Parties and Bureaucracy in Contemporary Japan – Since the Conservative Fusion in 1955*, Tokyo, Iwanami Shoten, 1967. In English, Chalmers Johnson's work has become the main study on the centrality of the bureaucracy, C. Johnson, *MITI and the Japanese Miracle: The Growth of Industrial Policy, 1925–1975*, Stanford, Stanford University Press, 1982.

3 By 1986 – the time of the Market-Oriented Sector-Selective (MOSS) talks – average tariff levels for manufactured products in Japan were reduced to 6.0 per cent, compared to 6.9 per cent in the EC and 5.7 per cent in the US (US Advisory Committee for Trade Policy and Negotiations, *Analysis of the US–Japan Trade Problem*, February 1989, p. 62.) As a result of the Uruguay Round trade talks, average tariff rates on Japan's manufactured product imports will be 1.5 per cent, *Nihon Keizai Shimbun*, 15 December 1993.

4 The SII talks began in May 1989 in order to eliminate the structural factors in both the US and Japan that contributed to trade and other economic problems. The final report of the negotiations was released in June 1990, after which several follow-up meetings were held. The 'Framework' talks aimed at expanding US exports through changes in the Japanese government's procurement policy, macro-economic policy and deregulation. The talks also included sector-specific negotiations on automobiles and auto-parts, insurance, and other areas. The first round of talks were concluded at the end of October 1994. While there were some achievements such as an agreement by the Japanese government to increase government procurement, whether the agreements will have a significant effect in increasing exports to Japan is unclear.

5 Reischauer's work is the classic study of Japanese socio-economic and political systems in light of this question. His answer is that Japan was not like us (i.e. America) but was gradually changing towards convergence, E. O. Reischauer, *The Japanese Today*, Cambridge MA, Harvard University Press, 1988, second edition. More recently, both van Wolferen and Fallows tried to show the sharp

contrasts between the Japanese and Western (American) political and economic systems, K. van Wolferen, *The Enigma of Japanese Power*, New York, Alfred A. Knopf, 1989 and J. Fallows, *More Like Us*, Boston, Houghton Mifflin Co., 1989. On economic systems, Bergsten and Noland ask the question whether American and Japanese systems are converging or not, C. F. Bergsten and M. Noland, *Reconcilable Differences? United States–Japan Economic Conflict*, Washington, DC, Institute for International Economics, 1993.

6 For classical studies of group theory, see A. Bentley, *The Process of Government*, Chicago, University of Chicago Press, 1908, and D. B. Truman, *The Governmental Process*, New York, Knopf, 1951.

7 J. Fallows, 'Containing Japan', *Atlantic Monthly*, May 1989, pp. 40–54.

8 Johnson, *MITI and the Japanese Miracle*, pp. 17–34.

9 Johnson, *MITI and the Japanese Miracle*, chapter 6.

10 For instance, see articles in C. Johnson L. D. Tyson, and J. Zysman (eds), *Politics and Productivity: How Japan's Development Strategy Works*, NY, HarperBusiness, 1989. The latest debate over policies to foster competitiveness unfolds in *Foreign Affairs*. As an opponent of such policies, see P. Krugman, 'Competitiveness: a dangerous obsession', *Foreign Affairs*, March/April 1994, vol. 73, no. 2. As an example of arguments displayed by proponents, see C.V. Prestowitz, Jr., L. C. Thurow *et al.*, 'The fight over competitiveness: a zero-sum debate?' *Foreign Affairs*, July/August 1994, vol. 73, no. 4, pp. 186–197.

11 For the structural reasons that the US has upheld free trade, see for instance R. A. Pastor, *Congress and the Politics of US Foreign Economic Policy*, Berkeley, University of California Press, 1980, R. E. Baldwin, *The Political Economy of US Import Policy*, Cambridge MA, The MIT Press, 1985 and J. Goldstein, 'Ideas, institutions, and American trade policy', *International Organization*, winter 1988, vol. 42, no. 1, pp. 179–218.

12 A report issued in the spring of 1986 by an advisory panel to Prime Minister Nakasone headed by Maekawa Haruo, former governor of the Bank of Japan. It proposed to expand domestic demand in order to reduce economic friction with other countries.

13 *Tsūshō Hakusho* 1993, chapter 1.

14 J. Bhagwati, *Protectionism*, Cambridge MA, The MIT Press, 1991, chapter 3, pp. 43–59.

15 In the Motorola–IDO agreement, the US and Japanese governments will enforce the agreement, thus making it a *de facto* market share agreement.

16 The American rationale for choosing these four sectors was that despite the international competitiveness of US firms in these sectors, US firms could not export to Japan because of Japanese governmental trade barriers. In addition to this rationale, the US used the following criteria to choose cases: 1 The sector had a history of wide-ranging trade complaints concerning either formal or informal trade barriers; 2 The products under discussion constituted a sector; 3 There was potential for increased US sales in Japan; 4 The US industry was interested in the talks and willing to provide backup information; and 5 There were good prospects for near-term, observable results (i.e., within three to five years.), US General Accounting Office (GAO), *US–Japan Trade: Evaluation of the Market-Oriented Sector–Selective Talks*, July 1988, p.11. In addition to these four sectors, auto parts were added in August 1986.

17 GAO, *US–Japan Trade: Evaluation*, p. 10.

18 The theory hypothesizes that Japan will protect industries that are less competitive in world markets, such as infant industries and sunset industries. In

addition, it is expected that the protection will be particularly strong for industries judged to be strategically important such as textiles, steel and automobiles in the past and high-technology industries today. To assist Japanese firms in their ever increasing competition abroad, the Japanese state is expected to protect the domestic markets of these firms.

19 For reasons of limited time and resources as well as the unavailability of laboratory experiments, most political scientists must base their work on a limited number of case studies, chosen *ex post facto*. Under this constraint, one effective way of choosing cases is to find 'crucial' cases, that is, to select the cases that are considered 'most-likely' or 'least-likely' cases. In other words, if a case is logically the 'most-likely' case to verify a postulate, and the finding proves contrary, the case study will be regarded as crucial to disconfirm the postulate. Conversely, if the case is the 'least-likely' case but turns out to prove the postulate, the postulate is strongly supported (Harry Eckstein, 'Case Study and Theory in Political Science', in F. I. Greenstein and N. W. Polsby (eds), *Strategy of Inquiry*, Handbook of Political Science Volume 7, Reading MA, Addison Wesley Publishing Co.,1975, pp. 113–123).

20 The *keiretsu* can perhaps best be described as business practices based on long-term relationships more than short-term economic rationality. There are both horizontal *keiretsu* typically consisting of companies mutually holding each others' stocks, and vertical *keiretsu*, grouping suppliers, wholesalers, retailers, and users. The US has charged that *keiretsu* foster exclusionary business practices.

21 Despite the claim of part of the US government that the trade balance is overdetermined by factors such as exchange rates (GAO, *US–Japan Trade: Evaluation*, p.5), the trade figures suggest that the MOSS talks did have a significant effect on the exports of the four sectors involved. For instance, in 1987, data obtained from the US Department of Commerce on US exports to Japan showed increases of 26.5 per cent in telecommunications, 31.6 per cent in electronics, 14.0 per cent in pharmaceuticals, and 28.7 per cent in forest products. These numbers are noticeably higher than the overall increase of US exports to Japan, which was only 4.5 per cent.

2 EXPLAINING JAPANESE FOREIGN ECONOMIC POLICY

1 Robert Keohane suggests four prerequisites for hegemon in the world political economy: access to crucial raw materials, control over major sources of capital, a large market for imports, and comparative advantages in high value added goods (R. O. Keohane, *After Hegemony: Cooperation and Discord in the World Political Economy*, Princeton, Princeton University Press, 1984, pp. 32–34). Also, C. P. Kindleberger, *The World in Depression, 1929–1939*, Berkeley, University of California Press, 1973; Robert Gilpin, *War and Change in World Politics*, Cambridge, Cambridge University Press, 1981, chapter 3, in particular, and S. D. Krasner, 'State power and the structure of international trade', *World Politics*, 1976, vol. 28, no.3, pp. 317–343. For a detailed evaluation of the theory of hegemonic stability, see Keohane, *After Hegemony*, chapter 3 and Gilpin, *The Political Economy of International Relations*, Princeton, Princeton University Press, 1987, pp. 72–80.

2 Keohane, *After Hegemony*, chapter 9; Gilpin, *War and Change in World Politics*, Epilogue; W. P. Avery and D. P. Rapkin (eds), *America in a Changing World Political Economy*, NY, Longman, 1982.

3 S. D. Krasner, 'Structural causes and regime consequences: regimes as intervening variables', in Krasner (ed.), *International Regimes*, Ithaca, Cornell University Press, 1983, p. 2. For theories of international regimes, see also other articles in this volume.

4 *Nihon Keizai Shimbun*, 15 December 1993.

5 Keohane and J. S. Nye, *Power and Interdependence: World Politics in Transition*, Boston, Little, Brown and Co., 1977, p. 8.

6 A. Stepan notes that J.P. Nettl's 'The State as a Conceptual Variable' (*World Politics*, July 1968, vol. 20, no.4) was the only article on the state in the period of 1958–1972 found in *World Politics* and *The American Political Science Review*. A. Stepan, *State and Society; Peru in Comparative Perspective*, Princeton: Princeton University Press, 1978, p. 3.

7 In addition to Stepan's book, see P. B. Evans, D. Rueschemeyer, and T. Skocpol (eds.), *Bringing the State Back In*, Cambridge, Cambridge University Press, 1985. This book was monumental in marking the reappearance of the state in American political science. Also, see Skocpol and K. Finegold, 'State capacity and economic intervention in the early New Deal', *Political Science Quarterly*, Summer 1982, vol. 97, no. 2, S. Skowronek, *Building a New American State: The Expansion of National Administrative Capacities 1877–1920*, Cambridge, Cambridge University Press, 1982, and I. Katznelson and K. Prewitt, 'Constitutionalism, class, and the limits of choice in US foreign policy', in R. R. Fagen (ed.) *Capitalism and the State in US–Latin American Relations*, Stanford, Stanford University Press, 1979.

8 For instance, Graham Allison's work on the Cuban Missile Crisis, which is considered as a cornerstone to the study of foreign policy, focused on the importance of state bureaucracies as well as political executives. G.T. Allison, *Essence of Decision: Explaining the Cuban Missile Crisis*, Boston, Little, Brown and Co., 1971. See also, M. H. Halperin, *Bureaucratic Politics and Foreign Policy*, Washington, DC: Brookings Institution, 1974.

9 See Krasner, *Defending the National Interest*, Princeton, Princeton University Press, 1978, and P. J. Katzenstein (ed.), *Between Power and Plenty: Foreign Economic Policies of Advanced Industrial States*, Madison, The University of Wisconsin Press, 1977. The state in these works seems to be defined loosely as institutions and actors that govern the society and make policy. In this book, when I refer to the state, I include administration (state bureaucracy), legislatures, courts, and parties with particular emphasis on the ministries within the bureaucracy.

10 See Katzenstein, *Between Power and Plenty*. For the strong state/weak state argument, see Krasner, *Defending the National Interest*, J. P. Nettl, 'The state as a conceptual variable,' and Katznelson and Prewitt, 'Constitutionalism'.

11 S. Haggard, 'The institutional foundations of hegemony: explaining the Reciprocal Trade Agreements Act of 1934', *International Organization*, winter 1988, vol. 42, no. 1, pp. 91–119.

12 For the evolution of approaches see H. Fukui, 'Studies in policymaking: a review of the literature', in T. J. Pempel (ed.), *Policymaking in Contemporary Japan*, Ithaca, Cornell University Press, 1977, pp. 22–59. Also see Nihon Seiji Gakkai (ed.) *Nihon no Atsuryoku Dantai*, Tokyo, Iwanami Shoten, 1960 and Nihon Seiji Gakkai (ed.), *Gendai Nihon no Seitō to Kanryō: Hoshu Gōdō Igo*, Tokyo, Iwanami Shoten, 1967. For more recent work that confirms the strength of the Japanese state, see, for instance, T. Inoguchi, *Gendai Nihon Seiji Keizai no Kōzu*, Tokyo, Toyo Keizai Shinpo-sha, 1983.

13 Fukui, 'Studies in policymaking'.

14 D. I. Okimoto, 'Political inclusivity: the domestic structure of trade', in T. Inoguchi and D. I. Okimoto (eds.), *The Political Economy of Japan Volume 2: The Changing International Context*, Stanford, Stanford University Press, 1988, p. 307. See also, J. C. Abegglen, 'The economic growth of Japan', *Scientific American*, March 1970, vol. 222, no. 3, pp. 31–37. For the academic elaborations of the 'Japan Inc.' model, see C. Yanaga, *Big Business in Japanese Politics*, New Haven, Yale University Press, 1968.

15 C. Johnson, *MITI and the Japanese Miracle: The Growth of Industrial Policy, 1925–1975*, Stanford, Stanford University Press, 1982, chapter 1.

16 Sato and Matsuzaki discuss the increased ability of the LDP in policymaking without reducing the power of the bureaucracy, *Jimintō Seiken*, Tokyo, Chūō Kōron-sha, 1986. Also, see M. Muramatsu and E. S. Krauss, 'Bureaucrats and politicians in policymaking: the case of Japan', *The American Political Science Review*, 1984, vol. 78, pp. 126–146 and T. Inoguchi, *Gendai Nihon Seiji*, chapter 6.

17 Okimoto, 'Political inclusivity'.

18 One of the recent offshoots of pluralist thinking is the studies done by economists to integrate rational-choice models into pluralist economic policymaking. In their explanation of US import policy, S. P. Magee and L. Young maintain that the level of tariffs is determined endogenously by the interest-maximizing activity of different kinds of economic actors such as 'economic agents, lobbies, political parties, and voters' (S. P. Magee and L. Young, 'Endogenous protection in the United States, 1900–1984', in R. M. Stern (ed.), *US Trade Policies in a Changing World Economy*, Cambridge MA, The MIT Press, 1987). See also S. P. Magee, W. A. Brock, and L. Young, *Black Hole Tariffs and Endogenous Policy Theory: Political Economy in General Equilibrium*, Cambridge University Press, 1989 and R. P. Lavergne, *The Political Economy of US Tariffs: An Empirical Analysis*, NY Academic Press, 1983.

The strength of theories based on rational choice are their parsimony as well as the formality of the models. However, the theories' assumptions face a number of problems because of their diversion from reality. (This is not to say that assumptions must be loyal to reality. Oftentimes, assumptions are made for the very reason of simplicity. However, assumptions need to be corrected when their diversion from reality becomes too obvious.) For instance, as John Odell points out, the commonly assumed conflict of interest between labour and capital does not always obtain, as seen in the case of Apple Computers' investors sharing common trade interests with the firm's workers. John S. Odell, 'Understanding international trade policies: an emerging synthesis', *World Politics*, October 1990, vol. 43, no. 1, p. 144.

19 See S. Skowronek, *Building a New American State: The Expansion of National Administrative Capacities 1877–1920*, Cambridge, Cambridge University Press, 1982.

20 E. E. Schattschnieder's work on the Smoot–Hawley Act of 1930 is still valid in contending that not all pressure groups are equally active and that the active ones tend to reap political benefits from favourable legislation. But we also have to be careful that Schattschnieder's methodology of interpreting testimony from interest groups in Congressional hearings as evidence that interest groups exert influence on US policymaking in general, was self–validating. Congress is, almost by definition, the arena where interest groups have the most influence on policymaking, so their activity in Congress comes as no great surprise. This method does not give a chance to focus on the other actors and institutions which play important roles in foreign economic policymaking

(E. E. Schattschneider, *Politics, Pressures and the Tariff: A Study of Free Private Enterprise in Pressure Politics, as shown in the 1929–1930 revision of the Tariff*, New York, Prentice Hall, Inc., 1935).

21 For instance, R. E. Baldwin, *The Political Economy of US Import Policy*, Cambridge MA, The MIT Press, 1985.

22 See Haggard, 'The Institutional Foundations of Hegemony'. Also, I. M. Destler, *American Trade Politics: System Under Stress*, Washington DC: Institute for International Economics, 1986.

23 Miyake I., Yamaguchi Y., Muramatsu M. and Shindō E., *Nihon Seiji no Zahyō: Sengo 40-nen no Ayumi*, Tokyo, Yōhikaku, 1985, p. 182. See for instance, Muramatsu, M., *Sengo Nihon no Kanryōsei*, Tokyo, Tōyō Keizai Shinpo-sha, 1981, and Ōtake H., *Gendai Nihon no Seijikenryoku Keizaikenryoku*, Tokyo, San-ichi Shobō, 1979.

24 Tsuji, S., *Nihon Kanryōsei no Kenkyū*, Tokyo, Tokyo Daigaku Shuppankai, 1969, chapter 7.

25 Murakami, Y., *Shin Chūkan Taishū no Jidai*, Tokyo, Chūō Kōron-sha, 1984, chapter 2.

26 This tendency is, however, gradually changing. For instance, with the decrease of financial dependence on the government, big business is beginning to vocalize its disagreement with government on issues regarding other sectors such as the protection of agriculture.

27 March and Olsen contrast the 'new' institutional approach with the earlier works on the state which centred around description of formal structures of traditional political institutions, such as legislatures and court systems (J. M. March and J. P. Olsen, 'The New Institutionalism: Organizational Factors in Political Life', *American Political Science Review*, September 1984, vol. 78, no. 3, pp. 734–749). For a detailed description of this approach, see G. J. Ikenberry, 'Conclusion: An Institutional Approach to American Foreign Economic Policy', *International Organization*, winter 1988, vol. 42, no. 1, pp. 219–243.

28 March and Olsen, 'The new institutionalism', p. 738.

29 Ikenberry, 'Conclusion', p. 223.

30 For a state-centred institutionalist argument, see Destler, *American Trade Politics*, Ikenberry, 'Market solutions for state problems: the international and domestic politics of American oil decontrol', *International Organization*, winter 1988, vol. 42, no. 1, pp. 151–177. Also, Haggard, 'The institutional foundations of hegemony' in the same volume. Skocpol and Finegold examined differences in the state capacity in the issues of industrial adjustment and agriculture based on resources of state institutions (Skocpol and Finegold, 'State capacity and economic intervention').

31 As J. S. Odell noted, ideas are more complex in origin than interests and have independent effects on policies (J. S. Odell, *US International Monetary Policy: Markets, Power, and Ideas as Sources of Change*, Princeton, Princeton University Press, 1982, p. 58).

32 The best examples are seen in J. Goldstein's 'The political economy of trade: institutions of protection', *American Political Science Review*, March 1986, vol. 80, no. 1, pp. 161–184 and 'Ideas, institutions, and American trade policy', *International Organization*, winter 1988, vol. 42, no. 1, pp. 179–216.

33 D. I. Okimoto, *Between MITI and the Market: Japanese Industrial Policy for High Technology*, Stanford: Stanford University Press, 1989, 1989 and R. J. Samuels, *The Business of the Japanese State*, Ithaca, NY, Cornell University Press, 1987. Also, J. O. Haley, 'Governance by negotiation: A reappraisal of

bureaucratic power in Japan', in K. B. Pyle (ed.), *The Trade Crisis: How Will Japan Respond?*, Seattle, Society for Japanese Studies, 1987, pp. 177–192.

34 The concept of capacity of ministries is in part based on Katzenstein's analytical framework (Katzenstein, 'Conclusion: domestic structures and strategies of foreign economic policy', in P. J. Katzenstein (ed.), *Between Power and Plenty*). However, note that Katzenstein assumes that a state is a unitary actor and assigns policy objectives to each state, while this book argues that policy objectives vary from one ministry to another.

35 Katzenstein, 'Conclusion', p. 303.

36 Kent E. Calder, 'International pressure and domestic policy response: Japanese informatics policy in the 1980s', Center of International Studies, Princeton University, Research Monograph no. 51, June 1989.

37 MHW (ed.), *Pharmaceutical Administration in Japan*, Tokyo, Yakuji Nippō-sha, 1988, p. 27.

38 Katzenstein, 'Conclusion', p. 303.

39 See Ikenberry, 'The irony of state strength: comparative responses to the oil shocks in the 1970s', *International Organization*, winter 1976, vol. 40, no. 1, pp. 105–137.

40 These categories resonate with Okimoto's distinction of promotional and regulatory activities, D. I. Okimoto, 'Political inclusivity', pp. 318–323.

41 Okimoto, *Between MITI and the Market*, chapter 2.

42 MPT, *Records*, 5 and 6 March 1985.

43 *Nihon Keizai Shimbun*, 5 November 1993.

44 *Nihon Keizai Shimbun*, 19 May 1994.

45 *Nihon Keizai Shimbun*, 4 April (evening edition), 13 and 17 May 1994.

46 *Nihon Keizai Shimbun*, 19 May 1994.

47 It would be difficult to argue, for example, that the Japanese government considered clean water and air to be public goods prior to the several pollution cases such as Minamata and Yokkaichi in the 1970s. The overriding goal of industrial development often took precedence over providing a safe environment.

48 The official view of the Cabinet Legislation Bureau states that *gyōsei shidō* (administrative guidance), which is a main means of promoting industrial growth, 'does not have coercive power but is intended to induce certain acts or non-acts of the private sector *with its cooperation* in order to attain administrative goals' [italics mine]. Quoted in E. Sugimoto (ed.), *Tsūshō Sangyō Shō Binran*, Tokyo, Kyōiku-sha, 1979, p. 149.

49 G. R. Winham and I. Kabashima, 'The Politics of US–Japanese Auto Trade', in I. M. Destler and H. Sato, *Coping with US–Japanese Economic Conflicts*, Lexington, Lexington Books, pp. 73–119.

50 During the early twentieth century, the *Naimushō*, using police force as its strong instrument, took part in severe oppression of the labour movement and freedom of thought and expression.

3 *GAIATSU* AND THE MOSS TALKS

1 For instance, see M. Yamamoto, ' "*Gaiatsu-hannō*" no junkan o koete', in Hosoya C. and Aruga, T. (eds.), *Kokusai Kankyō No Henyō To Nichibei Kankei*, Tokyo, Tokyo University Press, 1987, pp. 321–335; Funabashi Y., *Nichibei Keizai Masatsu*, Tokyo, Iwanami Shoten, 1987; Kōsaka M., 'The International Economic Policy of Japan', in R. A. Scalapino (ed.), *The Foreign Policy of Modern Japan*, Berkeley, University of California Press, 1977, pp. 207–226; K.

B. Pyle, *The Japanese Question, Power and Purpose in a New Era*, Washington DC, American Enterprise Institute, 1992, pp. 111–113.

2 See for instance, E. J. Lincoln, *Japan: Facing Economic Maturity*, Washington, DC, The Brookings Institution, 1988, F. M. Rosenbluth, *Financial Politics in Contemporary Japan*, Ithaca, Cornell University Press, 1989 and D. J. Encarnation and M. Mason, 'Neither MITI nor America: the political economy of capital liberalization in Japan', *International Organization*, winter 1990, vol. 44, no. 1, pp. 25–54.

3 The above studies indicate that many changes related to financial deregulation did not require *gaiatsu*.

4 L. J. Schoppa, 'Two-level games and bargaining outcome: why gaiatsu succeeds in Japan in some cases but not others', *International Organization*, summer 1993, vol. 47, no. 3, p. 383.

5 Johnson, *MITI and the Japanese Miracle: The Growth of Industrial Policy, 1925–1975*, Stanford, Stanford University Press, 1982, chapter 8.

6 In an interview, an MHW official mentioned that day-to-day tasks at the ministry require so much work that it left little room for the MHW officials to consider major policy changes.

7 I. M. Destler and H. Sato, 'Coping with economic conflicts', in Destler and Sato (eds), *Coping with US–Japanese Economic Conflicts*, Lexington, Lexington Books, 1982, p. 279, pp. 283–284.

8 Because 80 per cent of pharmaceutical sales is distributed through hospitals and medical institutions as prescription drugs, it is crucial for manufacturers that their products are given prices on the *yakka* list, which is used to determine reimbursement rates from the National Health Insurance system. To be sure, as in most other countries, drugs are also sold as over-the-counter drugs at pharmacies in Japan. However, the bulk of profit for Japanese pharmaceuticals companies is made from prescription drugs.

9 The National Health Insurance (NHI) system, established in 1961, covers nearly 100 per cent of the population. The two main pillars of the system are the firm-based system for employees and their families and the state-subsidized system that covers those who are not covered by the first system, such as self-employed workers, farmers, and retirees.

10 US manufacturers did not agree on what to do with the *yakka* system. According to a representative of an American pharmaceutical company, the effect of proposed reform of the *yakka* system, *iyaku bungyō* (separation of the practice of pharmacy from that of medicine in order to prevent unnecessary prescription of drugs by medical doctors), on US exports is not yet well understood by American manufacturers. An account offered by an official at the US Embassy in Japan was a little different. He said the US government avoided the issue of medical services because it did not want to make any request on issues that clearly belonged to the domain of domestic matters. An MHW official suggested the separation would lead to contraction of the market itself, which is not desirable to any manufacturers.

11 MHW (ed.), *Report on Medical Equipment and Pharmaceuticals Market–Oriented, Sector–Selective (MOSS) Discussions* by the US and Japan MOSS Negotiating Teams to Minister for Foreign Affairs Abe, Secretary of State Shultz, January 1986, Tokyo, Yakuji, Nippō-sha, 1986, pp. 24–25.

12 According to a former MHW official, it is not clear how serious the US was in bringing up kit products. Even after the streamlining of procedures, he said, no substantial amount of kit products had been introduced to Japan. It seems

likely the problem is not one of trade barriers, since no complaints were made by foreign manufacturers of kit products after the MOSS talks.

13 *Shōnin* is required for both foreign and domestic producers in order to bring a product to market. The issue of *shōnin* was about the problem of transferring *shōnin* from a Japanese company producing drugs under an American licence to the licence-holding American firm if it wanted to start its own production in Japan. The US requested that current requirements to obtain renewed *shōnin* be relaxed so that *shōnin* could be transferred automatically when the contractual relationship of the firms changed.

14 *Nihon Keizai Shimbun*, 26 April 1985.

15 *Report on Medical Equipment*, p. 21.

16 The US and Japan could not agree on the interpretation of the trade figures and thus could not agree whether Japan should unilaterally reduce tariffs or both Japan and the US should reduce tariffs. The US claimed that because of Japan's large trade surplus in electronics, Japan should reduce tariffs on a larger number of items, including peripherals, if the US were to agree to tariff reductions on computer parts, *Nihon Keizai Shimbun*, 19 June 1985. Therefore, the US refused Japan's suggestion of reciprocal elimination of tariffs on all computer products. On the other hand, Japan could not accept the US claim that Japan enjoyed an overwhelming trade surplus with the US. The Japanese point of view was based on the fact that the Japanese trade surplus included large procurements of finished products and parts in Japan by US firms, so that the aggregate data alone could not prove that there was a trade imbalance. Moreover, the Japanese thought that the imbalance must be investigated based on data including software and service trade, in which the US had a large trade surplus. The Japanese side also suggested that the recent growth of Japanese exports to the US was primarily caused by high demand in the US market which was not met by domestic production, *Nihon Keizai Shimbun*, 2 March 1985.

17 Interview with a MITI official.

18 T. Fukuzawa, ' "Misuteiku" hatsugen ni wa gakkuri' (Disappointing 'mistake' statement), *Sekai Shūhō*, 30 April/7 May 1985, p.23. According to a former USTR representative, the talks on telecommunications were separated from the rest of the electronics talks because telecommunications had already been dealt with in depth by the US–MPT discussions prior to the MOSS talks.

19 US General Accounting Office offers this data along with comparison of absolute values of US exports worldwide, to Japan, and to the EC (US General Accounting Office (GAO), *US–Japan Trade: Trade Data and Industry View on MOSS agreements*, February 1988).

20 Calculated from data in OECD, *Foreign Trade by Commodities*.

21 Calculated from data in United Nations, *International Trade Statistics 1984*.

22 31 trillion yen for 1990, estimated by the Japan Electronic Industry Development Association (JEIDA).

23 *US–Japan Joint Report on the Sector Discussions*, by Foreign Minister Shintaro Abe and Secretary of State George Shultz, New York, 26 September 1985, p. 80.

24 K. Takahashi, *Konpyūtā Gyōkai* (Computer Industry, Tokyo: Kyōiku-sha, 1987), chapter 4. According to Takahashi, computer dealers not only sell computer hardware but also develop software called 'system support' needed to adapt the function of hardware to specific business purposes, Takahashi, pp. 90–92.

25 JETRO, *Your Market in Japan, Computer Hardware*, March 1986.

26 Ministry of Posts and Telecommunications, *Records on the Telecommunications Talks*, 27 and 28 January 1985.

27 US Department of Commerce, MOSS Negotiating Team, *Report on Telecommunications Market-Oriented, Sector-Selective (MOSS) Discussions*, 1986, p. 3.

28 *Asahi Shimbun*, 3 March 1985.

29 *Nihon Keizai Shimbun*, 23 February 1985, *Denpa Shimbun*, 27 February 1985.

30 *Nihon Keizai Shimbun*, 5 March 1985.

31 Department of Commerce data.

32 *Denpa Shimbun*, 29 March 1985.

33 *The Washington Post*, 17 October 1985.

34 MPT, *Records*, 21 November 1985.

35 MPT, *Records*, 21 August 1985.

36 MPT, *Records*, 25 December 1985.

37 *Nihon Keizai Shimbun*, 3 January, 1985.

38 *Sekai Shūhō*, January 1985, Special Issue, p. 21.

39 US Congress, Senate Committee on Finance, *Hearings: State of the US Forest Products Industry*, ninety-ninth Congress, first session, 19 September 1985, p. 198. Also, President Reagan had a reason to be personally interested in the issue since he made a public commitment to resolve US–Japan forest products trade problems at Weyerhaeuser Co. in Tacoma, Washington. He stated that '[the administration] has discussed your keen interest in limiting Japan's tariffs on forest products but we are hoping very soon we'll have progress to report about that'. A copy of the speech held by the Forestry Agency.

40 *Asahi Shimbun*, 18 January, 1985.

41 *Nihon Keizai Shimbun*, 18 January 1985.

42 *Nihon Keizai Shimbun* (evening edition), 28 January 1985.

43 Forestry Agency document. Also, *Asahi Shimbun*, 10 April 1985.

44 A Forestry Agency official stated that, regarding building and fire codes, because the experts did not realize until close to the end of discussion that the locus of problems did not lie in the system of Japanese Agricultural Standard (JAS) but in these codes, it was agreed to continue discussions after the MOSS talks.

45 According to an official at the American Embassy in Tokyo, the US government had no clear idea which department would be in charge of the issue. After assigning the Department of State, Department of Commerce, and USTR for electronics, telecommunications, and forest products talks, the pharmaceuticals talks were assigned to the remaining department among the ones which deal with foreign trade, that is, the Treasury Department.

46 Even by this time, the US could not decide its representative and sent Michael Smith of the USTR. It was not until the second meeting on 25 April that David Mulford, the assistant secretary of the Treasury for International Affairs, took charge of the matter.

47 Prospects of increased sales were among the seven criteria used to select the sectors to be discussed at the MOSS talks (US General Accounting Office, *US–Japan Trade: Evaluation of the Market-Oriented Sector-Selective Talks*, July 1988, p. 11). Japan Pharmaceutical Manufacturers Association (JPMA) representatives agreed that this was the major reason for choosing the pharmaceuticals sector.

48 Interview with an official at the US Embassy in Japan.

49 *Nihon Keizai Shimbun*, 13 April 1985.

50 In an interview, a high MITI official said the decision was made sometime in

April. The reason for witholding the offer was that, according to the official, 'samidareshiki' (early summer rain in Japan) negotiation was no good, presumably meaning that giving what was asked instantly and continuously would induce the US to escalate its requests.

51 *Nihon Keizai Shimbun* (evening edition), 15 June 1985.

52 See Lincoln, *Japan: Facing Economic Maturity*, Rosenbluth, *Financial Politics*, and Encarnation and Mason, 'Neither MITI nor America'.

53 GAO, *US–Japan Trade: Evaluation of the Market-Oriented Sector-Selective Talks*, July 1988, p. 17.

4 THE THREE ELEMENTS OF THE CAPACITY OF MINISTRIES

1 K. E. Calder, 'Japanese foreign economic policy formation: explaining the reactive state', *World Politics*, July 1988, vol. 40, no. 4, p. 519. L. J. Schoppa proposes an interesting answer to the question how *gaiatsu* works. He maintains that foreign pressure only works to produce positive results (i.e. policy changes to meet demands placed by foreign opponents) when foreign pressure brings in large participation of elites and the general public into the policymaking process ('participation expansion') and works to 'spotlight policy alternatives that may not have been considered in the absence of foreign intervention' (L. J. Schoppa, 'Two-level games and bargaining outcome: why *gaiatsu* succeeds in Japan in some cases but not others', *International Organization*, summer 1993, vol. 47, no. 3, pp. 353–386).

2 Interview with a MHW official.

3 Although the terms VANs and type two telecommunications business are often used interchangeably, strictly speaking, VANs and type two telecommunications – both general and special businesses – are different. While VANs are services that enable connection of different types of terminals and delivery of messages and data such as electronic mail and packet switching services, type two telecommunications business provides telecommunications services using leased circuits.

4 For details of the 'VAN wars', see C. Johnson, 'MITI, MPT and the telecom wars: how Japan makes policy for high technology', Berkeley Roundtable on the International Economy (BRIE) Working Paper vol. 21, 1986.

5 For details about the collaboration between MITI and the US negotiators, see Kawakita T., *Tsūsan Yūsei Sensō* (MITI–PT War), Tokyo, Kyōiku-sha, 1985, pp. 29–43.

6 Tahara S., 'Nippon daikaizō 11', (Grand remodelling of Japan 11), *Shūkan Bunshun*, 16 May 1985, no. 2302, p. 46. The US–Japan Trade Study Group is 'a bilateral group, consisting mainly of Americans from the US business community in Tokyo and Japanese businessmen, all acting in an individual capacity', US–Japan Trade Study Group, *Progress Report 1984*, p. 1. The report addresses trade barriers in main industrial and service industries in detail. In addition, the report deals with trade problems associated with high technology industries, intellectual property, structurally depressed industries and investment policy.

7 Koyama's statement about MITI's collaboration with the US was, of course, denied by MITI officials. However, the information on which the US based its requests to the MPT was often identical to MITI's internal document presented to the MPT earlier, *Asahi Shimbun*, 8 March 1985.

8 A 'side-letter' was given to American negotiators from the Japanese Embassy in Washington D.C. stating that a high-speed information exchange (more than

1200 BPS) using a public switched telephone network (PSTN) circuit would still be counted as one circuit. The Japanese side also accepted the possibility of future amendment of the ordinances if market barriers became apparent for special type two business after 1 April (Ministry of Posts and Telecommunications, *Records on the Telecommunications Talks*, n.d.). Olmer complained that the 'side-letter' sent from Tokyo recording the agreement reached between him and Koyama had no address or signature (M. Ōmae, *Taimu Māchanto*, Tokyo, Tokuma Shoten, 1988, p. 186). At the same time, by 20 March, the MPT had decided that all the high-speed digital circuits that surpassed 12K BPS would be counted as 12K BPS (ten circuits of 1200 BPS) (MPT, *Records*, 20 March 1985).

9 The MPT also explained that if the MPT were to deny the registration, full reasons would be given within 30 days (Ōmae, *Taimu Māchanto*, p. 187, *Asahi Shimbun*, 3 April 1985). Also, US Department of Commerce, MOSS Negotiating Team, *Report on Telecommunications Market-Oriented, Sector-Selective (MOSS) Discussions*, 1986, pp. 42–49. A letter from Vice-Minister Koyama stated that 'special type-two enterprises may begin business 20 days after filing if they have heard nothing from the MPT within 15 days. If MPT sees a problem, the enterprise will be notified within 15 days and any rejection will be notified in 30 days. Any rejection will be accompanied by a written explanation of the reason for rejection' (US Department of Commerce, *Report on Telecommunications*, p. 44).

10 *Shōnin* is granted to each applicant that intends to manufacture in Japan or import drugs or medical equipment. The MHW grants *shōnin* based on consultations with the *Chūō Yakuji Shingikai*, or Central Pharmaceutical Affairs Council (CPAC). The CPAC is 'an advisory body to MHW which investigates from a scientific point of view whether it is appropriate to approve manufacturing or import of new pharmaceuticals or medical devices' (Ministry of Health and Welfare (ed.), *Report on Medical Equipment and Pharmaceuticals Market-Oriented, Sector-Selective (MOSS) Discussions* by the US and Japan MOSS Negotiating Teams to Minister for Foreign Affairs Abe, Secretary of State Shultz, January 1986, Tokyo, Yakuji Nippō-sha, 1986, p. 48).

11 *Kyoka* is the next step after receiving *shōnin*. The purpose of granting *kyoka* from the point of view of the MHW, is to ensure that the manufacturing plant or the importer meets appropriate safety and manufacturing standards, and that 'the board members of the manufacturer or importer are legally able to serve in that capacity' (*Report on Medical Equipment*, p. 4). Each manufacturing plant or importer's office must obtain a *kyoka* to do business in Japan.

12 According to a MHW official, current regulation of drug production is not rationally designed. The complex and often irrationally strict system of regulation was created as a reacton to a series of accidents caused by unexpected side effects of drugs such as thalidomide, chinoform, and streptomycin.

13 C. Johnson, 'MITI, MPT and the telecom wars: how Japan makes policy for high technology', Berkeley Roundtable on the International Economy (BRIE) Working Paper vol. 21, 1986, pp. 18–19.

14 The Management and Coordination Agency reported that as of March 1993, the number of MITI's *kyoninkaken* was 1893 while the Ministry of Transport, second in the ranking, held 1427, *Yomiuri Shimbun*, 15 December 1993.

15 As one MHW official stated, 'the MHW cannot protect the industry [from foreign competitors] because the world situation does not allow Japan to protect it' [and we must have a healthy competition].

16 Kyōiku-sha (ed.), *Kōseishō* (The Ministry of Health and Welfare), Tokyo Kyōiku-sha, 1979, pp. 57–60.
17 *Kōseishō* 1980 (The Ministry of Health and Welfare 1980), Tokyo, Gyōsei Shiryō Sentā, 1979, pp. 2–4.
18 Interview with a MHW official.
19 At the end of the MOSS talks, the problem of *shōnin* transfer was marked as an 'outstanding issue' and the US and Japan committed themselves to 'finding practical solutions to legitimate business problems', US General Accounting Office, *US–Japan Trade: Evaluation of the Market-Oriented Sector-Selective Talks*, July, p. 29.
20 MHW, *Report on Medical Equipment*, p. 21.
21 Interview with a former MHW official.
22 *Denpa Shimbun*, 29 March 1985.
23 Interviews with MPT officials.
24 MPT, *Records*, 15 March 1985.
25 *Yomiuri Shimbun*, 13 March 1985.
26 MPT, *Records*, 15 March 1985.
27 MPT, *Records*, 5 and 6 March 1985.
28 Although the MPT did not have a well-planned industrial policy, it had a clear interest in the growth of the telecommunications industry. The cellular phone market is a case in point. The MPT began to consider introducing a new system for cellular phones, which had a capacity larger than that of the NTT system, at the time of the MOSS talks. An MPT official said that the ministry had to consider a new system because the old system had a limit to the number of users to be provided with frequencies for cellular phones and the larger capacity system enabled the MPT to distribute finite frequencies more efficiently.
29 An example of a dispatcher and mobile stations is a pizza store and several delivery trucks communicating on directions to customers.
30 A non-profit organization that offered a semi-public service.
31 When the MPT began drafting the new Telecommunications Business Law, it decided to continue the current semi-public nature of the business instead of liberalizing it based on the assumption that the profitabilty of the business was not great enough to let private firms participate in the market.
32 MPT, *Records*, 22 and 23 November 1985.
33 US law, by contrast, has a third category called 'private carrier'.
34 Interview with an MPT official.
35 On this point, Murakami Yasusuke's work on Japan's state and market relationship is illuminating. He maintains that the Japanese economy is conceptualized as 'compartmentalized competition'. The role of state intervention was to create and to maintain such 'compartments' – groupings based on industries. Given the nature of state intervention, it is easily understandable why the MPT tried to avoid complete deregulation of the market but instead let one firm – Motorola – join the market. Y. Murakami, *Shin Chūkan Taishū no Jidai*, Tokyo, Chūō Kōron-sha, 1984.
36 Communication and Intelligence, *Jidōsha Denwa Sensō* (Automobile Phone War), Tokyo, Yell Books, 1989, p. 95. This is what Johnson might call a 'sweetheart' deal (C. Johnson, 'Trade, revisionism, and the future of Japanese–American relations', in K. Yamamura (ed.), *Japan's Economic Structure: Should It Change?* Seattle, Society of Japanese Studies, 1990).
37 Communication and Intelligence, *Jidōsha Denwa Sensō*, p. 79.

NOTES

38 The Forestry Agency is technically a branch agency of the MAFF with considerable decision-making independence due to its autonomy in appointing personnel.
39 Establishment Law of the Ministry of Agriculture, Forestry, and Fisheries, article
three.
40 Ōmiya T., 'Kome o daraku sasetanowa dareka', *Zaikai Tenbō*, August 1990, pp.
202–206.
41 *Nihon Keizai Shimbun*, 12 October 1978, quoted in H. Sato and T. J. Curran,
'Agriculture trade: the case of beef and citrus', in I. M. Destler and H. Sato,
Coping with US–Japanese Economic Conflicts, Lexington, Lexington Books,
1982, p. 161.
42 Sato and Curran, 'Agriculture trade', p. 175.
43 *New York Times*, 27 November 1991.
44 *Nihon Keizai Shimbun*, 27 March 1985.
45 *Nikkan Mokuzai Shimbun*, 24 January 1985, 28 March 1985.
46 *Nikkan Mokuzai Shimbun*, 28 March 1985.
47 *Nihon Keizai Shimbun*, 20 March 1985.
48 While the official position of the Japan Association of Laminated Lumber
Industries was opposition to the tariff reduction, the Association did not join
lobbying against proposed tariff cuts. The reason is that the sector could not
agree on the effect of reduced tariffs since the list of items on which tariffs
were to be reduced included spruce, pine and fir (SPF) lumber from the US,
which constituted about half of the raw materials used by Japanese firms in
manufacturing laminated lumber. As for particleboard, the relevant industrial
organization, the Japan Fiberboard and Particleboard Manufacturers Association (JFPMA), did not join lobbying because the organization was too weak for
effective lobbying. Unlike laminated lumber, most of the ingredients used to
manufacture particleboard were domestically supplied. Therefore, the sector
could have galvanized support against tariff reductions from the upstream
industry. However, the particleboard industry was regulated by two different
ministries. High-value particleboard products belong to the jurisdiction of
MITI, and the rest belong to the Forestry Agency. The division of jurisdiction
that cuts across the particleboard industry weakened the cohesiveness of the
JFPMA. Furthermore, the JFPMA included representatives from the fibreboard
industry which belongs to the jurisdiction of MITI. Because of the high cost of
keeping close relationships with two ministries, the JFPMA kept rather distant
relationships with both ministries. Also, according to a representative of the
JFPMA, the particleboard manufacturers did not join the lobbying activity in
opposition to tariff reductions, because they resented the strong leadership of
upstream industries.
49 Most of the technical standards issues were resolved by September except for
the ones that required drafting new procedures. The final draft of such
procedures was agreed by mid-December.
50 JETRO, *Your Market in Japan: Computer Hardware*, March 1986, pp. 23–24.
51 Interview with a MITI official.
52 Interview with a MITI official.

5 RELATIONSHIPS WITH THE PRIVATE SECTOR

1 Seo T., *Iyakuhin* (Pharmaceuticals), Tokyo, Nihon Keizai Shimbun-sha, 1987,
p. 26.
2 The members of the 'NTT family' remained NTT's exclusive suppliers until the

Japanese government agreed to open NTT's procurement to other manufacturers in late 1980.

3 Japan Plywood Manufacturer's Association, *Nihon no Gōhan Sangyō* (Japan's Plywood Industry) 1989, unpublished paper, p. 38.

4 Daniel Okimoto, 'Political inclusivity', pp. 323–325.

5 The political power of *Nihon Ishikai* is well known. Taguchi and Toshinai argue that its power derives from an abundance of financial resources, its ability to lobby extensively through its own *zoku* (see note 34) politicians in both the LDP and the Japan Socialist Party, and its cohesive organization which offers strong electoral support for political parties (Taguchi T. and Toshinai Y., 'Atsuryoku dantai toshiteno ishikai', (JMA as a pressure group) *Chūō Kōron*, April, 1959, p. 250. Also, Takahashi H., 'Nihon ishikai no seiji kōdō to ishi kettei', in M. Nakano (ed.), *Nihongata Ishi Kettei no Henyō* (Changes in Japanese Decision Making), Tokyo, Tōyō Keizai Shinpō-sha, 1986, pp. 237–266 and I. Neary, Research Note, 'Seiyakugyō ni kansuru sangyō seisaku' (Industrial policy for the pharmaceutical industry), *Leviathan*, spring 1990, vol. 6, p. 194).

6 'Used' here means that the JPMA waited until the American companies spoke up. There is no evidence that US and Japanese manufacturers coordinated efforts to influence the government for policy changes, however. The Pharmaceutical Manufacturers Association, the largest industrial association of the American pharmaceutical companies, and JPMA began having regular meetings only after they realized there were shared interests between them during the MOSS talks.

7 Actually, big pharmaceuticals manufacturers from the US, Europe and Japan shared this concern. Because coordinated regulatory requirements among these countries reduce the cost of data duplication, tripolar harmonization negotiations were planned for November 1991, *Yomiuri Shimbun*, 23 October 1990. By the end of the 1980s, major pharmaceuticals companies such as Takeda were changing their strategies to more aggressive export-oriented ones, *The Economist*, 6 May 1989, p. 65.

8 Japan Pharmaceutical Manufacturers Association, *DATA BOOK* 1989, p. 58.

9 Interview with a representative of JPMA.

10 For instance, by 1984, while Japanese manufacturers held 498 drug-related patents registered in Japan, American manufacturers held 1,119 drug-related patents registered in the US, JPMA, *DATA BOOK* 1989, pp. 72–73.

11 According to a former MHW official, new drug manufacturers, which diversified from other industries such as food, liquor and textiles had capital and technology to develop new drugs. They had been expressing strong interest in more frequent price listing for new drugs. Also, not all large drug manufacturers had clear interests in more frequent price listing because many large manufacturers produced generic drugs along with new drugs. The interest in more frequent listing was the function of the percentage of profits derived from new drugs.

12 Interview with an MHW official.

13 *Nihon Keizai Shimbun*, 10 April 1985.

14 *Nihon Keizai Shimbun*, 10 and 12 April 1985. *Asahi Shimbun*, 10 April 1985.

15 *IMR Profile: The Telecommunications Equipment Market in Japan*, Document prepared for US Department of Commerce, Tokyo, Pacific Projects, 1986, p. 21.

16 *Asahi Shimbun*, 22 February 1985.

17 In an interview with *Denpa Shimbun*, Ozawa Haruo, a representative of the

CIAJ, emphasized the importance of increasing imports (to avoid protectionism abroad), *Denpa Shimbun*, 24 July, 1985. In 1984, Tōyō Tsushinki and Nihon Musen, respectively, relied on exports for 11 per cent and 31 per cent, Yamaichi Securities, *Kaisha Shikihō*, fall 1984.

18 *Nihon Keizai Shimbun*, 12 April 1985; *Asahi Shimbun*, 22 February and 10 April 1985; *Denpa Shimbun*, 20 December 1985.

19 *IMR Profile*, p. 21.

20 *Jōhō Tsūshin Nenkan '91* (Information Communications Almanac '91), Tokyo, InfoCom Research Inc., pp. 314–318.

21 There are two ways to operate international VAN business. One is to tie up with overseas firms. The other is to establish an overseas subsidiary. In the case of US–Japan international VANs, Japanese firms preferred to exploit US firms' expertise in their business in the US. In 1985, out of nine VAN firms, seven registered for international VANs. Among the seven firms, all but one (The Japan Research Institute) tied up with US firms for their international business (interview with a representative of Special Type II Telecommunications Carriers Association).

22 Takahashi K. and Odawara S., *Jōhō Tsūshin Gyōkai* (Information Communication Industry), Tokyo, Kyōiku-sha, 1988, pp. 82–86.

23 Interview with a representative of Special Type II Telecommunications Carriers Association.

24 J. O. Haley, 'Governance by negotiation; a reappraisal of bureaucratic power in Japan', in K. Pyle (ed.), *The Trade Crisis: How Will Japan Respond?* Seattle, Society of Japanese Studies, 1987, p. 186.

25 C. Johnson, *MITI and the Japanese Miracle: The Growth of Industrial Policy, 1925–1975*, Stanford, Stanford University Press, 1982, p. 260.

26 Haley, 'Governance by negotiation', p. 189.

27 However, recently, there is a rising awareness among firms that commercial practices that 'in effect' create obstacles to market access must change. For instance, three large automobile manufacturers decided to loosen their relationships with dealers, through changes such as reducing the period within which commissions are given for sales of cars manufactured by the main maker, *Nihon Keizai Shimbun*, 7 May 1994.

28 MITI made its own decisions as regards these sectors. In addition, MITI was in charge of higher value-added particleboard. But presumably because of the lack of strategic importance, MITI did not intervene in the Forestry Agency's decisions on particleboards. Officials from both ministries acknowledged that the Agency made the decisions on particleboard and MITI merely approved them.

29 Nishio T., *Nihon Shinrin Gyōseishi no Kenkyū*, Tokyo, Tokyo University Press, 1988, p. 1. pp. 288–289.

30 Plywood manufacturers included veneer manufacturers.

31 *Nikkan Mokuzai Shimbun*, 11 January 1985, 20 March 1985.

32 Interview with a representative of Japan Plywood Manufacturer's Association.

33 *Nihon Keizai Shimbun* (evening edition), 11 January 1986.

34 According to Satō Seizaburō and Matsuzaki Tetsuisa, *zoku* (literally, tribes) politicians are 'legislators who exert strong influence on policymaking of given issue areas defined by the division of ministries. Also, to become a *zoku* member, one must have occupied a ministerial position for at least one term or be expected to join the next cabinet' [translation mine]. Satō S. and Matsuzaki T., *Jimintō Seiken*, Tokyo, Chūō Kōron-sha, 1986, p. 265.

140

35 *Nihon Keizai Shimbun*, 9 March 1985.

36 Nakasone did not clarify what 'the sector' meant, and there was no specification among the leaders of the party either. The party's Secretary-General Kanemaru and the chairman of the LDP Policy Affairs Research Council (PARC) Chairman Fujio Masayuki (these are two of the four top positions in the LDP) suggested a comprehensive compensation programme to rescue the forestry industry as a whole, whereas Finance Minister Takeshita Noboru showed some reluctance about including the upstream industries such as raw materials (logs) and semi-finished (lumber) industries. It was agreed that the programme would be reviewed in detail by the PARC and related ministries, *Nihon Keizai Shimbun*, 26 March 1985.

37 Meeting with Kanemaru, Agricultural Minister Satō Moriyoshi said that as compensation for tariff reduction, a medium-term programme for forestry promotion costing approximately 300 billion yen was necessary. Responding to this concern, Kanemaru, at a press conference, stated that 'the Satō (Eisaku) cabinet spent 200 billion yen for the domestic industry to solve the US–Japan fibre negotiation. Because the value of money has declined, we must use more money. In sum, we must implement a permanent policy to promote forestry. The expenditure must not be paid for with general account funds' [but should be defrayed through a special account] (*Yomiuri Shimbun* (evening edition), 1 April 1985). While LDP's consensus shifted toward reducing tariffs, strong opposition was still expressed by the *Nōrin zoku* of the ruling party. Hata Tsutomu, the chairman of the LDP Research Commission on Forestry and Tamazawa Tokuichirō, the chairman of the LDP Agriculture and Forestry Division, told Nakasone 'the sectors like plywood are suffering from recession so that they need protection. It is an absurd idea to reduce tariffs' (*Asahi Shimbun*, 2 April 1985).

38 *Nikkan Mokuzai*, 11 April 1985.

39 *Nikkan Mokuzai*, 11, 13 and 19 April 1985.

40 *Nihon Keizai Shimbun*, 7 April 1985.

41 *Asahi Shimbun*, 4 April 1985.

42 Ogura K., *Nichibei Keizai Masatsu* (US–Japan Economic Friction), Tokyo, Nihon Keizai Shimbun-sha, 1982, pp. 162–163.

43 *Yomiuri Shimbun*, 12 January 1985; *Asahi Shimbun*, 5 April 1985.

44 At the final stage of the MOSS talks, unfinished pine timber and finished SPF (spruce, pine and fir) timber were included in order to increase the number of items listed in the final offer. These two items plus hardwood unfinished timber were the only ones with tariffs (7 to 10 per cent) among semi-finished products. All raw material, i.e. logs, were tax free. The US was interested in pine unfinished and finished timber. Separate to the MOSS talks, Canada was interested in SPF finished timber and New Zealand was asking for tariff reductions on pine unfinished timber.

45 *Nikkan Mokuzai Shimbun*, 11 January 1985.

46 *Nikkan Mokuzai Shimbun*, 20 March 1985, also 'Towareru shinrin, ringyō, sanson eno kihonshisei' (Basic attitude toward forests, forestry, and rural villages questioned), Gendai Ringyō (ed.), *Gendai Ringyō*, May 1985, p. 22.

47 *Yomiuri Shimbun*, and *Asahi Shimbun*, 9 April 1985.

48 *Nikkan Mokuuzai Kōgyō*, 30 March 1985, 19 April 1985; Gendai Ringyō, 'Towareru shinrin', p. 22. In an interview, a JPMA representative denied that the plywood manufacturers invited the upstream sector to obtain greater political leverage.

49 Gendai Ringyō, 'Towareru shinrin', pp. 20–24.

50 During the war wood was used for ships, aircraft, and piles to support trenches made along sea shores to prepare for the war on the mainland. During the period immediately following the end of the war, when Japan needed to reconstruct housing but lacked foreign exchange to import wood, domestically produced wood was used to build shacks on the incinerated land.

51 *Asahi Shimbun*, 13 April 1985; *Yomiuri Shimbun*, 11 April 1985; *Nikkan Mokuzai Kōgyō*, 18 May 1985.

52 *Ringyō Hakusho* (Forestry White Paper), p. 10, p. 118.

53 Gendai Ringyō, 'Towareru shinrin', p. 22.

54 *Nikkan Mokuzai Shimbun*, 1 May 1985.

55 This figure of downstream workers includes only plywood and veneer manufacturing (the Forestry Agency, *Mokuzaijukyū to Mokuzaikōgyō no Genjō*, 1986, p. 139; *Ringyō Hakusho*, p. 22). The number of workers in forestry includes those who are also engaged in farming (*Nihon Kokusei Zue*, 1988, p. 92).

56 Matsuda T., Katayama M., *et al.*, 'Shinrin no sōgō riyō to ringyō kasseika eno hōsaku', in *Nōrinsuisanshō sono Yakuwari to Seisaku*, Tokyo, Sangyō Seisaku Kenkyūjo, 1988; *Nikkan Mokuzai Kogyō*, 25 April 1985.

57 According to the Forestry Agency plan, the 8.5 billion yen and 1.3 billion yen from the national account would be used as two-thirds of a fund that the government and the private sector would establish in order to support interest payments for the funding needed by the manufacturers who were converting to other business and by those who were disposing of excess capacity (*Nikkan Mokuzai Shimbun*, 9 and 28 November, 1985).

58 *Nihon Keizai Shimbun*, 26 March 1985.

59 *Nikkan Mokuzai Kōgyō*, 25 April 1985.

60 *Yomiuri Shimbun*, 26 March 1985.

61 *Nikkan Mokuzai Shimbun*, 22 June 1985.

62 *Nikkan Mokuzai Shimbun*, 31 July 1985.

63 *Nikkan Mokuzai Shimbun*, 15 June, 13 August, 26 September 1985.

64 *Nikkan Mokuzai Kōgyō*, 27 September 1985, 2 October 1985, 16 October 1985, 9 November 1985, 25 December 1985.

65 Minister of Agriculture Satō's statement after the Forestry Agency's submission of the final draft of the *Gokanen Keikaku* (Table 5.3) indicates that the allocation of subsidies was closely linked to the size of tariff reductions to be made. Satō promised that the size of tariff reduction would not be determined before the compensation programme was formulated (*Nikkan Mokuzai Kogyō*, 28 March 1985). When the LDP and the MOF finally settled over the size of the compensation on 17 December, Satō showed his willingness to present a tariff reduction plan to the US 'before the end of the year' (*Asahi Shimbun*, 18 December 1985). By 20 December, the Forestry Agency decided that the general size of reduction would be approximately 30 per cent (*Asahi Shimbun*, 21 December 1985).

6 CONCLUSION

1 'Neo-mercantilism' appears to be a twentieth-century version of the mercantilism exemplified by Japan, in which a nation does not 'concern themselves with international hegemony, but focused instead on extracting maximum benefits from the international political economy' (P. J. Katzenstein, Introduction: 'Domestic and international forces and strategies of foreign economic

policy', Katzenstein (ed.) *Between Power and Plenty: Foreign Economic Policies of Advanced Industrial States*, Madison, The University of Winconsin Press, 1977, p. 21).

2 T. J. Pempel, 'Japanese foreign economic policy: the domestic bases for international behavior', in Katzenstein (ed.), *Between Power and Plenty*, pp. 139–190.

3 See, for instance, W. J. Holstein, *The Japanese Power Game: What It Means for America*, NY, Macmillan Publishing Co., 1990, chapter 6.

4 Multi-media is an information system that enables reciprocal communication of letters, symbols, graphics, and sounds through computer networks, *Nihon Keizai Shimbun*, 23 February 1994.

5 *Imidas* 1994, Tokyo, Shūei-sha, 1994, p. 712.

6 *Yomiuri Shimbun* (evening edition), 10 May 1994; *The Japan Times*, 11 May 1994.

7 D. I. Okimoto, *Between MITI and the Markets: Japanese Industrial Policy for High Technology*, Stanford, Stanford University Press, 1989, chapter 3; T. Inoguchi, *Gendai Nihon Seiji Keizai no Kōzu*, Tokyo, Tōyō Keizai Shinpō-sha, 1983, chapter 1; Satō S. and Matsuzaki T., *Jimintō Seiken*, Tokyo, Chūō Kōron-sha, 1986, chapter 8.

8 Satō and Matsuzaki, *Jimintō Seiken*, chapter 4; G. Curtis, *Japanese Way of Politics*, New York, Columbia University Press, 1988, chapter 3; M. Muramatsu and E. S. Krauss, 'The conservative policy line and the development of patterned pluralism', in K. Yamamura and Y. Yasuba (eds), *The Political Economy of Japan, Volume 1: The Domestic Transformation*, Stanford, Stanford University Press, 1987.

9 Satō and Matsuzaki, *Jimintō Seiken*, p. 127.

10 I. Murakawa, *Jimintō no Seisaku Kettei Shisutemu*, Tokyo; Kyōiku-sha, 1989, pp. 299–300.

11 For instance, after the ten-year fifth generation computer project ended with no clear sign of success in 1992, MITI launched another ten-year project called the Real World Computing Project. The project aims at developing computers that resemble the function of human brains, *Nihon Keizai Shimbun*, 7 February 1994.

12 *Nihon Keizai Shimbun*, 23 February 1994.

13 In the case of copyrights for software, MITI and the Ministry of Education fought over the shape of a new bill. In the case of telecommunications (VANs), MITI and the MPT struggled over its jurisdiction. In both cases, MITI lost. For details, see K. E. Calder, 'International pressure and domestic policy responses'.

14 The SDPJ changed its policy programme related to defence and other issues on 3 September 1994 at a party convention primarily because of the need to maintain its coalition with the LDP. For instance, in the new policy programme, the SDPJ's traditional stance toward the Self Defense Force was reversed and the party acknowledged its constitutionality. More importantly, the SDPJ abandoned the central pillar of its programme, that is, neutrality and non-alliance. However, the adoption of this programme did not come easy or without reservations. For instance, nearly 40 per cent of the members voted for the *revision* of the executive committee's proposal. In fact, very strong opposition was expressed by representatives of local party organizations. Also the new programme still shows the SDPJ's reservations against adopting active defence policy. For instance, the SDF is accepted as constitutional but with the condition that it will remain at the minimal scale needed for self-defence,

Yomiuri Shimbun, 4 September 1994. Because the SDPJ changed its policy programme and not the party platform, which is more permanent and binding, the underlying strong opposition to the change in policy programme as well as the general reservation toward drastic change in Japan's defence policy will remain as a cause of disagreement between the LDP and the SDPJ.

15 Political reform bills intend to change various aspects of the Japanese political system. Measures to be implemented include: a change from the current multi-member electoral districts to a combination of single-member districts and proportional representation in the House of Representatives, restrictions on financial contributions to political parties, and national subsidies for political parties. The core of the political reform is the new electoral system. The 500 seats in the new House of Representatives are divided into 300 that are elected through single-member districts and 200 that are elected through proportional representation. Currently, 512 seats for the House are elected through multi-member districts that elect between two and six legislators.

16 It seems that to some US trade negotiators, these two are not mutually exclusive choices. However, as Avinash Dixit points out, 'management [through results-oriented trade strategy] does imply cartelization'. If market share is guaranteed, foreign firms do not need to fear losing customers even if they decide to raise prices. Under such circumstances, a prerequisite for an open market, that is, free market competition, is unlikely to occur, 'Avinash K. Dixit, 'Discussion by Avinash K. Dixit', in R. Z. Lawrence and C. L. Schultze (eds), *An American Trade Strategy: Options for the 1990s*, Washington DC, The Brookings Institution, 1990, pp. 185–194.

17 Kent E. Calder, 'International pressure and domestic policy response: Japanese informatics policy in the 1980s'. Center of International Studies, Princeton University, June 1989, Research Monograph no. 51.

18 Nomura Research Institute and Booz Allen and Hamilton reported that in the case of automobiles trade, *keiretsu* is one of the major obstacles to market access. The report said in addition to a change in *keiretsu*, there are four problems that auto dealers faced in Japan: personnel, space, funds, and efforts by American manufacturers to adapt to the Japanese market. The report said that if these four problems are resolved without a change in the *keiretsu* system, there would be a 57,000 annual increase in the number of American cars exported to Japan. (An additional 37,000 cars would be exported if *keiretsu* were disbanded.) In addition, if the price of US-made cars is reduced by 10 to 25 per cent, the report stated that an annual increase of 6,000 to 22,000 US-made car imports would be expected (*Nihon Keizai Shimbun*, 14 February 1994).

19 *Nihon Keizai Shimbun*, 11 October 1993.

20 *Nihon Keizai Shimbun*, 12 November 1993.

21 Jagdish Bhagwati recommends the use of multilateral measures such as the GATT article twenty-three in order to correct market access problems related to *keiretsu* (*Nihon Keizai Shimbun*, 14 February 1994).

22 The structural budget balance is the budgetary position that would be observed if the level of actual output coincided with potential output (IMF, *World Economic Outlook*, October 1993, p. 103, May 1994, p. 43).

23 In October 1994, the Murayama government approved a revision of the ten year programme for public works – originally proposed under the Kaifu government in 1990 – that should maintain a high level of growth of public works in the mid-1990s. The overall size of the programme was changed from

430 trillion yen (Fiscal Years 1991–2000) to 630 trillion yen (Fiscal Years 1995–2004 (*Nihon Keizai Shimbun* (evening edition), 7 October 1994).

24 For instance, the *Yomiuri Shimbun* conducted an opinion survey covering senior bureaucrats, business leaders, politicians, and academics, on the question of politicians' ability to govern. Excepting the bureaucrats, many responded that currently the bureaucracy has more power than the politicians (*Yomiuri Shimbun*, 19 June 1994).

25 Salomon Brothers, *The Week in Prospect and Review*, 26 September 1994 (unpublished), p. 2.

26 See for instance, *Nihon Keizai Shimbun*, 1 and 4 February, and *Nihon Keizai Shimbun* (evening edition) 3 February 1994.

27 In April 1992, 16,242,000 (13.1 per cent of the population) were over 65 years old. Given the current rate of birth (average 1.50 children per woman) and life expectancy (male: 76.09 years, female: 82.22 years), by 2014, over 30,000,000 (23.5 per cent of the population) will be over 65 years old (*Kōsei Hakusho* 1993, p. 41 and p. 90).

28 *Nihon Keizai Shimbun* (evening edition), 7 October 1994.

29 Some specialists on bureaucratic reform suggest formation of a similar ministry such as *Seikatsu-shō* (Life Ministry) or *Shimin-shō* (Citizens Ministry) (*Nihon Keizai Shimbun*, 29 June 1994).

30 Murakawa, *Jimintō no Seisaku Kettei Shisutemu*, Part III, pp. 178–248.

31 For instance, the MHW's share fluctuated only 1.9 percentage points between 1980 and 1991.

BIBLIOGRAPHY

Abegglen, J. C., 'The economic growth of Japan', *Scientific American*, March 1970, vol. 222, no. 3, pp. 31–37.

Allison, G. T., *Essence of Decision: Explaining the Cuban Missile Crisis*, Boston, Little, Brown and Co., 1971.

Andō Y., 'Shijō kaihō seisaku no tenkai to mokuzai mondai' (The Evolution of Market Liberalization Policy and the Issue of Forest Products), *Ringyō Keizai*, September 1985, pp. 1–7.

Arai Y., 'Mada tsuzuku? Shijō kaihō yōkyū' (Will it Continue? Demands for market liberalization), *Sekai Shūhō*, 30 April/7 May 1985, pp. 12–15.

Asaoka H., *Kami, Parupu* (Pulp and Paper), Tokyo, Nihon Keizai Shimbun-sha, 1989.

Ashizaki T., *Kōseishō Zankoku Monogatari* (Horror Stories of the Ministry of Health and Welfare), Tokyo, Yell Books, 1980.

Avery, W. P. and D. P. Rapkin, *America in a Changing World Political Economy*, NY, Longman, 1982.

Baldwin, R. E., *The Political Economy of US Import Policy*, Cambridge, MA, The MIT Press, 1985.

Bentley, A., *The Process of Government*, Chicago, University of Chicago Press, 1908.

Bergsten, C. F. and M. Noland, *Reconcilable Differences? United States–Japan Economic Conflict*, Washington DC, Institute for International Economics, 1993.

Bhagwati, J., *Protectionism*, Cambridge, MA, The MIT Press, 1991.

Borrus, M., 'Japanese telecommunications: reforms and trade Implications', *California Management Review*, Spring 1986, vol. 28, no. 3, pp. 43–61.

Buckley, R., *Japan Today*, Cambridge, Cambridge University Press, 1990, second edition.

Calder, K. E., *Crisis and Compensation, Public Policy and Political Stability in Japan, 1949–1986*, Princeton, Princeton University Press, 1988.

—— 'International pressure and domestic policy response: Japanese informatics policy in the 1980s', Center of International Studies, Princeton University, June 1989, Research Monograph no. 51.

—— 'Japanese foreign economic policy formation: explaining the reactive state', *World Politics*, July 1988, vol. 40, no. 4, pp. 517–541.

Caves, R. E., 'Economic models of political choice: Canada's tariff structure', *Canadian Journal of Economics*, May 1976, vol. 9, no. 2, pp. 278–300.

Communication and Intelligence, *Jidōsha Denwa Sensō* (Automobile Phone War), Tokyo, Yell Books, 1989.

Curtis, G., *The Japanese Way of Politics*, New York, Columbia University Press, 1988.

Destler, I. M., *American Trade Politics: System Under Stress*, Washington DC, Institute for International Economics, 1986.

Destler, I. M. and Hideo Sato (eds), *Coping with US–Japanese Economic Conflicts*, Lexington, Lexington Books, 1982.

Dixit, Avinash, K., 'Discussion by Avinash K. Dixit', in R. Z. Lawrence and C. L. Shulze (eds), *An American Trade Strategy: Options for the 1990s*, Washington DC, The Brookings Institution, 1990.

Eckstein, H., 'Case study and theory in political science', in F. I. Greenstein and N.W. Polsby (eds), *Strategy of Inquiry*, Handbook of Political Science Volume 7, Reading MA, Addison Wesley Publishing Co., 1975, pp. 79–137.

Eguchi N., 'Shushō no "tosshutsu" ga "tōnai masatsu" o manēkū' ('Protrusion' of the Prime Minister invites 'intra-party friction'), *Sekai Shūhō*, 30 April/7 May 1985, pp. 24–27.

Encarnation, D. J. and M. Mason, 'Neither MITI nor America: the political economy of capital liberalization in Japan', *International Organization*, Winter 1990, vol. 44, no. 1, pp. 25–54.

Enoto I., 'Nichibei bōeki masatsu (mokuzai) no hāikei' (The background to the US–Japan (forest product) trade friction), *Ringyo Keizai*, September 1985, pp. 12–16.

Evans, P. B., D. Rueschemeyer, and T. Skocpol (eds), *Bringing the State Back In*, Cambridge, Cambridge University Press, 1985.

Fallows, J., 'Containing Japan', *Atlantic Monthly*, May 1989, pp. 40–54.

—— *More Like Us*, Boston, Houghton Mifflin Co., 1989.

Fujii Y., 'Trade friction', *Japan Economic Almanac*, 1985.

Fukui H., 'Studies in policymaking: a review of the literature', in T. J. Pempel (ed.), *Policymaking in Contemporary Japan*, Ithaca, Cornell University Press, 1977, pp. 22–59.

Fukuzawa T., ' "Misuteiku" hatsugen ni wa gakkuri' (Disappointing 'mistake' statement), *Sekai Shūhō*, 30 April/7 May, 1985, pp. 22–23.

Funabashi Y., *Nichibei Keizai Masatsu* (US–Japan Economic Conflict), Tokyo, Iwanami Shoten, 1987.

Gaizai Kenkyūkai, 'Wagakuni no mokuzai sangyō to kanzei hikisage' (Forest products industry and tariff reduction in our country), n.p., 1986.

Gendai Ringyō (ed), 'Towareru shinrin, ringyō, sanson eno kihonshisei' (Basic attitude toward forests, forestry, and rural villages questioned), *Gendai Ringyō*, May 1985.

Gilpin, R., *War and Change in World Politics*, Cambridge, Cambridge University Press, 1981.

—— *The Political Economy of International Relations*, Princeton, Princeton University Press, 1987.

—— 'Where does Japan fit in?', *Millennium: Journal of International Studies*, 1989, vol. 18, no. 3, pp. 329–342.

Goldstein, J., 'The political economy of trade: institutions of protection', *American Political Science Review*, March 1986, vol. 80, no. 1, pp. 161–184.

—— 'Ideas, institutions, and American trade policy', *International Organization*, Winter 1988, vol. 42, no. 1, pp. 179–218.

Gourevitch, P., 'The second image reversed: the international sources of domestic politics', *International Organization*, autumn 1978, vol. 32, no. 4, pp. 881–912.

Haggard, S., 'The institutional foundations of hegemony: explaining the Reciprocal Trade Agreements Act of 1934', *International Organization*, winter 1988, vol. 42, no. 1, pp. 91–119.

Haley, J. O., 'Governance by negotiation: a reappraisal of bureaucratic power in Japan', in K. B. Pyle (ed.), *The Trade Crisis: How Will Japan Respond?*, Seattle, The Society of Japanese Studies, 1987, pp. 177–192.

Halperin, M. H., *Bureaucratic Politics and Foreign Policy*, Washington DC, Brookings Institution, 1974.

Harris, R. G., 'Telecommunications policy in Japan: lessons for the US', *California Management Review*, Spring 1989, pp. 113–131.

Higashi E., *Iyakuhin Sangyō Gekidō no Mirai* (Dynamic Future of Pharmaceuticals Industry), Tokyo, Nihon Nōritsu Kyōkai, 1989.

—— *Seiyaku Gaisha ga Abunai* (Pharmaceutical Companies in Danger), Tokyo, Yell Books, 1990.

Hirschman, A. O., *National Power and the Structure of Foreign Trade*, Berkeley, University of California Press, 1945.

Holstein, W. J., *Japanese Power Game: What It Means for America*, New York, Macmillan Publishing Co., 1990.

Igarashi J., 'Study on the leadership of former Prime Minister Nakasone', *Leviathan* 5, Fall 1989, pp. 167–182.

Ikenberry, G. J., 'The irony of state strength: comparative responses to the Oil Shocks in the 1970s', *International Organization*, Winter 1986, vol. 40, no. 1, pp. 105–137.

—— 'Conclusion: an institutional approach to American foreign economic policy', *International Organization*, Winter 1988, vol. 42, no. 1, pp. 219–243.

—— 'Market solutions for state problems: the international and domestic politics of American oil decontrol', *International Organization*, winter 1988, vol. 42, no. 1, pp. 151–178.

Inoguchi T., *Gendai Nihon Seiji Keizai no Kōzu* (The Contemporary Japanese Political Economy), Tokyo, Tōyō Keizai Shinpō-sha, 1983.

Inoguchi T. and Iwai T., *'Zoku Giin' no Kenkyū* (A Study on Tribal Politicians), Tokyo, Nihon Keizai Shimbun-sha, 1987.

Inoguchi T. and D. I. Okimoto (eds), *The Political Economy of Japan Volume 2: The Changing International Context*, Stanford, Stanford University Press, 1988.

Johnson, C., 'Japan: who governs? An essay on official bureaucracy', *Journal of Japanese Studies*, Autumn 1975, vol. 2, no. 1, pp. 1–28.

—— *MITI and the Japanese Miracle: The Growth of Industrial Policy, 1925–1975*, Stanford, Stanford University Press, 1982.

—— 'MITI, MPT and the telecom wars: how Japan makes policy for high technology', Berkeley Roundtable on the International Economy (BRIE) Working Paper vol. 21, 1986.

—— 'Trade, revisionism, and the future of Japanese–American relations', Kozo

Yamamura (ed.), *Japan's Economic Structure: Should It Change?*, Seattle, Society of Japanese Studies, 1990.

Johnson, C., L. D. Tyson, and J. Zysman (eds), *Politics and Productivity; How Japan's Development Strategy Works*, New York, HarperBusiness, 1989.

Jussawalla, M., 'The race for telecommunications technology: The USA vs. Japan', *Telecommunications Policy*, September 1987, pp. 297–307.

Katzenstein, P. J. (ed.), *Between Power and Plenty: Foreign Economic Policies of Advanced Industrial States*, Madison, The University of Wisconsin Press, 1977.

Katznelson, I. and K. Prewitt, 'Constitutionalism, class, and the limits of choice in US foreign policy', R. R. Fagen (ed.), *Capitalism and the State in US–Latin American Relations*, Stanford, Stanford University Press, 1979, pp. 25–40.

Kawakita S., 'Mokuzai kanzei mondai ni tsuite' (On problems of tariffs on forest products), *Nōrinsuisanshō Kōhō*, February 1986, vol. 17, no. 2, pp. 28–31.

Kawakita T., *Tsūsan Yūsei Sensō* (MITI–MPT War), Tokyo Kyōiku-sha, 1985.

Keohane, R. O., *After Hegemony: Cooperation and Discord in the World Political Economy*, Princeton, Princeton University Press, 1984.

Keohane, R. O. and J. S. Nye, Jr., *Power and Interdependence: World Politics in Transition*, Boston, Little, Brown and Co., 1977.

Kindleberger, C. P., *The World in Depression 1929–1939*, Berkeley, University of California Press, 1973.

Kobayashi S., 'Esukarēto suru bōeki masatsu' (Escalating trade friction), *Rippō to Chōsa*, June 1985, vol. 128, pp. 41–50.

Kōsaka M., 'The international economic policy of Japan', in R. A. Scalapino (ed.), *The Foreign Policy of Modern Japan*, Berkeley, University of California Press, 1977.

Krasner, S. D., 'State power and the structure of international trade', *World Politics*, April 1976, vol. 28, no. 3, pp. 317–343.

—— *Defending the National Interest: Raw Materials Investments and US Foreign Policy*, Princeton, Princeton University Press, 1978.

—— 'Structural causes and regime consequences: regimes as intervening variables', in S. D. Krasner (ed.), *International Regimes*, Ithaca, Cornell University Press, 1983, pp. 2–21.

Krugman, P., 'Competitiveness: a dangerous obsession', *Foreign Affairs*, March/ April 1994, vol. 73, no. 2, pp. 28–44.

Kuroda M., 'Talking tough about trade', *Journal of Japanese Trade and Industry*, 1988, no. 6, pp. 30–32.

Kyōiku-sha (ed.), *Kōseishō* (The Ministry of Health and Welfare), Tokyo, Kyōiku-sha, 1979.

Lake, D. A., *Power, Protection, and Free Trade: International Sources of US Commercial Strategy, 1887–1939*, Ithaca, Cornell University Press, 1988.

Lavergne, R. P., *The Political Economy of US Tariffs: An Empirical Analysis*, New York, Academic Press, 1983.

Lawrence, R. Z. and C. L. Schultze (eds), *An American Trade Strategy: Options for the 1990s*, Washington DC, The Brookings Institution, 1990.

Leslie, E., 'MOSS talks remove barriers to sales in four Japanese sectors', *Business America*, 17 March 1986, pp. 23–24.

Lincoln, E. J., *Japan: Facing Economic Maturity*, Washington DC, The Brookings Institution, 1988.

Lowi, T. J., 'American business, public policy, case-studies, and political theory', *World Politics*, July 1964, vol. 16, no. 4, pp. 677–715.

—— *The End of Liberalism: The Second Republic of the United States*, New York, W. W. Norton and Co., 1979, second edition.

Maeno K., 'Scramble for a share of the telecom trade', *Journal of Japanese Trade and Industry*, 1987, no. 6, pp. 24–26.

—— 'Turf battles and telecom', *Journal of Japanese Trade and Industry*, 1988, no. 5, pp. 47–50.

Magee, S. P. and L. Young, 'Endogenous protection in the United States, 1900-1984', in R.M. Stern (ed), *US Trade Politics in a Changing World Economy*, Cambridge MA, The MIT Press, 1987, pp. 145–206.

Magee, S. P., W. A. Brock and L. Young, *Black Hole Tariffs and Endogenous Policy Theory: Political Economy in General Equilibrium*, Cambridge, Cambridge University Press, 1989.

March, J. M. and J. P. Olsen, 'The new institutionalism:organizational factors in political life', *American Political Science Review*, September 1984, vol. 78, no. 3, pp. 734–749.

Maswood, S. J., *Japan and Protection: The Growth of Protectionist Sentiment and the Japanese Response*, New York, Routledge, 1989.

Matsuda T., Katayama M. *et al.*, 'Shinrin no sōgō riyō to ringyō kasseika eno hosaku' (General utilization of forestry and a programme for revitalization of forestry), *Nōrinsuisanshō sono Yakuwari to Seisaku* (MAFF: Its Role and Policy), Tokyo, Sangyō Seisaku Kenkyūjo, 1988, pp. 122–141.

Maurer, R. P., *Nihon Shijō deno Kyōsō* (Competing in High-Tech Japan), Tokyo, The Simul Press, 1989.

MITI (ed.), *Nihon no Sentaku* (Japan's Choices), Tokyo, Tsūshō Sangyō Chōsa-kai, 1988.

Miyake I., Yamaguchi Y., Muramatsu M. and Shindō E. (eds), *Nihon Seiji no Zahyō: Sengo 40-nen no Ayumi* (Dimensions of Japanese Politics: Progress in the Forty Years' Postwar Period), Tokyo, Yūhikaku, 1985.

Morita A. and Ishihara S., *'No' to Ieru Nippon* (Japan that Can Say 'No'), Tokyo, Kobun-sha, 1989.

Murakami Y., *Shin Chūkan Taishū no Jidai* (The Age of the New Middle Mass), Tokyo, Chōō Kōron-sha, 1984.

Murakawa I., *Jimintō no Seisaku Kettei Shisutemu* (The LDP's Policymaking System), Tokyo, Kyōiku-sha, 1989.

Muramatsu M., 'Min'eika, kiseikanwa to saikisei no kōzō' (Structure of privatization, deregulation and reregulation), *Leviathan*, Spring 1988, no. 2, pp. 118–135.

—— *Sengo Nihon no Kanryōsei* (The Bureaucracy in Postwar Japan), Tokyo, Tōyō Keizai Shinpō-sha, 1981.

Muramatsu M. and E. S. Krauss, 'Bureaucrats and politicians in policymaking: the case of Japan', *The American Political Science Review*, 1984, vol. 78, pp. 126–146.

—— 'The conservative policy line and the development of patterned pluralism', in K. Yamamura and Y. Yasuba (eds), *The Political Economy of Japan, Volume 1: The Domestic Transformation*, Stanford, Stanford University Press, 1987.

Murashima Y., *Mokuzai Sangyō no Keizaigaku* (Economics of the Forest Products Industry), Tokyo, Nihon Ringyō Chōsa-kai, 1987.

Nakano M. (ed.), *Nihongata Seisaku Kettei no Henyō* (Changes in Japanese Decision Making), Tokyo, Tōyō Keizai Shinpō-sha, 1986.

Namiki N., *Tsūsanshō no Shūen* (End of MITI), Tokyo, Daiyamondo-sha, 1989.

Neary, I., Research Note, 'Seiyakugyō ni kansuru sangyō seisaku' (Industrial policy for the pharmaceuticals industry), *Leviathan*, Spring 1990, vol. 6, pp. 186–196.

Nettl, J. P., 'The state as a conceptual variable', *World Politics*, July 1968, vol. 20, no. 5, pp. 559–592.

Nihon Hyōron-sha, *Nichibei Kankei Hakusho 1985–86.*

Nihon Keizai Shimbun-sha (ed.), *Gekishin Dokyumento NTT* (Document NTT), Tokyo, Nihon Keizai Shimbun-sha, 1989.

Nihon Seiji Gakkai (ed.), *Gendai Nihon no Seitō to Kanryō: Hoshu Gōdō Igo* (The Parties and Bureaucracy in Contemporary Japan – Since the Conservative Fusion in 1955), Tokyo, Iwanami Shoten, 1967.

—— *Nihon no Atsuryoku Dantai* (Pressure Groups in Japan), Tokyo, Iwanami Shoten, 1960.

Nishio T., *Nihon Shinrin Gyōseishi no Kenkyū* (The History of Japanese Forestry Administration), Tokyo, Tokyo University Press, 1988.

Nordlinger, E., *On the Autonomy of the Democratic State*, Cambridge MA, Harvard University Press, 1981.

Nye, J. S., Jr., *Bound to Lead: The Changing Nature of American Power*, New York, Basic Books, 1990.

Odell, J.S., *US International Monetary Policy: Markets, Power, and Ideas as Sources of Change*, Princeton, Princeton University Press, 1982.

—— 'Understanding International Trade Policies: An Emerging Synthesis', *World Politics*, October 1990, vol. 43, no. 1, pp. 139–167.

Ogura K., *Nichibei Keizai Masatsu* (US–Japan Economic Friction), Tokyo, Nihon Keizai Shimbun-sha, 1982.

Ōhashi I., 'Terecomu kisei kanwa no eikyō' (Effects of telecommunications deregulation), in Ezra Vogel (ed.), *Mosaku, nichibei shinjidai* (New epoch for the US–Japan relationship), Tokyo, Nihon Hyōron-sha, 1984.

Ohira S., 'Mondai o sakiokuri shita "tamamushi iro" no kecchaku' (Equivocal resolution avoiding the real problems), *Sekai Shūhō*, 1985, 30 April/7 May 1985, pp. 18–19.

Okimoto, D. I., 'Political inclusivity: the domestic structure of trade', in T. Inoguchi and D. I. Okimoto (eds), *The Political Economy of Japan Volume 2: The Changing International Context*, Stanford, Stanford University Press, 1988, pp. 305–344.

—— *Between MITI and the Market: Japanese Industrial Policy for High Technology*, Stanford, Stanford University Press, 1989.

Olmer, L. H. (interview) 'Nichibei keizai masatsu no sainen wa fukahi ka?' (Inevitable reheating of US–Japanese trade friction?), *Sekai Shūhō*, 1985, pp. 20–24.

Olson, M., *The Logic of Collective Action: Public Goods and the Theory of Groups*, Cambridge MA, Harvard University Press, 1965.

Ōmae M., *Taimu Māchanto* (Time Merchant), Tokyo, Tokuma Shoten, 1988.

Ōmiya T., 'Kome o daraku sasetanowa dareka' (Who corrupted 'rice'?), *Zaikai Tenbō*, August 1990, pp. 202–206.

Omura K., 'Hihan ga nokoru kōyōju gōban no kanzei hikisage' (Remaining criticism against reduction on tariffs on hardwood plywood), *Sekai Shūhō*, 30 April/7 May 1985, pp. 38–39.

Orr, R. M. Jr., *The Emergence of Japan's Foreign Aid Power*, New York, Columbia University Press, 1990.

Ōtake H., *Gendai Nihon no Seijikenryoku Keizaikenryoku* (Political Power and Economic Power in Contemporary Japan), Tokyo, San-ichi Shobō, 1979.

151

Pastor, R. A., *Congress and the Politics of US Foreign Economic Policy*, Berkeley, University of California Press, 1980.

Pempel, T. J., 'Japanese foreign economic policy: the domestic bases for international behavior', in P. J. Katzenstein (ed.), *Between Power and Plenty: Foreign Economic Policies of Advanced Industrial States*, Madison, The University of Wisconsin Press, 1977, pp. 139–190.

—— *Policy and Politics in Japan: Creative Conservatism*, Philadelphia, Temple University Press, 1982.

Prestowitz, C. V., Jr., *Trading Places: How We Allowed Japan to Take the Lead*, New York, Basic Books, 1988.

Prestowitz, C. V., Jr., L. C. Thurow *et al.*, 'The fight over competitiveness: a zero-sum debate?', *Foreign Affairs*, July/August 1994, vol. 73, no. 4, pp. 186–197.

Pyle, K. B., *The Japanese Question, Power and Purpose in a New Era*, Washington DC, American Enterprise Institute, 1992.

Reich, M. R., 'Why the Japanese don't export more pharmaceuticals: health policy as industrial policy', *California Management Review*, Winter 1990, pp. 124–150.

Reich, R. B., 'Members only', *The New Republic*, 26 June, 1989, pp. 14–18.

Reischauer, E. O., *The Japanese Today*, Cambridge MA, Harvard University Press, 1988, second edition.

Rosenbluth, F. M., *Financial Politics in Contemporary Japan*, Ithaca, Cornell University Press, 1989.

Saitō M., 'Towareru shinrin, ringyō, sanson eno kihonshisei' (Basic attitude toward forests, forestry, and rural villages questioned), *Gendai Ringyō*, May 1985, pp. 20–24.

Sakai T., 'Mokuzai to kanzei mondai no kokunai gyōkai e no eikyō ni tsuite' (on the effect of forest products tariffs on domestic industries), *Ringyō Keizai*, September 1985, pp. 8–11.

Salvaggio, J. L., *The Computer and Telecommunications Industry in Japan, 1986: Analysis*, Arlington, Virginia: Telecom Publishing Group, 1986.

Samuels, R. J., *The Business of the Japanese State: Energy Markets in Comparative and Historical Perspective*, Ithaca, Cornell University Press, 1987.

Sangyō Seisaku Kenkyūjo, *Tsūsanshō sono Yakuwari to Seisaku* (MITI, Its Role and Policy), 1988.

—— *Nōrinsuisanshō sono Yakuwari to Seisaku* (MAFF, Its Role and Policy), 1988.

Saruwatari J., 'Yonbunya kyōgi (MOSS) to nihon sangyōkai no dōkō' (MOSS talks and the trend in Japanese industries), *Kokusai Mondai*, December 1985, no. 309, pp. 32–44.

Satō B., *Nihon no Yūsei Senryaku* (The Strategy of the Ministry of Posts and Telecommunications in Japan), Tokyo, Bijinesu-sha, 1987.

Satō I., 'Gōban kanzei hikisage no ura ni ugomeku amerika shinrin mejā' (Forest major acting behind the scenes of tariff reduction for plywood), *Asu no Nōson*, September 1985, no. 130, pp. 92–97.

Satō M., *Tsūshin wa Jidai o Tsukuru* (Telecommunication Makes a New Era), Tokyo, Bijinesu-sha, 1985.

Satō S. and Matsuzaki T., *Jimintō Seiken* (LDP in Power), Tokyo, Chūō Kōron-sha, 1986.

Saxonhouse, G., 'The micro- and macro- economics of foreign sales in Japan', in R. Cline (ed.), *Trade Policy in the 1980s*, Washington DC, Institute for International Economics, 1983.

Schattschneider, E. E., *Politics, Pressures and the Tariff: A Study of Free Private*

Enterprise in Pressure Politics, as shown in the 1929–1930 revision of the Tariff, New York, Prentice Hall, Inc., 1935.

Schoppa, L. J., 'Two-level games and bargaining outcome: why gaiatsu succeeds in Japan in some cases but not others', *International Organization*, summer 1993, vol. 47, no. 3, pp. 353–386.

Seki H., *Terekomu Kyojin no Sekai Senryaku* (Global Strategy of Telecom Giant), Tokyo, Nihon Keizai Shimbun-sha, 1987.

Seo T., *Iyakuhin* (Pharmaceuticals), Tokyo, Nihon Keizai Shimbun-sha, 1987.

Shakai Keizai Kokumin Kaigi (ed.), *Kokusai Masatsu o Kiru* (Japan's Choices for Avoiding Crises), Tokyo, Shakai Keizai Kokumin Kaigi, 1988.

Shibukawa F., 'Nichibei tsūshin masatsu no yukue' (Future of the US–Japan telecommunications friction), *Rippō to Chōsa*, June 1985, no. 128, pp. 45–50.

Shikano S., 'Mokuzai no shijō kaihō mondai o megutte' (On the problems of forest products market liberalization), *Rippō to Chōsa*, June 1985, pp. 51–56.

Shiose Y., *Yūseishō no Gyakushū* (The Ministry of Posts and Telecommunications Retaliate), Tokyo, Bijinesu-sha, 1986.

Sigur, G. J., Jr., 'Perspective and proportion for US–Japanese relations', *Department of State Bulletin*, October 1986, pp. 24–25.

Singer, J. D., 'The level-of-analysis problem in international relations', in K. Knorr and S. Verba (eds), *The International System: Theoretical Essay*, Princeton, Princeton University Press, 1961, pp. 77–92.

Skocpol, T. and K. Finegold, 'State capacity and economic intervention in the early New Deal', *Political Science Quarterly*, Summer 1982, vol. 97, no. 2, pp. 255–278.

Skowronek, S., *Building a New American State: The Expansion of National Administrative Capacities 1877–1920*, Cambridge, Cambridge University Press, 1982.

Stepan, A., *State and Society: Peru in Comparative Perspective*, Princeton, Princeton University Press, 1978.

Stigler, G. J., 'The theory of economic regulation', *The Bell Journal of Economics and Management Science*, Spring 1971, vol. 2, no. 1, pp. 3–21.

Sugimoto E. (ed.), *Tsūshō Sangyō Shō Binran* (Handbook of MITI), Tokyo, Kyōiku-sha, 1979.

Suguro T., *Iyakuhin Gyōkai* (Pharmaceutical Industry), Tokyo, Kyōiku-sha, 1987.

Tabuchi Y., 'Kaiho saretemo "Jisseki no tsumimashi" teido' (Liberalization adds little to the end result), *Sekai Shūhō*, 30 April/7 May 1985, pp. 15–17.

Taguchi T. and Toshinai Y., 'Atsuryoku dantai toshiteno ishikai' (Association of medical doctors as a pressure group), *Chūō Kōron*, April 1959, pp. 246–268.

Tahara S., 'Nippon daikaizo 11' (Grand remodelling of Japan 11), *Shūkan Bunshun*, 16 May, 1985, no. 2302, pp. 42–47.

Takahashi H., 'Nihon ishikai no seiji kōdō to ishi kettei' (JMA's political activities and decision making), in M. Nakano (ed.), *Nihongata Ishi Kettei no Henyō* (Changes in Japanese Decision Making), Tokyo, Tōyō Keizai Shinpō-sha, 1986, pp. 237–266.

Takahashi K., *Konpyūta Gyōkai* (Computer Industry), Tokyo, Kyōiku-sha, 1987.

Takahashi K. and Odawara S., *Jōhō Tsūshin Gyōkai* (Information Communication Sector), Tokyo, Kyōiku-sha, 1988.

Takahashi M., 'High tech development hindered by government regulations', *Nikkei High Tech Report*, November 1985.

Takeda H., 'Shijō kaihōka ni okeru mokuzai mondai' (The issue of forest products under market liberalization), *Ringyō Keizai Kenkyū*, November 1986, pp. 50–58.

Truman, D. B., *The Governmental Process*, New York, Knopf, 1951.

Tsuji S., *Nihon Kanryōsei no Kenkyū* (Studies in Japanese Bureaucracy), Tokyo, Tokyo Daigaku Shuppankai, 1969.

Tyson, L. D. and J. Zysman, 'Developmental strategy and production innovation in Japan', in C. Johnson, L.D. Tyson, and J. Zysman (eds), *Politics and Productivity: How Japan's Development Strategy Works*, New York, HarperBusiness, 1989, pp. 59–140.

Unger, D. and P. Blackburn (eds), *Japan's Emerging Global Role*, Boulder, Lynne Rienner Publishers, 1993.

van Wolferen, K., *The Enigma of Japanese Power*, New York, A. A. Knopf, 1989.

Watanabe H., 'MOSS kyōgi to rinsanbutsu no kijun, ninshō' (MOSS talks and standards and approval of forest products), *Mokuzai Kōgyō*, vol. 40-10, pp. 34–37.

Winham, G. R., *International Trade and the Tokyo Round Negotiation*, Princeton NJ, Princeton University Press, 1986.

Winham, G. R. and I. Kabashima, 'The politics of US–Japanese auto trade', in I. M. Destler and H. Sato, *Coping with US–Japanese Economic Conflicts*, Lexington, Lexington Books, 1982, pp. 73–119.

Yamaichi Securities, *Kaisha Shikihō*, Fall 1984.

Yamakawa H., 'Miryoku aru 4 chō en no nihon shijō' (Enchanting ¥ 4 trillion Japanese market), *Sekai Shūhō*, 30 April/7 May 1985, pp. 20–21.

Yamamoto M., ' "Gaiatsu-hannō" no junkan o koete' (Beyond the cycle of 'pressure-reaction'), in C. Hosoya and T. Aruga (eds), *Kokusai Kankyō no Henyō to Nichibei Kankei* (Change in International Environment and the US–Japan Relationship), Tokyo, Tokyo University Press, 1987, pp. 321–335.

Yanaga, C., *Big Business in Japanese Politics*, New Haven, Yale University Press, 1968.

Yanagisawa K., 'Nōrin suisan bunya mo shijō kaihō suishin no seiiki de wa nai' (Agricultural, forestry, and fishery sectors are no longer considered off-limits for market liberalization), *Nōsei Chōsa Jihō*, May 1985, no. 344, pp 2–20.

Yeutter, C., 'Improved market access to Japan', *Department of State Bulletin*, October 1985, pp. 27–29.

GOVERNMENT DOCUMENTS AND PUBLICATIONS

Forestry Agency, *Mokuzai Jukyū to Mokuzai Kōgyō no Genjō* (Supply and demand of forest products and the state of the forest products industry), 1986, 1990.

—— 'Mokuzai seihin no kanzei hikisage' (Tariff reduction of forest products). Gyōsei Kōhō Shiryō Sentā, *Kōseishō 1980*.

IMR Profile: The Telecommunications Equipment Market in Japan, Document prepared for US Department of Commerce, Tokyo, Pacific Projects, 1986.

Informatization White Paper, 1989.

JETRO, *Your Market in Japan, Computer Hardware*, March 1986.

Kōsei Hakusho (Health and Welfare White Paper), 1993.

Kōseisho 1980 (The Ministry of Health and Welfare 1980), Tokyo, Gyōsei Shiryō Sentā, 1979.

Ministry of Health and Welfare (MHW) (ed.), *Report on Medical Equipment and Pharmaceuticals Market-Oriented, Sector-Selective (MOSS) Discussions* by the US and Japan MOSS Negotiating Teams to Minister for Foreign Affairs Abe, Secretary of State Schultz, January 1986, Tokyo, Yakuji Nippō-sha, 1986.

—— *Pharmaceutical Administration in Japan*, Tokyo, Yakuji Nippō-sha, 1988.

Ministry of Posts and Telecommunications (MPT), *Records on the Telecommunications Talks*.

MITI, *Kami Parupu Sangyō no Genjō* (Current State of the Paper and Pulp Industries).

Ringyō Hakusho (Forestry White Paper).

Tsūshō Hakusho (Trade and Commerce White Paper).

US Advisory Committee for Trade Policy and Negotiations, *Analysis of the US–Japan Trade Problem*, February 1989.

US Congress, House, Subcommittee on Asian and Pacific Affairs and on International Economic Policy and Trade of the Committee on Foreign Affairs, *Hearings*, ninety-ninth Congress, 17 April, 9 and 14 May 1985.

US Congress, House, Subcommittee on Economic Stabilization of the Committee on Banking, Finance, and Urban Affairs, *Hearings*, ninety-ninth Congress, 30 April 1985.

US Congress, House, Subcommittee on Telecommunications, Consumer Protection, and Finance and the Subcommittee on Commerce, Transportation, and Tourism of the Committee on Energy and Commerce, ninety-ninth Congress, 27 and 28 March 1985.

US Congress, Senate, Committee on Finance, *Hearings: State of the US Forest Products Industry*, ninety-ninth Congress, first session, 19 September 1985.

US Congress, Senate, Subcommittee on International Finance and Monetary Policy of the Committee on Banking, Housing, and Urban Affairs, ninety-ninth Congress, 30 July 1985.

US Congress, Senate, Subcommittee on International Trade of the Committee on Finance, ninety-ninth Congress, 8 March 1985.

US Congress, Subcommittee on Economic Goals and Intergovernmental Policy of the Joint Economic Committee, *Hearings*, ninety-ninth Congress, 20 March 1985.

US Department of Commerce, MOSS Negotiating Team, *Report on Telecommunications Market-Oriented, Sector-Selective (MOSS) Discussions*, 1986.

US Department of State Bulletin.

US General Accounting Office, *US–Japan Trade: Evaluation of the Market-Oriented Sector-Selective Talks*, July 1988.

US General Accounting Office, *US–Japan Trade: Interim Report on Sector-Selective Agreements*, July 1987.

US General Accounting Office, *US–Japan Trade: Trade Data and Industry Views on MOSS Agreements*, February 1988.

US–Japan Joint Report on Sectoral Discussions by Secretary of State George Schultz and Foreign Minister Shintaro Abe, Washington DC, 10 January 1986.

US–Japan Joint Report on the Sector Discussions, by Foreign Minister Shintaro Abe and Secretary of State George Schultz, New York, 26 September 1985.

Wertman, P., 'The MOSS talks: success or failure?' Congressional Research Service, Report no. 85-1129 E, 19 December 1985.

Young, J. D., *Japanese Standards of Living and US Approaches to Japan*, Congressional Research Service, Report for Congress, 22 April 1992.

NEWSPAPERS AND PERIODICALS

Asahi Shimbun
Denpa Shimbun
Japan Times
The Journal of Commerce
Mainichi Shimbun
The New York Times
Nihon Keizai Shimbun
Nihon Nōgyō Shimbun
Nikkan Mokuzai Shimbun (Japan Forest Products Journal)
Sankei Shimbun
Wall Street Journal
The Washington Post
Yomiuri Shimbun

American Political Science Review
Asu no Nōson
Atlantic Monthly
Bell Journal of Economics and Management Science
Business America
Business Asia
California Management Review
Chemical Marketing Reporter
Chemical Week
Chūō Kōron
Denshi Kōgyō Nenkan (Electronics Industry Almanac), 1990
Ekonomisuto
FAO, *Yearbook of Forest Products*
Foreign Affairs
IMF, *World Economic Outlook*

Imidas 1994
International Organization
Japan Economic Almanac
Japan Economic Journal
Jihyō
Jōhō Tsūshin Nenkan '91 (Information Communications Almanac '91)
Journal of International Studies
Journal of Japanese Trade and Industry
Kokusai Mondai
Leviathan
Mokuzai Kōgyō
Mokuzai Nooto
Nihon Kokusei Zue
Nihon Seiyaku Kōgyō Kyōkai Gaido, 1985
Nikkei High Tech Report
Nōrinsuisanshō Kōhō
Nōsei Chōsa Jihō
OECD, *Foreign Trade by Commodities*
Ringyō Keizai
Scientific American
World Politics
Ringyō Keizai Kenkyū
Rippō to Chōsa
Sekai Shūhō
Shūkan Bunshun
Telecommunications Policy
The Economist
United Nations, *International Trade Statistics Yearbook*
Zaikai Tenbō

UNPUBLISHED PAPERS AND OTHERS

Anderson, S., 'Chapter five: biotechnology', in K. E. Calder (ed.), *Japan in the Global Political Economy: International Pressure and Domestic Policy Formation*, manuscript.

Cho S., Manuscript for the speech delivered at Zenkoku Gyōsei Kenshūkai, 13 June 1990.

Japan Paper Association, 'Nichibei MOSS kyōgi keika hōkoku' (Progress report of the US–Japan MOSS talks).

Japan Pharmaceutical Manufacturers Association, *DATA BOOK*, 1989.

Japan Plywood Manufacturer's Association, *Nihon no Gōhan Sangyō* (Japan's Plywood Industry), 1989.

Nikkei Telecom (On-line database).

Salomon Brothers, *The Week in Prospect and Review*, 26 September 1994.

US–Japan Trade Study Group, *Progress Report: 1984.*

INTERVIEWS AND ASSISTANCE*

Abe Michiharu Pharmaceutical Affairs Bureau, Ministry of Health and Welfare (MHW).

Abelson, Donald S. Deputy Assistant, United States Trade Representative (USTR).

Achilles, Norman. Office of Japan, Department of State.

Agress, Philip. Office of Japan, Department of Commerce.

Aoyagi Tomoo. Forestry Agency.

Aritomi Kanichiro. Director, Telecommunications Bureau, Ministry of Posts and Telecommunications (MPT).

Asami Hiroshi. Deputy Director, Communications Policy Bureau, MPT. .

Blum, Larry. Forest Products Division, Department of Agriculture.

Cho Susumu. Executive Vice President, Nippon Motorola, Ltd.

Dai Yutaka. Pharmaceutical Affairs Bureau, MHW.

Fujisue Kenzō. Machinery and Information Industries Bureau, Ministry of International Trade and Industry (MITI).

Fukushima, Glen S. Director, AT & T Japan, Ltd. .

Gotō Kenji. Deputy Director, Agency of Industrial Science and Technology.

Gradowille, James. Director of International Trade, Motorola, USA.

Himeno Tomiyuki. Director, Japan Fiberboard and Particleboard Manufacturers Association.

Hoshino Shinyasu. Vice-Minister, Economic Planning Agency.

Inamura Kōbō. Director, Communications Policy Bureau, MPT.

Irisawa Hajime. Deputy Director General, Forestry Agency.

Ishida Tooru. Councilor, Minister's Secretariat, MITI.

Kaji Shigenori. General Manager, Japan Paper Association.

Kamiya Kazuko. Manager, MSD (Japan) Co., Ltd.

Kaneko Yoshihiro. Director, Japan Laminated Wood Products Association.

Kawakita Susumu. Deputy Director, Forestry Agency.

Kayukawa Masatoshi. Councilor. Cabinet Legislation Bureau.

Kimura Masaaki. Deputy Director, Petroleum Department, Agency of Natural Resources and Energy.

Kimura Saburō. Commerce Section, American Embassy, Japan.

Kita Shūji. Member of the Upper House, LDP.

Kobayashi Satoshi, Telecommunications Bureau, MPT.

Koito Masaki, Deputy Director, Consumer Goods Industries Bureau, MITI.

Koizumi Toshizō. Deputy Director, Communications Policy Bureau, MPT.

Kōno Takeshi. Manager, Japan Pharmaceutical Manufacturers Association (JPMA).

Kumaki Tokichi. Director, INTEC, Inc.

Kuroiwa Satoshi. Deputy Director, Machinery and Information Industries Bureau, MITI.

Kurokawa Tatsuo. Deputy Director, Pharmaceutical Affairs Bureau, MHW.

Matsui Tetsuo. Deputy Director, Machinery and Information Industries Bureau, MITI.

Matsumoto Shinji. Director General, International Procurement Office, Nippon Telegraph and Telephone Co. (NTT).

Matsumura Atsushi, Board Director, MSD (Japan) Co., Ltd. .

Maurer, P. Reed. Pharmaceutical Manufacturers Association.

Miyata Isamu. Yakuji Nippō-sha.

Mochinaga Tetsuji. Industrial Policy Bureau, MITI.

*These positions are those held at the time of the interviews (January to August 1990).

Nagai Kōji. Professor, Hoshi College of Pharmacy.
Nakamura Yoshio. Deputy Director, Pharmaceutical Affairs Bureau, MHW.
Niiya Tetsurō. Managing Director, JPMA.
Nozoe Yutaka. Telecommunications Bureau, MPT.
Porges, Amelia. Assistant General Council, USTR.
Tabiki Seirō. Assistant to President, ICI-Pharma.
Tanahashi Yūji. Director General, Industrial Policy Bureau, MITI.
Teshima Reishi. Ambassador to Italy, Ministry of Foreign Affairs.
Toda Hideaki. Associate Vice-President, NTT.
Toshida Seiichi. Director, Economic Planning Agency.
Wetzel, Hayden M. International Trade Administration, Department of Commerce.
Wright, Bryan O. President, MSD (Japan) Co., Ltd.
Yamamoto Akito. Chief, Research Section, Japan Plywood Manufacturer's Association.
Yokoo Hidehiro. Deputy Director, Machinery and Information Industries Bureau, MITI.

INDEX

Note: Most references are to Japan, unless otherwise stated.

Abe Shintarō 47, 49
accountability, political 114
administrative guidance, MITI 83–4
aerospace industry 8
ageing population 107, 109, 113
agencies 7; *see also* FA (Forest
   Agency), Science and Technology
   Agency
agenda formation 52, 101–2, 103;
   MOSS talks 39–45
agriculture 70; European Union
   subsidies 4; and forest products
   tariffs 88–90
anti-dumping measures 12, 20–1
Anti-Monopoly Law 104, 111
APEC 12, 106
approval grants 60, 61; for drugs 30,
   41–2, 59, 64–5, 77–9
automobiles 4, 5, 8, 13, 94, 103–4
autonomy of ministries 27, 28–9,
   35–6, 54–8, 84, 102

Baldridge, Malcolm 44, 47
barriers, trade 4, 6, 98, 108;
   electronics 44–5, 52, 73, 83–4, 100;
   in regional integration 12; types of
   30–1; *see also* market liberalization;
   regulations; tariffs
beef 6, 70
Boren, David L. 47, 66
boxes 31
Brock, William 44, 46
budgets 110–11

bureaucracy *see* ministries
Bush, George 49

capacity of ministries 27–31, 35–7,
   54–73, 84–5, 102–3; MITI 95
car industry 4, 5, 8, 13, 94, 103–4
Clinton, Bill 9–10, 106
commercial practices: electronics 45,
   52, 73, 83, 84, 100; *keiretsu* 31,
   103–5
Common Agricultural Policy (CAP) 4
compensation, forest products 82,
   85–92
competition, compartmentalized 24–5,
   96
computer industry 108: distribution
   45; relationship with MITI 76; tariffs
   42–3, 51–2, 72–3
computer software industry 8
conflict, inter-ministry 28–9, 55–8, 73,
   99, 108, 111
consumer policies 95–6, 113–14
consumer protection 33, 66–7, 96,
   102
Curran, Timothy 70

Danforth, John H, 47, 66
deregulation 10–11, 113–14, *see also*
   market liberalization
developmental state model 8, 22, 39,
   97
distribution system 45, 100
drugs: approval grants 30, 41–2, 59,

64–5, 78–9; generic 78; pricing 41, 55–6, 59, 77–9; role of MHW 29–30; safety 59, 63, 64, 74–5

economic growth 100; policy change from 93–5
economic policies: approaches to 19–37; global 9–14; Japan 4–7, 8–9, US 5–7, 9–10, 101–13; see also market liberalization; MOSS talks
electronics 14, 16, 74; agenda formation 42–5; chronology of talks 123–4; effects of foreign pressure 51–2, 53; and market liberalization 83; and MITI 76, 96, 97, 103; trade barriers 45, 52, 73, 83, 84, 100; see also MITI
Electronics Industries Association (EIA) 47
elitist model of policymaking 22–3, 26, 93–4
European Union (EU) 11, 13, 106; agricultural subsidies 4
exclusive trading relationships see commercial practices

FA (Forest Agency) 89; autonomy 54–5, 84; and forest products subsidies 91–2; institutional objectives 70–2; and market liberalization 82; policy instruments 61–2, 84; relationship with forest products industry 74, 75–6, 84–5
fiscal policy 109
Forest Agency see FA
forest products industry 14, 16; chronology of talks 121–3; effects of foreign pressure 48–50, 52; and market liberalization 82, 84–92; politicization 102; relationship with FA 74, 76, 84–5; standards 50, 71–2; subsidies 82–3, 85–92; tariffs 48–50, 61–2, 71, 82–3, 85–92; see also FA
Framework talks 5, 9–10, 15, 16, 40
Fujinaka Akio 86
Fujio Masayuki 91

gaiatsu (foreign pressure) 94, 98, 101–2, 114; effects of 38–53; reasons for Japan's response to 19–21; response of ministries to 26–7
GATT 11, 12, 13–14, 20–1, 105

global policies 9–14; Japan 3–4, 114
government procurement 108
group theory 7–8; see also interest groups

Harbinger Party 1, 99, 107
Hata Tsutomu 1, 96
hegemony, US 20, 106
Hideo Sato 70
Hosokawa Morihiro 1, 11, 96, 109

IDO (Nippon Idō Tsūshin) 12, 13
Ikeda Hayato 100
Indonesia, timber imports 76, 82, 87
inflation 10
institutional objectives: ministries 27, 28, 29–30, 62–73, 102–3; MITI 95
institutional structure approach, economic policy 25
interest groups 7–8, 96, 107; approach to economic policy 23–5
interests, shared, between ministries and private sector 76–83, 84
international regimes theory 20
issue specification, in MOSS talks 40–5

Japan Fair Trade Commission (JFTC) 104, 111
Japan Forestry Association 88
Japan Medical Association 77
Japan Pharmaceuticals Manufacturers Association (JPMA) 77, 91
Japan Plywood Manufacturers' Association (JPMA) 86–7
Johnson, Chalmers, developmental state model 8, 22, 39, 97

Kanemaru Shin 49, 91
Kasumigaseki 97
Katzenstein, Peter 93
keiretsu relationships 31, 103–5
kisei kanchō (regulator ministries) 34, 67
kit products 41
Koomoto Toshio 86
Koyama Moriya 48, 57–8
kyoka (drug licences) 59
kyoninkaken (approval grants) 60, 61

laminated timber, tariffs 71
LDP 3, 26, 77, 107; decline in power 26, 107; forest products tariffs 49,

86–7, 90–1; relationships with ministries 97–8; role in policymaking 22–3, 26, 93–4
LDP–Socialist coalition 1, 99, 109, 112
leaders and leadership, political 107–9, 114; and commercial practices 103–4; need for 112–13; relationship with ministries 97–8, 99–101
licences, drug 59

macro-economic policy 106–7, 109, 112
MAFF (Ministry of Agriculture, Forestry and Fisheries) 23, 84, 88; forest products subsidies 91; institutional objectives 70–1
Mansfield, Michael 49
market liberalization: demanded by US 9–10; and ministries 7–8, 18, 30, 36–7, 94–5; need for 4–5, 10–11, 12–13; US 105–6; see also Framework talks; MOSS talks
Matsushita 69
mercantilism 15, 93; neo-mercantilism 93–5
MHW (Ministry of Health and Welfare) 6–7, 34; agenda formation 39–42; autonomy 54–6; institutional objectives 63–5; and market liberalization 78–9; and pharmaceuticals 29–30, 36, 74–5, 94, 97; policy instruments 58–60
military role 3–4
ministries: agenda-setting 39–42; autonomy 27, 28–9, 35–6, 54–8, 84, 102; institutional objectives 27, 28, 62–73, 102–3; inter-ministry conflict 28–9, 55–8, 73, 99, 108, 111; jurisdiction 6–7; and market liberalization 7–8, 18, 30, 36–7, 94–5; need for reorganization 100, 110–11; policy instruments 27, 28, 30–1, 37, 58–62, 73, 103; policy-oriented 34, 35, 67; and regulations 4–5; regulator 34, 67; relationship with political leaders 97–8, 99–101; relationship with private sector 31–7, 74–92, 96–7, 98–9, 111; role in policymaking 2, 5, 22–3, 24, 26–37, 93–4; in study 7; see also specific ministries e.g. MITI

Ministry of Agriculture, Forestry and Fisheries see MAFF
Ministry of Construction 6–7, 34, 36
Ministry of Finance see MOF
Ministry of Foreign Affairs 5
Ministry of Health and Welfare see MHW
Ministry of International Trade and Industry, see MITI
Ministry of Labour 36
Ministry of Posts and Telecommunications see MPT
Ministry of Transportation 34
MITI (Ministry of International Trade and Industry) 22, 23, 100, 104; autonomy 54–5; institutional objectives 72–3, 95; jurisdiction of 6–7; and market liberalization 83–4; policy instruments 61; policy-oriented 34, 35; and private sector 32, 35–36, 39, 74; promotive relationships 98–9; relationship with electronics industry 76, 96, 97; role in policymaking 5, 9, 26, 94
Mitsubishi 80
Miyazawa Kiichi 95
Mobile Radio Center 68, 69, 82
MOC (Ministry of Construction) 6–7, 34, 36
MOF (Ministry of Finance) 5, 22, 23, 34, 104; budgets 110; fiscal policy 109; forest products subsidies 85; 91; inter-ministry conflict 29; and pharmaceuticals 55–6; role in policymaking 26
MOFA (Ministry of Foreign Affairs) 5
MOL (Ministry of Labour) 36
MOSS (Market-Oriented Sector-Selective) talks 5–6, 31, 108; agenda formation 39–45; effects of gaiatsu 45–53; in study 14–17
MOT (Ministry of Transportation) 34
Motorola 11, 13, 68, 69
MPT (Ministry of Posts and Telecommunications) 9, 28; agenda formation 39–40; autonomy 54–5, 56–8; institutional objectives 65–9; policy instruments 58–9, 60–1; and telecommunications 47–8, 75, 94–5
Murayama Tomiichi 1, 96

NAFTA (North American Free Trade Agreement) 5–6, 9, 11, 13, 106

Nakasone, Yasuhiro 49, 86–7, 90–1
National Federation of Forest Owners' Association 89
neo-mercantilism 93–5
New Frontier Party 1, 100, 107, 112, 113
Nihon Musen 80
Nikaidō Susumu 49
NTT (Nippon Telegraph and Telephone Corporation) 6, 33, 46, 60–1; relationship with MPT 75; VANs 82
NTT family 80, 82

Okimoto, Daniel 23
Olmer, Lionel 47
oranges 6, 70
Ozawa Ichirō 112–13

paper products 50
particleboard, tariffs 71
paternalism, of ministries 33–4, 102–3
peace, global 3–4
Pharmaceutical Affairs Law 65
pharmaceuticals 14, 16; agenda formation 39–42; chronology of talks 115–16; effects of foreign pressure 50–1, 52–3; and market liberalization 77–9; and MHW 29–30, 36, 74–5, 94, 96–7; see also MHW
plywood manufacturers, and market liberalization 86–7, 89–90
policy instruments: FA 84; meaning of 27, 28, 30–1; ministries 37, 58–62, 73, 103
policy-oriented ministries 34, 35, 67
political system: and bureaucracy 99–100, 101, 107–8; changes 1–2, 93–4, 112, 113–14; see also leaders
politicization and forest products industry 85–92, 102
post-promotive relationships 84, 98, 103; meaning of 32, 34–5; MITI 36, 74, 76, 97; and policy instruments 37
pressure, foreign see gaiatsu
price listing: drugs 55–6, 59, 78–9
private sector: relationship with ministries 31–7, 74–92, 96–7, 98–9, 111; role in policymaking 24–5; see also commercial practices
Product Liability Law (1994) 96

promotive relationships 31–2, 34–6, 37, 76, 98–9
public goods 32–3, 35, 102
public services, fee rises 34
Public Telecommunications Law (1953) 80
public works 109, 112

quality of life 95–6, 113–14
quotas 4, 27, 30, 61

Radio law 69
radio services, third party 68–9, 82
radio telecommunications 67–8, 75–6
recession 10
regional economic integration: global 11–12; Japan's response to 12–13
regulations 4–5, 28, 30–1, 98, 108; effect of foreign pressure 39–42; and ministries 32–4
regulatory relationships 74; and autonomy 36; FA 76, 84–5; and foreign pressure 39–40, 98; and market liberalization 37; meaning of 32–4, 35; MHW 75, 96–7
relationships, of ministries and private sector 74–92; see also post-promotive; regulatory; restructuring
restructuring relationships 84–5, 98; and autonomy 36–7; FA 76; meaning of 32, 35
ruling triad model of policymaking 22–3, 26, 93–4

satellites 9
Satō Moriyoshi 86, 88
Schoppa, Leonard 38–9
Science and Technology Agency 9
SDPJ 3; coalition with LDP 1, 99, 109
sector specific talks 16–17
security policy 3–4
seisaku kanchō 34, 35, 67
Semiconductor Industry Association (SIA) (US) 52
semiconductors 13, 42–3, 52, 76
shōnin (approval grants) 30, 41–2, 59, 64–5, 78
SII talks 5, 15, 16, 45
Smith, Michael 46
SMON disease 64, 75
Socialist party 107, 112
society, relationship with state 7–8, 93–7

stagflation 10
standards: forest products 50, 71–2; telecommunications 67–8
state: active and passive 8; approach to economic policy 21–3; relationship with society 7–8, 93–7; strong and weak 21–2; and VANs 82; *see also* political system
steel 5, 8, 94
Structural Impediments Initiative (SII) talks 5, 15, 16, 45
subsidies: export 4, 27; forest products 83, 85–92

Tanabu Masami 70
tariffs 4, 27, 30, 61; computers 42–3, 51–2, 72–3; forest products 48–50, 61–2, 71, 82–3, 85–92
telecommunications 9, 14, 16, 108; agenda formation 39–40; chronology of talks 117–21; deregulation 113–14; effects of foreign pressure 46–8, 52, 53; and market liberalization 78–82; as public good 33–4; relationship with MPT 75–6, 94–5; separated from electronics 43; standards 67–8; *see also* MPT
Telecommunications Business Law 56, 57, 60–1, 68–9
telecommunications service, type-two 80–2
Teshima Reishi 47
textiles 5, 8
thalidomide 59, 64, 75

timber growers, and market liberalization 88–90
Toshiba 80
Toyō Tsūshinki 80
trade; managed 13, 105–6
trade imbalance; US 43–4
trade policy: US 5–7, 9–10, 101–13; *see also* market liberalization

United Nations, Japan in 3–4
Uruguay Round 6, 9–10, 11, 20–1
US: hegemony 20, 106; and Japan 4, 21; market liberalization 105–6; regional economic integration 11; suggestions for future trade policy 101–13; trade policies 5–7, 9–10; as weak state 21–2, 23–4
US–Japan negotiations 13, 40, 108; *see also* MOSS talks

value added networks (VANs) 28, 56–8; market liberalization 80–2
voluntary export restraints (VERs) 4, 12, 94
voluntary import expansion 12

Wakasugi Kazuo 51
welfare provisions 107, 109–10
World Trade Organization (WTO), 6, 12

yakka (drug pricing) 41, 55, 59, 77-8
Yamamoto Takuma 79
Yoshida Shigeru 100